SKYSCRAPERS_GRATTACIELI_WOLKENKRABBERS

SKYSCRAPERS_GRATTACIELI_WOLKENKRABBERS

Coordination • Coordinazione • Auteur
Ariadna Àlvarez Garreta (architect • architecte • architect)

Texts • Testi • Teksten
Ariadna Àlvarez Garreta
Joaquim Ballarín Bargalló (architect • architecte • architect)

Translation • Traduzione • Vertaling
Peter Miller (English)
Raffaella Coia / Franco Balduzzi (Italiano)
Sabine Schaub (Nederlands)

Design and layout • Design e grafica • Design en lay-out
Manel Peret Calderón

Production • Produzione • Productie
Juanjo Rodríguez Novel

Copyright © 2004 Atrium Group

Published by: Atrium Group de
ediciones y publicaciones, S.L.
C/ Ganduxer, 112
08022 Barcelona

Telf: +34 932 540 099
Fax: +34 932 118 139
e-mail: atrium@atriumgroup.org
www.atriumbooks.com

ISBN: 84-95692-25-2
Dep. Leg.: B-13167-2004

Printed in Spain

Copyright © 2004 Atrium Group

Pubblicato da: Atrium Group de
ediciones y publicaciones, S.L.
C/ Ganduxer, 112
08022 Barcelona

Telf: +34 932 540 099
Fax: +34 932 118 139
e-mail: atrium@atriumgroup.org
www.atriumbooks.com

ISBN: 84-95692-25-2
Dep. Leg.: B-13167-2004

Stampato in Spagna

Copyright © 2004 Atrium Group

Publishing project: Atrium Group de
ediciones y publicaciones, S.L.
C/ Ganduxer, 112
08022 Barcelona

Telf: +34 932 540 099
Fax: +34 932 118 139
e-mail: atrium@atriumgroup.org
www.atriumbooks.com

ISBN: 84-95692-25-2
Dep. Leg.: B-13167-2004

Gedrukt in Spanje

INDEX-INDICE-INDEX

INTRODUCTION

This book proposes a non-historical vision of the most representative tall buildings of the last decade of the 20th Century reflecting current architecture in different realities, cultures and cities throughout the world, from twenty-floor buildings to the utopian eighty meter-tall skyscrapers.

The choice has been made to include some emblematic buildings from the second half of the last century, taking architecture to be an artistic discipline tied to history. Going through the book chronologically, we observe that the starting point is established in the fifties as a reference to the technical and formal evolution of skyscrapers. Between the 80s and the 90s we find a greater number of examples to reach the central axis of the book, the 90s. As its character is not historical, the buildings have been ordered alphabetically with the intention of facilitating an efficient form of consultation and handling of the information for the reader. Each reader will be able to plan routes, according to their interests, through an ample and objective vision, leaving the more technical analysis and information to other publications.

Following a geographic trajectory, we can see how the period established in this volume coincides in many cases with the economic and constructive expansion of the Asian continent. These cities, over a period of ten years, have seen their traditional silhouette transformed by big towers in a vertiginous race lacking in town planning to regulate their implantation on urban land. The relationship between man and architecture has been the greatest preoccupation of the architect, but in the case of tall buildings this goes beyond the human dimension, establishing a level of relationship at city scale. In this case, the problem of representation covers the relationship between the public space/constructed space, the contact of the building with the ground, the volumetry and choice of materials. How to make compatible the scale of skyscrapers with the traditional city is the architectural investigation proposed by this compilation.

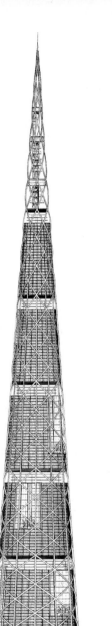

The date of each project corresponds to the year in the period of construction comes to an end, which could be past, present or future with the incorporation of proposals for buildings for the cities of the new millennium.

This book is dedicated to all those people who perished in the attacks of September 11th 2001 which destroyed the Twin Towers of New York and part of the Pentagon building in Washington. We also want to remember all those who lost their lives in the rescue tasks and those who die on a daily basis all over the world as victims of economic avarice and the intolerance of some governments.

Ariadna Àlvarez Garreta

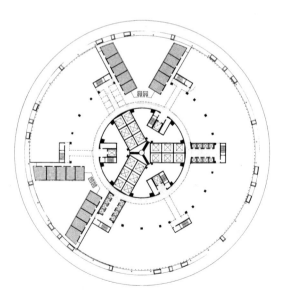

INTRODUZIONE

Questo libro propone un panorama dei grattacieli più rappresentativi dell'ultimo decennio del xx secolo, non sulla base di un criterio storico, ma studiando gli esempi dell'architettura odierna in contesti, culture e città differenti di tutto il mondo, dagli edifici di venti piani fino agli utopici grattacieli alti ottocento metri.

Abbiamo ritenuto opportuno occuparci, inoltre, di alcuni edifici emblematici della seconda metà dello scorso secolo, dal momento che consideriamo l'architettura una disciplina artistica legata alla storia. Se seguiamo un ordine cronologico, noteremo che il decennio degli anni cinquanta viene preso come punto di partenza dell'evoluzione tecnica e formale dei grattacieli. Negli anni ottanta e novanta troveremo un maggior numerodi esempi, che ci porteranno al nucleo centrale del libro, ossia il decennio degli anninovanta. Dal momento che non viene seguito un criterio storico, gli edifici sono presentati in ordine alfabetico, con l'intenzione di renderne facile e pratica la consultazione e lo studio. Ciascun lettore potrà seguire un percorso a seconda delle sue inquietudini in questo vasto ed obiettivo panorama che lascia l'analisi ed i dati tecnici ad un altro tipo di pubblicazioni.

Da un punto di vista geografico, potremo osservare che il periodo trattato in questovolume corrisponde, in molti casi, all'espansione economica ed edilizia del continenteasiatico. Queste città hanno visto cambiare completamente, nel giro di dieci anni, il lorotradizionale aspetto da alte torri costruite in una corsa vertiginosa e priva di qualsiasicriterio urbanistico che regolasse la crescita della città. Il rapporto tra l'uomo e l'edificioè la maggiore preoccupazione dell'architetto, tuttavia, per quanto riguarda edifici di grande altezza, questo trascende la dimensione umana per stabilire una relazione con la città.

In questo caso, la questione della rappresentazione comprende il rapporto tra lo spaziopubblico e lo spazio costruito, il contatto dell'edificio con il terreno, la volumetriae la scelta dei materiali. L'indagine architettonica proposta in questa raccolta riguarda la compatibilità della dimensione del grattacielo con la città tradizionale.

La data di ogni progetto si riferisce all'anno –passato, presente o futuro- in cui ne è stata ultimata la costruzione, l'aggiunta di alcuni progetti edilizi per le città del nuovo millennio lasciano il libro aperto al futuro.

Questo libro è dedicato alle vittime dell'attentato dell'11 settembre 2001 contro le Torri Gemelle di New York e l'edificio del Pentagono a Washington. Vorremmo ricordare inquesta sede tutti coloro che persero la vita durante i tentativi di salvataggio e tutti coloro che soccombono ogni giorno in tutto il mondo vittima dell'avarizia e dell'intolleranza dei governi.

Ariadna Àlvarez Garreta

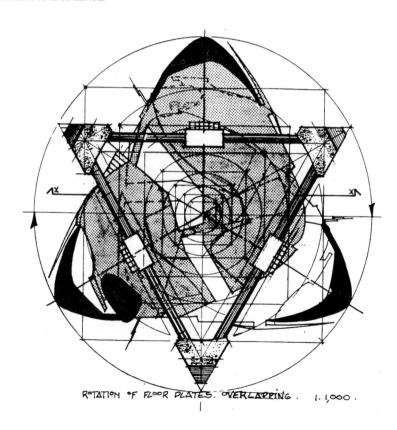

ROTATION OF FLOOR PLATES. OVERLAPPING. 1. 1,000.

INLEIDING

Dit boek biedt een overzicht van de meest markante hoge gebouwen uit het laatste decennium van de 20e eeuw, met hun architectonische actualiteit in uiteenlopende landschappen, culturen en steden over de hele wereld – van gebouwen met 20 verdiepingen tot utopische wolkenkrabbers van 800 meter hoogte.

Er is voor gekozen om ook enkele emblematische gebouwen uit de tweede helft van de vorige eeuw op te voeren, aangezien architectuur een artistieke discipline is die met de geschiedenis is verbonden. Wanneer men dit boek in chronologische volgorde doorloopt, stelt men vast dat om deze reden de jaren '50 als het uitgangspunt zijn genomen voor de technische en vormende ontwikkeling van wolkenkrabbers. Tussen 1980 en 1990 neemt het aantal wolkenkrabbers toe, om uit te monden in de kernperiode van dit boek, de jaren '90. Aangezien het boek niet historisch van opzet is, zijn de gebouwen alfabetisch gerangschikt, zodat de lezer gemakkelijker informatie kan opzoeken en raadplegen. Iedere lezer kan zich naar eigen voorkeur een uitgebreid en objectief overzicht verschaffen, waarbij analyses en uitgebreidere technische informatie aan andere publicaties worden overgelaten.

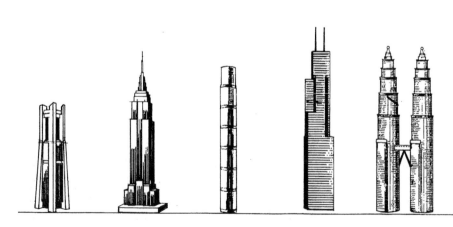

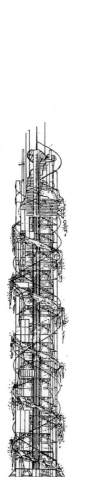

Bij deze geografische reis stellen we vast dat de in dit boek behandelde periode in veel gevallen samenvalt met de economische en architectonische opkomst van het Aziatische continent. Binnen een tijdsbestek van 10 jaar is in een duizelingwekkend tempo en zonder enige stadsplanning het traditionele silhouet van deze steden door gigantische torens drastisch veranderd. De relatie tussen mens en architectuur heeft de architect altijd het meest beziggehouden, maar de dimensies van wolkenkrabbers overstijgen het bevattingsvermogen van de mens en veranderen zo de relatie van de mens tot de stad. In dit geval beslaat de kwestie van vertegenwoordiging de relatie tussen de openbare ruimte/bebouwde ruimte, het contact van het gebouw met de grond, de ruimtelijke omvang en de keuze van de materialen. Deze compilatie biedt een architectonisch onderzoek naar de vraag hoe de schaal van wolkenkrabbers te verenigen is met de traditionele stad.

Het jaartal dat bij elk gebouw wordt vermeld heeft betrekking op het jaar van voltooiing. Dit kan in het verleden, heden of de toekomst zijn, waarbij tegelijkertijd bebouwingvoorstellen voor steden in het nieuwe millennium worden gedaan.

Dit boek is opgedragen aan alle mensen die omkwamen bij de aanslagen van 11 september 2001, die de Twin Towers van New York en een deel van het Pentagon in Washington verwoestten. Ook gedenken we allen die het leven lieten bij de reddingsacties en al diegenen die dagelijks over de hele wereld omkomen als slachtoffers van economische hebzucht en de intolerantie van sommige regeringen.

Ariadna Àlvarez Garreta

53ʳᵈ AT THIRD

PHILIP JONSON & JOHN BURGEE ARCHITECTS

CLIENT / CLIENTE / OPDRACHTGEVER: GERLAD D.HINES INTERESTS	**1986**
TOTAL AREA / SUPERFICIE / TOTALE OPPERVLAKTE: 54.495 m²	
FLOORS / PIANI / VERDIEPINGEN - HEIGHT / ALTEZZA / HOOGTE: 34 fl / 138 m	

Also known as Lipstick, this is an emblematic building in the city because of its characterstic volumetry and architectural quality which was projected for the company Revlon. The contact with the ground on pillars provides a porch on the ground floor and the triple staggering with which it rises is the result of the urban planning rule which characterizes the speculative buildings of New York. The eliptical form of the ground plan (and the location of the structure) gives a spatial distribution which is more interesting with respect to a traditional office building, guaranteeing total views of the exterior. The facade is treated like a luxurious skin in bands of polished Imperial Swedish red granite, stainless steel and glass.

Conosciuto anche come Lipstick, questo è un edificio emblematico della città per la sua caratteristica volumetria e qualità architettonica che venne progettato per la compagnia Revlon. Il contatto con il suolo attraverso pilastri offre un portico a piano terra e il triplice scaglionamento con cui si eleva è il risultato della normativa urbanistica che caratterizza gli edifici speculativi di uffici newyorkini. La forma ellittica della pianta (e l'ubicazione della struttura) offrono una distribuzione spaziale più interessante rispetto a un edificio tradizionale per uffici, garantendo vedute totali verso l'esterno. La facciata si presenta come una pelle lussuosa in forma di frange rosse di granito Imperiale Svedese lucido, acciaio inossidabile e vetro.

Dit gebouw werd ontworpen voor het bedrijf Revlon en staat ook bekend onder de naam 'Lipstick'. Het is een van de emblematische gebouwen in de stad vanwege de karakteristieke vorm en architectonische kwaliteit. De constructie rust op pilaren die op de begane grond een overdekte hal vormen. De drievoudige fasering is het resultaat van een bouwverordening van de stad, die de spectaculaire kantoorkolossen van New York kenmerken. Door de elliptische vorm van het ontwerp (en de locatie van het gebouw) ontstaat een interessantere ruimtelijke verdeling dan in een traditioneel kantoorgebouw, hetgeen rondom een vrij uitzicht garandeert. De façade bestaat uit stroken gepolijst Zweeds graniet, roestvrij staal en glas.

The elliptical shape of the ground plan (atypical in the city's architecture) rising from the ground floor with a porch and the desire to distinguish itself from neighbouring buildings allows it to gain public space. The corners on the block are enlarged where there is more pedestrian traffic.

La forma ellittica della pianta (così atipica nell'architettura della città) che si alza a piano terra con un portico e la volontà di distinguersi dagli edifici vicini, permettono di guadagnare spazio pubblico. Gli angoli dell'isolato si ampliano nel punto di maggior traffico pedonale.

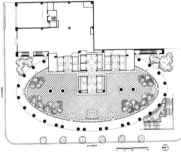

Extra vrije ruimte wordt verkregen door de elliptische vorm van het ontwerp (atypisch voor de architectuur van de stad), dat vanaf de begane grond begint met een overdekte portiek, om zich op deze wijze te onderscheiden van omringende gebouwen. De hoeken van de blokken worden groter op plaatsen waar meer voetgangersverkeer is.

The two-storey foyer was decorated with great sobriety. The façades are made up of two strips of reflecting glass, polished red granite and aluminium. The elliptical curve is tangent to the pavement at its centre and creates an illusion of spatial continuity.

Il vestibolo di due piani di altezza è stato decorato con grande sobrietà, le facciate si compongono di due frange di cristallo riflettente, granito rosso lucido e alluminio. La curva ellittica tangente nel suo centro al marciapiede, crea una sensazione spaziale di continuità.

De foyer uit twee verdiepingen is met een sobere elegantie ingericht. De façaden zijn opgebouwd uit twee stroken reflecterend glas, gepolijst rood graniet en aluminium. De elliptische curve raakt in het midden het trottoir en wekt de illusie van een ruimtelijke continuïteit.

Projected for a well-known American brand of cosmetics, the shape of this building recalls a tube of lipstick. The architects used pop iconography to reflect their idea of an American city, made up of a mixture of buildings and styles, images, people, shapes and colours.

La forma di questo edificio, progettato per una famoso firma americana di cosmetici, ricorda un rossetto per le labbra. Gli architetti utilizzarono una iconografia pop per rispoecchiare la loro idea della città americana, composta a partire dalla mescolanza di edifici e tipologie, di immagini, di gente, di forme e colori.

De vorm van het gebouw, dat voor het Amerikaanse cosmeticabedrijf Revlon werd ontworpen, lijkt op een lippenstift. De architecten maakten gebruik van popiconografie om hun opvatting van een Amerikaanse stad tot uiting te brengen, bestaand uit een mengeling van gebouwen en stijlen, beelden, mensen, vormen en kleuren.

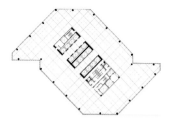

101 PARK AVENUE

ELI ATTIA ARCHITECTS

CLIENT / CLIENTE / OPDRACHTGEVER: H.J KALIKOW & CO. INC.	**1982**

TOTAL AREA / SUPERFICIE / TOTALE OPPERVLAKTE: 111.524 m²

FLOORS / PIANI / VERDIEPINGEN - HEIGHT / ALTEZZA / HOOGTE: 50 fl / 183 m

Designed as an efficient office building destined to attract high level clients, its shape and orientation are a direct answer to the conditioning factors of its location, pre-existing factors and planning conditions of the city. The building is oriented diagonally to allow access through the lots only point of contact with Park Avenue. To respect the schematic continuity and that of adjacent buildings, the lines which limit the streets and other existing buildings were maintained, creating a podium upon which the structure of the tower is raised. The building's shape reduces the visual mass of the construction.

Concepito come un moderno edificio di uffici destinato ad attirare clienti di alto livello, la sua forma e la sua posizione rispondono alle esigenze dettate dal luogo e dalla situazione urbanistica preesistente. L'edificio è collocato di traverso per consentire l'entrata dall'unico punto di incontro dell'edificio con Park Avenue. Allo scopo di mantenere la continuità della struttura e delle edificazioni adiacenti, furono mantenuti gli allineamenti che delimitavano le strade e venne costruito un basamento sul quale sorge la struttura della torre. La forma dell'edificio riduce la massa visibile della costruzione.

Het is ontworpen als efficiënt kantoorgebouw om belangrijke klanten aan te trekken. De bouwstijl en oriëntatie zijn optimaal afgestemd op de locatie, de reeds bestaande bebouwing en de voorwaarden van de stadsplanning. Het gebouw staat diagonaal op de hoek Park Avenue, waar zich ook de enige ingang van het gebouw bevindt. Om toch rekening te houden met de schematische continuïteit en de aangrenzende gebouwen werd een soort podium geconstrueerd waarop de toren rust. De vorm van het gebouw verkleint het zichtbare deel van de constructie.

The location of the public squares related to the access and the section of the project in this area help the transition between interior and exterior.

L'ubicazione delle piazze pubbliche relative all'ingresso e a quest'area del progetto favoriscono il passaggio dall'interno all'esterno.

De ligging van openbare pleinen en de toegang en vormgeving van het gebouw in deze zone bevordert de overgang tussen interieur en exterieur.

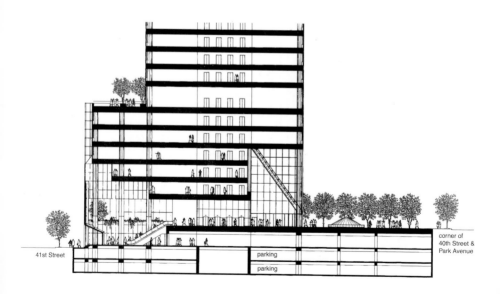

41st Street

parking

parking

corner of
40th Street &
Park Avenue

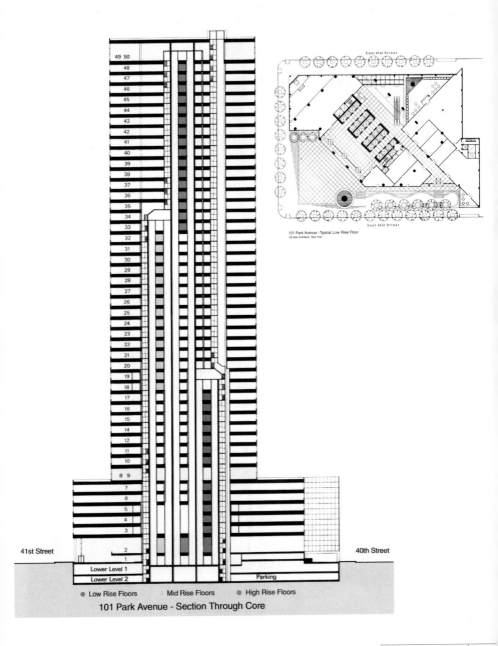

49 50
48
47
46
45
44
43
42
41
40
39
38
37
36
35
34
33
32
31
30
29
28
27
26
25
24
23
22
21
20
19
18
17
16
15
14
12
11
10
8 9
7
6
5
4
3
2
1

41st Street

40th Street

Lower Level 1
Lower Level 2

Parking

● Low Rise Floors   ● Mid Rise Floors   ● High Rise Floors

101 Park Avenue - Section Through Core

East 41st Street

East 40st Street

101 Park Avenue - Typical Low Rise Floor
Eli Attia Architects, New York

The fragmented façade helps break up the shape and widens visuals, making the building lighter and less imposing.

La frammentazione della facciata contribuisce a romperne la forma e ad aumentarne la visuale, rendendo l'edificio meno imponente e più leggero.

De gefragmenteerde façade maakt de vorm losser en het blikveld groter; hierdoor wordt het gebouw lichter en minder overheersend.

The project emphasizes the singularity of the meeting between Park Avenue and 44th Street, drawing back the building by means of the chamfered facade and locating the access and a public square.

Questo progetto sottolinea il peculiare Incrocio tra Park Avenue e la 44ª strada, ritirando l'edificio per mezzo dello scantonato della facciata e situandone l'ingresso in una piazza pubblica.

Het project bewerkstelligt een bijzonder samenkomen van Park Avenue en 44th Street. Door de afgeschuinde façade wijkt het gebouw terug. Ervoor bevindt zich een plein met de ingang naar het gebouw.

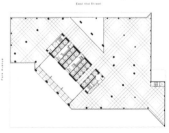

101 Park Avenue - 2nd Floor

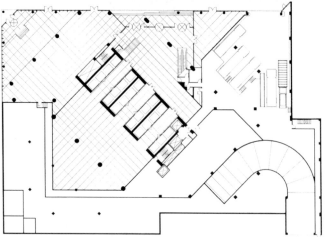

The project places great importance on its effect on the surroundings, attempting to control its areas of shadow and creating free spaces.

Il progetto conferisce grande importanza all'impatto sull'ambiente cerca di controllare le zone d'ombra e creare spazi aperti.

Er is sterk rekening gehouden met het effect van het gebouw op zijn omgeving. Schaduwwerking wordt zoveel mogelijk ingeperkt en er zijn open ruimten gecreëerd.

181 WEST MADISON

CESAR PELLI & ASSOCIATES INC.

CLIENT / CLIENTE / OPDRACHTGEVER: MIGLIN-BEITLER DEVELOPMENTS

1990

TOTAL AREA / SUPERFICIE / TOTALE OPPERVLAKTE: 97.370 m²

FLOORS / PIANI / VERDIEPINGEN - HEIGHT / ALTEZZA / HOOGTE: 50 fl / 184 m

This office tower found on the Chicago Loop was designed with the style of those sculptural skyscrapers of the 20s in the city where these buildings were constructed for the first time. With a square plan, it rises describing an elegant silhouette which, when it reaches the upper part, is breeched, thus losing part of its volume, and is topped with an elegant crown which distinguishes it from the city skyline. The vertical rhythm of the façade is made up of strips of granite combined with the glass of the windows, and the stainless steel mullions which reinforce the ascending character of the building.

Questa torre di uffici, situata nel Loop di Chicago, la città che vide nascere questo tipo di edifici, venne progettata nello stile dei maestosi grattacieli degli anni venti. Di base quadrata, si erge stagliando contro il cielo la sua elegante sagoma che, nella parte superiore, si ritrae perdendo cosi parte del voume; è sormontata da un elegante corona che spicca nel panorama dello skyline della città. Il ritmo verticale della facciata è costituito da fasce di granito combinate con il vetro delle finestre e da fasce di acciaio inossidabile che accentuano la natura ascendente dell'edificio.

Deze kantoorkolos bevindt zich aan de Chicago Loop en werd ontworpen in de stijl van de jaren 1920, in de stad waar dit soort gebouwen voor het eerst verrezen. Het elegante silhouet verheft zich vierkant tot het gebouw in het bovenste gedeelte door meerdere trapsgewijze constructies aan omvang afneemt. Bovenop bevindt zich een elegante 'kroon', waardoor het gebouw gemakkelijk te herkennen is in de skyline van de stad. Het gelijkmatige ritme van de façade bestaat uit stroken graniet, afgewisseld door het glas van de ramen en de dragers van roestvrij staal, die het verticale karakter van het gebouw sterk benadrukken.

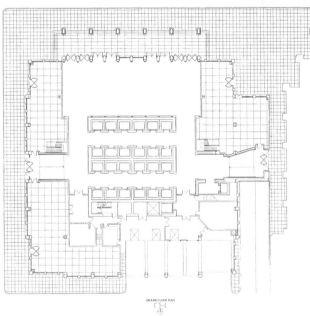

GROUND FLOOR PLAN

Above, main access to the building marked by a metallic pergola. Below, ground floor of the building. The structure of the tower responds to a central core of vertical communications and services, thus freeing the perimeter for office space.

In alto, l'ingresso principale dell'edificio ricoperto da un pergolato metallico. In basso, il pianterreno. La struttura della torre è costituita dal nucleo verticale di comunicazioni e di servizi al centro che lascia libero il perimetro per la distribuzione degli uffici.

Boven: hoofdingang met aangebouwde metalen overkapping.
Onder: de begane grond van het gebouw. Door centraal geplaatste liften en andere voorzieningen is er meer ruimte voor kantoorruimte.

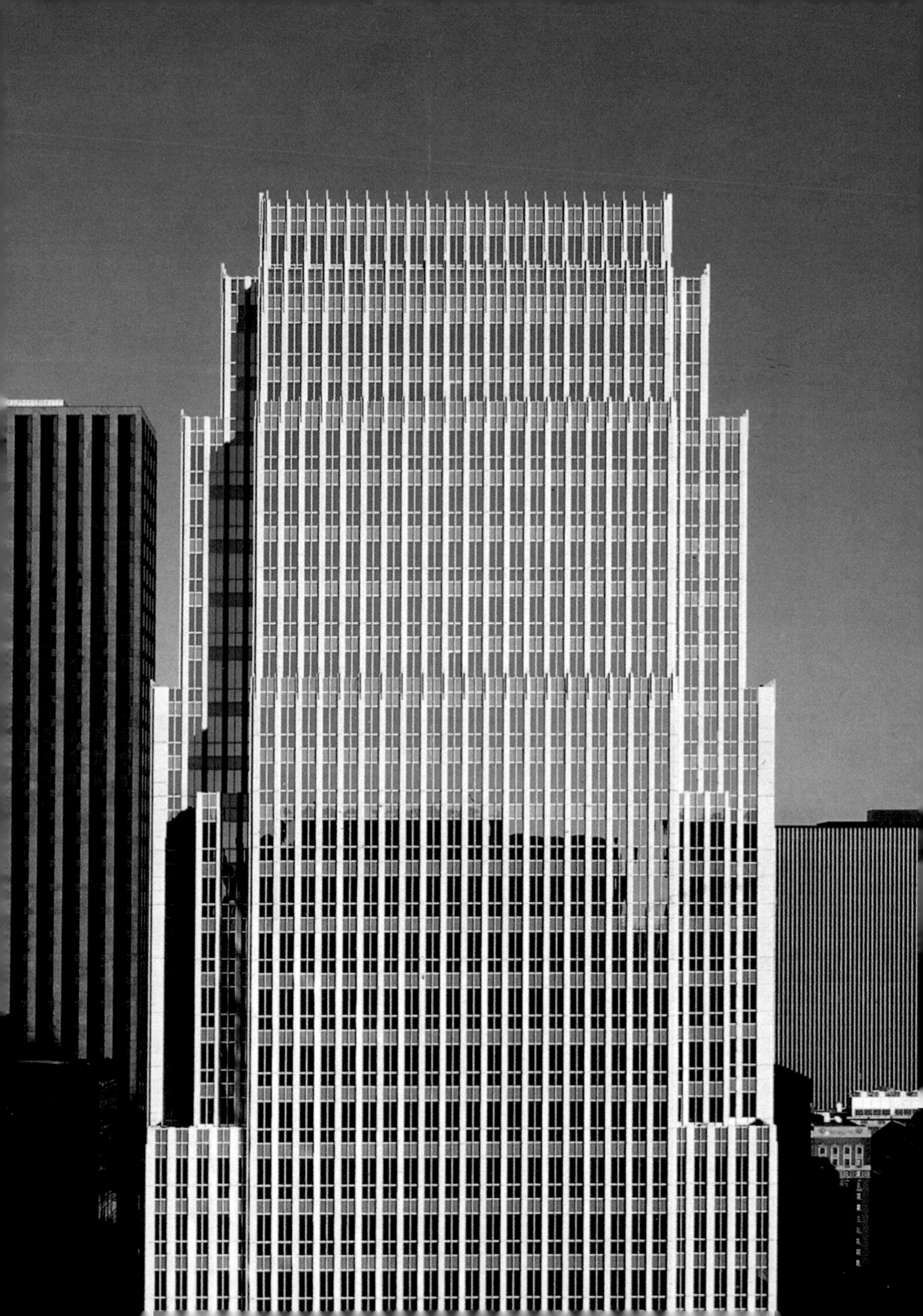

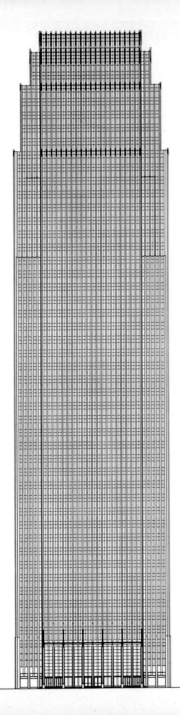

The interior lobby is a four-floor high loggia (it forms part of the base of the building) with large windows. It was thought of as a space which would receive a lot of light from outside which was decorated with gray and green marble.

L'atrio interno, e una loggia alta quattro piani (fa parte della base dell'edificio) con enormi finestre. Venne concepito come una zona adornata da marmi grigi e verdi e intensamente illuminata dall'esterno.

De toegangshal is vier verdiepingen hoog (onderdeel van de basis van het gebouw) met hoge ramen die veel daglicht toelaten. De decoratie bestaat uit grijs en groen marmer.

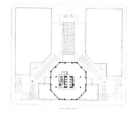

311 SOUTH WACKER DRIVE

KOHN PEDERSEN FOX ASSOCIATES PC (KPF)

CLIENT / CLIENTE / OPDRACHTGEVER: LINCOLN PROPERTY COMPANY	**1991**
TOTAL AREA / SUPERFICIE / TOTALE OPPERVLAKTE: 130.000 m²	
FLOORS / PIANI / VERDIEPINGEN - HEIGHT / ALTEZZA / HOOGTE: 65 fl / 293 m	

This building, contiguous to the well-known Sears Tower, was the first of a group of three towers situated around a winter garden, conceived as pedestrian core and linked with different systems of transport concentrated in this area. The large public space is organized by means of two large squares crossed by a covered pedestrian area. The winter garden is also the lobby through which the octagonal office tower is accessed. Its bulky volume is decomposed in different elements. It culminates with a large translucent glass cylinder which is lit up at night, making the building stand out from the Chicago landscape.

Questo edificio, situato accanto allafamosa Sears Tower, fu il primo di un complesso di tre torri che si innalzano intorno ad un giardino invernale. Venne concepito come zona pedonale e centro di collegamento dei vari mezzi di trasporto ubicati in quest'area. L'ampio spazio pubblico è organizzato in due grandi piazze attraversate da un'area pedonale coperta. Il giardino invernale, inoltre, è anche l'ingresso della torre ottagonale di uffici. La robusta struttura è costituita da vari elementi ed è coronata da un grande cilindro di vetro semitrasparente che, di notte, quando è illuminato, spicca nel panorama di Chicago.

Dit gebouw grenst aan de beroemde Sears Tower en vormde de eerste van een groep van drie torens rondom een wintertuin, die werd aangelegd als een voetgangerszone en tegelijk als verbinding met verscheidene transportmiddelen die zich in dit gebied bevinden. De grote openbare ruimte bestaat uit twee grote pleinen, waarover een overdekte voetgangerszone loopt. De wintertuin is ook de lobby die toegang verleent tot het achthoekige kantoorgebouw. Verschillende elementen van uiteenlopende hoogte maken de toren minder volumineus. Bovenop staat een doorzichtige glazen cilinder, die 's nachts wordt verlicht. Zo valt het gebouw sterk op in het stedelijke landschap van Chicago.

The treatment of the façades is horizontal with vertical stripes which mark the concrete structure. The most stand out material is the red granite from Texas which forms a contrast with the neighboring Sears Tower.

La lavorazione della facciata è a fasce orizzontali e verticali, che sottolineano la struttura di cemento. Il materiale che risalta, il granito rosso del Texas, contrasta con l'edificio della vicina Sears Tower.

De façaden zijn samengesteld uit horizontale en verticale verbindingen, die de betonstructuur benadrukken. Het meest opmerkelijke materiaal is het rode graniet uit Texas, dat contrasteert met de aangrenzende Sears Tower.

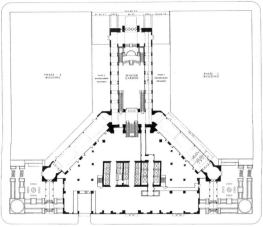

777 TOWER

CESAR PELLI & ASSOCIATES INC.

CLIENT / CLIENTE / OPDRACHTGEVER: SOUTH FIGUEROA PLAZA ASSOCIATES

1990

TOTAL AREA / SUPERFICIE / TOTALE OPPERVLAKTE: 102.200 m²

FLOORS / PIANI / VERDIEPINGEN - HEIGHT / ALTEZZA / HOOGTE: 53 fl / 221 m

Located in the business area of Los Angeles, it is one of the most graceful buildings in the area and a landmark in the city. The building, a square prism with the corners rounded, diminishes arching towards the east and west, maintaining the same façade plan towards the south and north. This is covered with lightly colored metal, with special attention to the treatment of the details, generating shadows and volumes which break up the monotony of the plan. The building's access lobby, at triple space, leaves its east and south façades completely glass-covered, so that the building is arrived at through an area bathed in sunlight.

Situato nel quartiere degli affari di Los Angeles, è uno degli edifici più esili della zona ed un vero e proprio simbolo della città. L'edificio, un prisma quadrato dagli spigoli arrotondati, decresce inarcandosi su lato est ed ovest, mentre conserva la stessa superficie sulle superfici sud e nord. La facciata, nella quale è stata dedicata un'attenzione particolare alla lavorazione delle rifiniture, con la creazione di ombre e volumi che rompono la monotonia della superficie, è ricoperta da un metallo leggermente colorato. L'atrio di accesso, disposto su tre aree, lascia le facciate est e sud interamente vetrate, in modo che la visione dell'edificio è anticipata da un bagno di luce.

Dit gebouw geldt als een van de meest elegante in de zakenwijk van Los Angeles en is een herkenningspunt in de stad. Het is een vierkante prismavorm met afgeronde hoeken, die naar het oosten en westen toe afneemt en een gelijke façade in het zuiden en noorden handhaaft. De façade wordt bedekt door licht gekleurd materiaal, met bijzondere aandacht voor details als schaduwwerking om de monotonie van de vlakken te doorbreken. De toegangshal bestaat uit drie verdiepingen en is aan de oostelijke en zuidelijke façade volledig opgebouwd uit glas, zodat de ingang baadt in het zonlicht.

The bulky zones of the
façade develop a volumetric
capacity which breaks up the
monotony of the curtain wall.

*Le zone piene della facciata
sviluppano una capacità
volumetrica che rompe
la monotonia della parete
a cortina.*

De uitstekende delen van de
façade verlenen het gebouw
volume en onderbreken de
monotonie van de buitenkant.

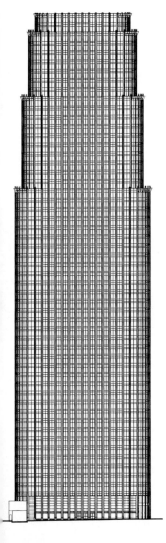

The lobby, at triple height, is bathed in sunlight thanks to the liberation of the façade, completely glass-covered.

L'atrio, di triple altezza, è inondato dalla luce del sole grazie alla lavorazione della facciata, interamente di vetro.

De lobby van drie verdiepingen baadt in het zonlicht dankzij de volledig glazen wand van de façade.

ABN-AMRO BANK WORLD HQTRS.

PEI COBB FREED & PARTNERS

CLIENT / CLIENTE / OPDRACHTGEVER: ABN-AMRO BANK N.V

1999

TOTAL AREA / SUPERFICIE / TOTALE OPPERVLAKTE: 105.000 m²

FLOORS / PIANI / VERDIEPINGEN - HEIGHT / ALTEZZA / HOOGTE: 24 fl / 96 m

Located next to an important communications junction in the southern sector of the center of Amsterdam, the building aims to be representative, providing an image for the firm. The project folds out in three directions: the 24-floor building, which contains offices and marks the importance of the urban axis, a 7-floor building, which contains the areas of relation – central lobby, auditorium, conference hall, center and meeting halls and a restaurant for 500 diners surrounding a garden park, and finally a 17-floor building which has an employees canteen on the top floor. In the basement there is a large car park and the plumbing and electrical systems areas.

Situato accanto ad un importante nodo delle comunicazioni nel quartiere a sud del centro di Amsterdam, l'edificio vorrebbe rappresentare ed essere l'immagine della compagnia. Il progetto si sviluppa in tre direzioni; l'edificio di ventiquattro piani, che ospita uffici e conferisce importanza al nucleo urbano, un edificio di sette piani, che accoglie le aree di relazione –l'atrio centrale, l'auditorium, la sala riunioni, un centro ed una sala per assemblee ed un ristorante per 500 convitati- intorno ad un parco, ed infine un edificio alto diciassette piani con un ristorante per gli impiegati all'ultimo piano. Nel sottosuolo si trova un grande parcheggio e la zona degli impianti.

Dit gebouw, gelegen aan een belangrijk verkeersknooppunt in het zuidelijke deel van het centrum van Amsterdam, vormt het visitekaartje voor de bank. Het ontwerp loopt in drie richtingen: een gebouw met 24 verdiepingen met kantoren, als belangrijke stedelijke as van de stad. Daarnaast een gebouw van zeven verdiepingen met toegangshal, auditorium, congrescentrum en vergaderruimten en een restaurant voor vijfhonderd gasten. Alles wordt omringd door een parkeerplaats. Tot slot is er een gebouw van zeventien verdiepingen met restaurant voor de werknemers op de bovenste verdieping. Onder de grond bevindt zich naast de elektriciteits- en watervoorzieningen een grote parkeerplaats.

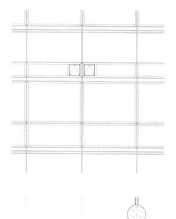

The general plan
combines an orthogonal
organization with circular
forms.
High up, some blocks
form a slight incline in
its façade.

*La pianta generale è
costituita da una
struttura ortogonale e
forme circolari. Alcuni
dei blocchi sono
leggermente inclinati
verso la facciata.*

Het totale ontwerp is een
combinatie van rechte
hoeken en halve cirkels.
Enkele gebouwen buigen
naar boven toe licht af.

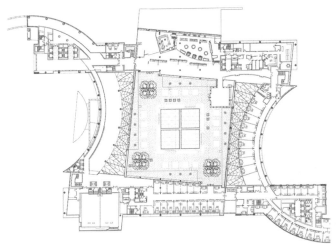

The façade presents differently paced gaps and colored finishes in the different projected volumes.

La facciata presenta vari vuoti intercalati e rifiniture variopinte dei vari volumi progettati.

Het uiterlijk van het ontwerp toont een afwisselende uitvoering en kleurgebruik.

Despite the extension and magnitude of the complex, the design has been kept in the scale closest to the users.

Nonostante l'estensione e la grandezza del complesso, il design è stato mantenuto a dimensioni il più possibile vicine agli utenti.

Ondanks de uitgestrektheid en grootte van het complex is de schaal van het ontwerp dicht bij de menselijke maat gebleven.

The interior decoration of
the building, sober and
contemporary, expresses
the power and dynamism
of
the bank.

*La decorazione interna
dell'edificio, semplice e
moderna, vuole esprimere
il potere ed il dinamismo
della banca.*

De decoratie van het
gebouwinterieur is sober
en modern, als uitdrukking
van de macht en de
dynamiek van de bank.

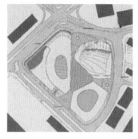

AL ASIMA SHOPPING VILLAGE

T.R. HAMZAH & YEAN SDN BHD

2000

CLIENT / CLIENTE / OPDRACHTGEVER: SALHIA REAL ESTATE COMPANY K.S.C.

TOTAL AREA / SUPERFICIE / TOTALE OPPERVLAKTE: 44.000 m²

FLOORS / PIANI / VERDIEPINGEN - HEIGHT / ALTEZZA / HOOGTE: 40 fl / 157,5 m

The client for this building wanted a shopping and office complex which proposed a different concept from the American classic, the concept drifts towards a "Retail Village" characterized by the incorporation of vernacular elements. Organized starting out from three units, each of them organized starting out from a ring around a core, they are inter-related by means of another larger core. The result is an entity formed by a tower and a four-floor building of offices and a three-floor shopping base which, like a jellyfish, absorbs and unifies the surface area of the complex. The formal result and the bioclimatic design of the building have turned it into a reference point in the city.

Il cliente di questo edificio voleva un complesso commerciale e di uffici che proponesse un concetto differente dal classico americano; il concetto tende verso un "Retail Village" caratterizzato dall'incorporazione di elementi vernacolari. Organizzato a partire da tre unità, ognuna delle quali strutturata a partire da un anello attorno a un nucleo, si rapportano tra loro attraverso un altro nucleo maggiore. Il risultato è un'entità formata da una torre e un edificio di 4 piani di uffici e uno zoccolo commerciale di tre piani di altezza che come una medusa assorbe e unifica tutta la superficie del complesso. Il risultato finale e il disegno bioclimatico dell'edificio lo hanno trasformato in una referenza della città.

De opdrachtgever van dit gebouw wenste een winkel- en kantorencomplex dat zich zou onderscheiden van het klassieke Amerikaanse concept. Het ontwerp neigt naar een 'Retail Village', gekenmerkt door de opname van plaatselijke elementen. Het complex is opgebouwd uit drie eenheden, die elk een ring rond een kern vormen. Ze worden onderling verbonden door een andere, grotere kern. Het resultaat is een complex dat bestaat uit een toren, een kantoorgebouw van vier verdiepingen en een basis van drie verdiepingen met een winkelcentrum, die als een octopus het oppervlak omspant en verenigt. De vormgeving en het bioklimatologisch ontwerp hebben dit gebouw tot een herkenningspunt van de stad gemaakt.

The part of the building complex at ground level establishes
a connection with the exterior, and the shopping plaza
ceilings are immense skylights, giving shoppers the feeling
of walking on a street rather than the inside of a building.

*La parte del complesso che si trova nell'edificio zoccolo
ha una grande rrelazione con l'esterno, e i tetti delle
piazze si coprono con grandi lucernari in modo che il
passante abbia la sensazione che si trova in una via e no
all'interno di un edificio.*

Het lager gelegen deel van het complex is sterk verbonden
met het exterieur. De plafonds van het winkelcentrum zijn
uitgerust met grote lampen die de bezoeker het gevoel
geven zich op straat in plaats van in een gebouw te
bevinden.

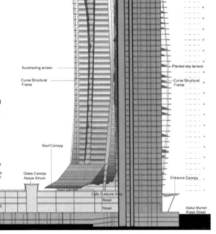

The tower consists of a series of membranes that envelop the structure, which is the skeleton of the building, and protect it from the exterior.

La tour fonctionne à partir de membranes qui recouvrent la structure, elles sont le squelette du bâtiment et le protègent de l'extérieur.

De toren is opgebouwd uit een reeks 'membranen' die het skelet van de structuur omhullen en tegen invloeden van buiten beschermen.

AL FAISALIAH COMPLEX

FOSTER & PARTNERS

CLIENT / CLIENTE / OPDRACHTGEVER: KING FAISAL FOUNDATION	**2000**
TOTAL AREA / SUPERFICIE / TOTALE OPPERVLAKTE: 240.000 m²	
FLOORS / PIANI / VERDIEPINGEN - HEIGHT / ALTEZZA / HOOGTE: 40 fl / 267m	

This office tower is a key point in the planning development of the city, because it is also the first skyscraper in Saudi Arabia. Stands out because of a profile that rises gently towards the sky, containing the golden sphere where an exclusive restaurant offers views of the city and environs. The complex also houses a luxury hotel, a banquet and conference center, up-market apartments and three commercial floors. The project, which aspires to a balance between the cost of the building and its effectiveness, flexibility, environmental and architectural harmony, develops interesting proposals in the treatment of façades and layout of the building.

Questa torre di uffici rappresenta un momento decisivo dello sviluppo urbanistico della città, dal momento che si tratta del primo grattacielo dell'Arabia Saudita. L'edificio, che si innalza delicatamente verso il cielo, spicca per la sua bella sagoma e cela al suo interno una sfera dorata nella quale un esclusivo ristorante offre uno splendido panorama della città e dei suoi dintorni. Il complesso ospita inoltre un albergo di lusso, un centro banchetti e congressi, appartamenti di alto standing e tre piani di locali commerciali. Il progetto, che aspira a raggiungere un equilibrio tra il costo dell'edificio e la sua produttività, presenta interessanti proposte nella lavorazione della facciata e nella distribuzione dell'edificio.

Dit kantoorgebouw vormt een cruciaal punt in de ontwikkeling van de stadsplanning, want het is tevens de eerste wolkenkrabber in Saoedi-Arabië. Het geleidelijk naar de hemel reikend profiel is zeer opvallend. In de goudkleurige bol onder de spits bevindt zich een exclusief restaurant met uitzicht over de stad en de omgeving. Het complex herbergt naast een luxe hotel een centrum voor banketten en congressen, luxe appartementen en drie commerciële verdiepingen. De bouw tracht een balans tussen kosten en effectiviteit, flexibiliteit, harmonie met de omgeving en de architectuur te creëren. Hierbij zijn interessante oplossingen ontwikkeld voor de uitwerking van façaden en de lay-out.

Above, in the base of the tower, a five-floor high lobby links towards the north with the hotel and towards the south with the apartments and the shopping area. On the left, detail of the façade of the tower where it meets the base. Panels of aluminum regulate the solar radiation of the façade and prevent its reflection.

In alto, nella base della torre, un atrio alto cinque piani collega l'albergo a nord con gli appartamenti e la zona commerciale situata a sud. A sinistra, particolare della facciata della torre nel punto di congiungimento con la base. I pannelli di alluminio regolano le radiazioni solari della facciata e ne evitano il riflesso.

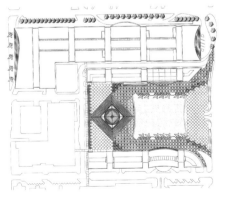

Boven: in de voet van de toren bevindt zich een lobby van vijf verdiepingen, die naar het noorden verbonden is met een hotel en naar het zuiden met de appartementen en het winkelcentrum.
Links: detail van de façade van de toren op de grens tussen toren en basis. Aluminium panelen reguleren de straling van de zon op de façade en reflecteren zo min mogelijk.

The square plan is laid out from a central structural core of vertical communications and services. The rest of the structure is located in the corners tethering the building.

La distribuzione della pianta quadrata si basa su un nucleo strutturale al centro per le comunicazioni verticali e le zone di servizio. Le zone rimanenti sono disposte agli angoli ed occupano il resto dell'edificio.

In het vierkante ontwerp bevinden zich in het centrum liften en voorzieningen. Het overige deel van de structuur wordt door vier hoeken bijeengehouden.

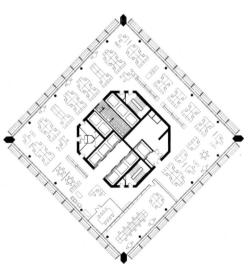

AURORA PLACE

RENZO PIANO BUILDING WORKSHOP

CLIENT / CLIENTE / OPDRACHTGEVER: LEND LEASE DEVELOPMENT

1996

TOTAL AREA / SUPERFICIE / TOTALE OPPERVLAKTE: 49.000 m²

FLOORS / PIANI / VERDIEPINGEN - HEIGHT / ALTEZZA / HOOGTE: 44 fl / 200 m

Built to coincide with the Sydney Olympics, its program combines residential use, in a 17-floor building and the office tower, of 44 floors. Its location in a district whose origin dates back to the mid-19th century, with all the contextual weight that this implies, its proximity to the Sydney Opera House by Jorn Urzon, with which it does not shy away from dialogue, the social intention of provoking the relationship between the work and residential areas, by means of shared public leisure areas and special attention to the climatic conditions and the physical environment in which it is located, constitute the bases of the development of the project.

Costruito in occasione delle olimpiadi di Sidney, questo progetto combina l'uso residenziale di una costruzione di 17 piani con una torre di uffici, di 44. L'ubicazione in una zonale cui origini risalgono a metà del XIX secolo, contutto ciò che questo rappresenta, la vicinanza all'Opera di Sidney di Jorn Urzon, con la quale cerca il dialogo, l'intenzione di stabilire una relazione tra le zone di uffici e quelle residenziali, con spazi pubblici ricreativi comuni ed un'attenzione particolare per le condizioniclimatologiche e dell'ambiente nel quale si inserisce, costituiscono le basi dello sviluppodi questo progetto.

Dit complex werd opgericht naar aanleiding van de Olympische Spelen in Sydney. In een gebouw van zeventien verdiepingen bevinden zich woningen en in een toren van 44 verdiepingen met kantoren. De ligging in een wijk die halverwege de 19e eeuw ontstond zorgt voor een beduidende context. Het beroemde operagebouw van Jorn Urzon is niet ver weg, en Aurora Place schuwt de dialoog met dit gebouw niet. Door gemeenschappelijke openbare ontspanningsgebieden, bijzondere aandacht voor klimatologische omstandigheden en de omgeving wordt getracht een sociale relatie te leggen tussen woon- en werkgebieden.

The project emphasizes the delicate and free aspects of
the form, as shown by the closures of the main façades.

*Il progetto enfatizza le forme fragili e libere,come
mostrano i tetti delle facciate principali.*

Het ontwerp benadrukt de delicate en vrije aspecten van
de vorm. Dit is vooral te zien aan de uiteinden van de
hoofdfaçaden.

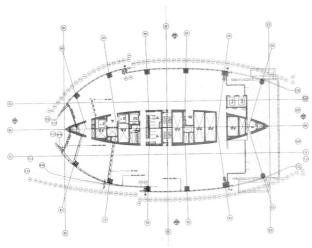

The design of the building has an ethereal quality, to diminish its capacity to impose itself on the built-up surroundings.

Questo edificio ha un aspetto eterea, che ne attenua l'impatto sulle costruzioni che lo circondano.

Het ontwerp van het gebouw heeft een bijzondere etherische kwaliteit en vermindert op deze wijze de bebouwde omgeving te domineren.

The glass skin of the building regulates the rays of the sun and the temperature of the walls, at the same time as it confers a misty tonality.

La superficie di vetro dell'edificio regola i raggi del sole e la temperatura delle facciate ed allo stesso tempo gli conferisce una tonalità grigiastra.

De glazen omhulling van het gebouw reguleert de zonnestralen en de temperatuur van de muren, maar zorgt tegelijkertijd voor een mat karakter.

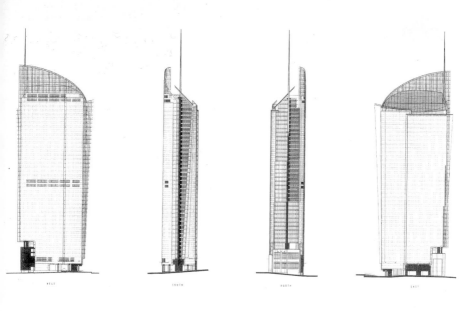

The curtain wall spreads beyond the volume of the building, dissolving its limits and accentuating its light appearance.

Il muro-cortina si estende oltre la struttura dell'edificio, dissolvendone i limiti ed enfatizzandone la leggerezza.

De buitenwand strekt zich uit tot voorbij het volume van het gebouw, waardoor het grensvlak minder scherp wordt en een licht voorkomen wordt geaccentueerd.

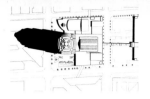

BANK OF AMERICA CORPORATE CENTER

CESAR PELLI & ASSOCIATES INC.

1992

CLIENT / CLIENTE / OPDRACHTGEVER: NATIONSBANK CORPORATION, CHARTER PROPIERTIES & LINCOLN PROPERTY CO.

TOTAL AREA / SUPERFICIE / TOTALE OPPERVLAKTE: 126.000 m²

FLOORS / PIANI / VERDIEPINGEN - HEIGHT / ALTEZZA / HOOGTE: 60 fl / 265,5 m

Known as NationsBank, this building, which houses the central offices of the bank, is found in the geographical, historical and economic center of Charlotte. Its construction responded to both the economic profitability of the promoter and the possibility of culturally and economically revitalizing the city center, forming part of the public complex. Two garden squares and the Founders Hall (a civic and shopping center) are found in the base of the tower. Its silhouette, which is characterized by the breeching towards the interior in ascending direction of the curved façades, is a landmark in the cityscape.

Noto con il nome di Nations-Bank, questo edificio che ospita il quartier generale di questa banca si trova nel centro geografico, storico ed economico di Charlotte. Il motivo di questo progetto fu sia la redditività economica per l'imprenditore che la possibilità di rivitalizzare culturalmente ed economicamente il centro della città, come parte del complesso pubblico. Alla base della torre si trovano due piazze con giardini ed il Founders Hall, un centrocommerciale e civico. Il suo profilo particolare è caratterizzato dalla rientranza, in senso ascendente, delle facciate ricurve.È un punto di riferimento nel panorama della città.

Dit gebouw staat bekend als NationsBank, waarin de hoofdkantoren van de bank zijn ondergebracht. Het bevindt zich in het geografische, historische en economische centrum van Charlotte. De bouw beantwoordde zowel aan het economische potentieel van de opdrachtgever als aan de mogelijkheid om het stadscentrum cultureel en economisch te revitaliseren. Het maakt deel uit van een openbaar complex. Aan de voet van de toren liggen twee parken en de Founders Hall (een winkel- en gemeentelijk centrum). Het silhouet wordt gekenmerkt door de geleidelijk naar binnen lopende bovenkant en geldt als herkenningspunt in het stedelijke landschap.

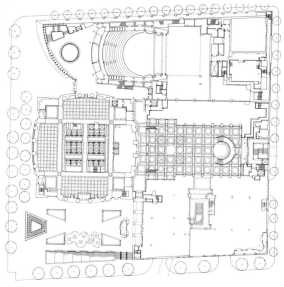

Above, one of the accesses to the tower next to the waterfall which opens out on the squares. The base is cased in dark granite with marble columns at the entrances.

In alto, uno degli ingressi della torre accanto alla cascatache si apre verso la piazza. La base è avvolta da granito scuro con colonne di marmo agli ingressi.

Boven: een van de ingangen tot de toren aan de watercascade die op de pleinen uitkomt. De basis is gehuld in donker graniet, met marmeren zuilen bij de ingangen.

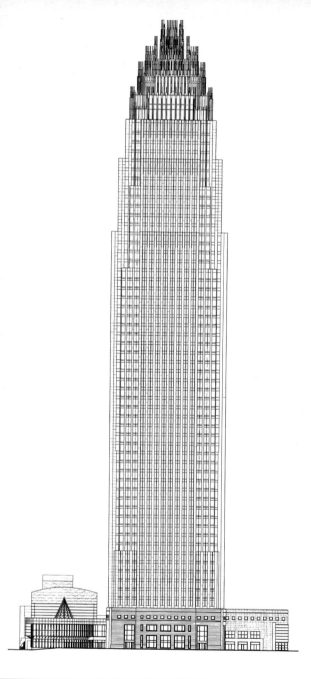

The composition of the façades
is based on horizontal and
vertical bands where granite
predominates over the windows.

*La struttura delle facciate è
costituita da fasce orizzontali
e verticali, il granito prevale
nelle finestre.*

De opbouw van de façaden is
gebaseerd op horizontale en
verticale stroken, waarbij het
graniet meer op de voorgrond
treedt dan de vensters.

Above, view of the main lobby from which the elevator lobbies open out, also shown in detail on the left.

In alto, veduta dell'atrio principale da cui emergono gli atrii degli ascensori, anche a sinistra.

Boven: blik op de voornaamste toegangshal die uitkomt op ruimten met de liften, links in groter detail te zien.

BIONIC TOWER

CERVERA-PIOZ & CELAYA

CLIENT / CLIENTE / OPDRACHTGEVER: THE CHINESE GOVERNMENT	**1992**
TOTAL AREA / SUPERFICIE / TOTALE OPPERVLAKTE: 275.000.000 m²	
FLOORS / PIANI / VERDIEPINGEN - HEIGHT / ALTEZZA / HOOGTE: 300 fl / 1.230 m	

Based on the development of Bionic Architecture, a science which unites Architecture with Engineering and Biology, proposes the use of a highly resistant reinforced concrete microstructure capable of supporting 2,000 Kg/cm² (currently 250 Kg/cm2 is in use), a floating foundation (which maintains the weight of the building isolated from contact with the earth by means of plastic fluids) and a structure which imitates the internal formation of trees, with multiple vertical capillary vessels which complete a building with a stylized cereal shape whose elliptical floors have an area of 223,450 m² (45 soccer pitches).

L'edificio, che si basa sugli ultimi progressi dell'Architettura Bionica, una scienza che fonde l'architettura, l'ingegneria e la biologia, prevede l'uso di un tipo di cemento armato microstrutturato ad alta resistenza, in grado di sostenere un peso di 2.000 Kg/cm² (attualmente si usa il cemento di 250 Kg / cm²), fondamenta fluttuanti (che impediscono il contatto diretto del peso dell'edificio con il terreno grazie a fluidi plastici) e ad una struttura simile a quella interna degli alberi, con numerosi vasi capillari verticali che gli danno la forma di spiga stilizzata; l'estensione delle piante dell'edificio a forma ellittica ricoprono fino a 223.450 m² (che corrispondono a quarantacinque campi di calcio).

Gebaseerd op de bionische architectuur, die biologie en bouwkunst verenigt. Hiertoe werd de toepassing voorgesteld van versterkt gewapend beton met een microstructuur dat een draagkracht van 2000 kg/ cm² bezit (tegenwoordig gebruikt men 250 kg/cm²), een drijvende basis (die het gewicht van het gebouw niet in contact laat komen met de aarde door middel van plastic vloeistoffen) en een structuur die het innerlijk van bomen imiteert, met vele verticale 'haarvaten' die resulteren in een gebouw met gestileerde vorm van een korenaar. De elliptische verdiepingen bieden een totale oppervlakte van 223.450 m² (dit komt overeen met 45 voetbalvelden).

Typical section of the Bionic city, commercial, cultural and leisure uses in the interior, offices and residences in the exterior. Below, the floor structural concept.

Sezione-tipo della città bionica che prevede attività commerciali, culturali e ricreative al suo interno, uffici e una residenza all'esterno. In basso: il progetto della struttura della pianta.

Typische doorsnede van de bionische stad. Het midden is bestemd voor commerciële, culturele en vrijetijdsdoeleinden, terwijl de buitenrand woningen en kantoren herbergt. Onder: concept van de bouwstructuur.

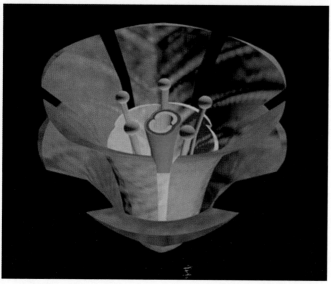

Section of a tree showing the micro-fragmented structure which gives rigidity
to the conducts which transport fluids.

Sezione di un albero che mostra la struttura microframmentata che conferisce rigidità ai condotti che trasportano i fluidi.

Doorsnee van een boom, die de microfragmentarische structuur toont die de vaten, waar de sappen door stromen, stevigheid verleent.

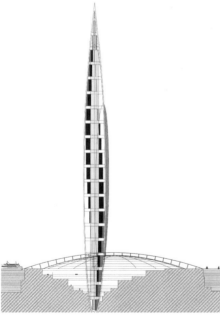

Figurative elevation locating the building in Hong Kong and section showing the heliocoidal distribution of levels and anchorage of the tower.

Prospetto simulato che raffigura l'edificio ad Hong Kong e una sezione che mostra la disposizione elicoidale dei livelli e l'ancoraggio della torre.

Gesimuleerd uitzicht op het gebouw in Hongkong en schets met de weergave van de schroefvormige verdeling van de niveaus en de verankering van de toren met de bodem.

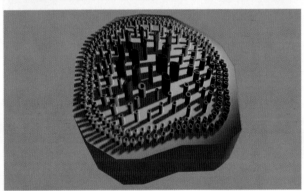

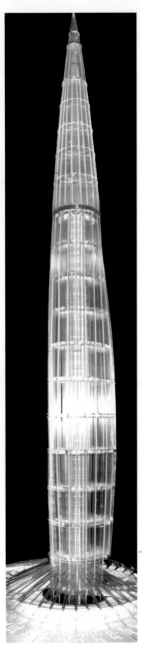

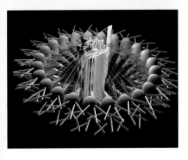

Structural and mock-up
representations of the
completed building.

*Raffigurazione strutturale e
plastico dell'edificio ultimato.*

Afbeeldingen van de
structuren en het model van
het voltooide gebouw.

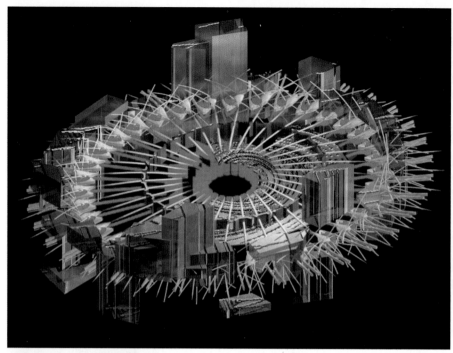

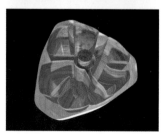

Representation of the fractal layout
of the vertical quarters and structural
schemes.

*Raffigurazione della distribuzione
frattale dei quartieri verticali
e gli schemi strutturali.*

Doorsneden van de fractalvormige
vlakverdeling van de verticale
ruimten en structuurschema's.

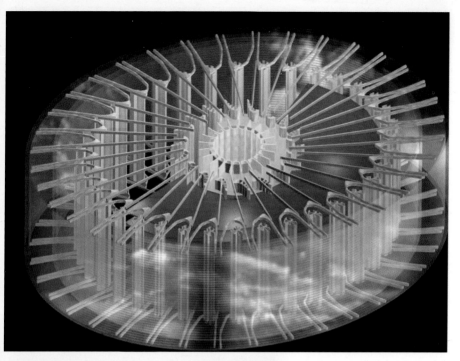

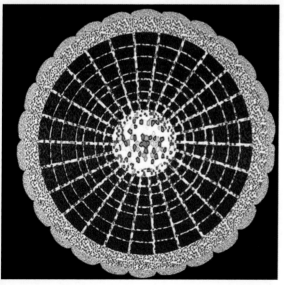

Sketch of the "multi-radial flotation system" earthquake resistant foundations.

Schema della struttura delle fondamenta resistente ai terremoti chiamata "sistema di flottazione multiradiale".

Schets van het aardbevingbestendige fundament, het 'multiradiale drijfsysteem'.

BNI CITY

ZEIDNER GRINNELL PARTNERSHIP

1996

CLIENT / CLIENTE / OPDRACHTGEVER: PT LYMAN INVESTINDO
TOTAL AREA / SUPERFICIE / TOTALE OPPERVLAKTE: 522.000 m²
FLOORS / PIANI / VERDIEPINGEN - HEIGHT / ALTEZZA / HOOGTE: 46 fl / 250 m

The firm of architects conceived the general plan of the project for this mixed use superblock, situated in a lot of 15 hectares in the center of Jakarta and later developed the 46 floor office tower, currently the highest in Indonesia. With its characteristic deck topped with a mast and its volumetry of light granite and the blue reflective curtain wall, this building is the most significant landmark of the Jakarta skyline. The regular shape of the plan, which introduces the solid façade treatment, complements the design of the coronation of the building.

Gli autori idearono le linee generali di questo immenso centro destinato a vari usi e costruito su quindici ettari nel centro di Jacarta, ed in seguito realizzarono la torre di 46 piani destinata ad ospitare uffici e che attualmente è la più alta del paese. Con il suo peculiare tetto, sormontato da un'asta, con la struttura di granito chiaro ed il muro-tenda riflettente color celeste, questo edificio è un elemento di fondamentale importanza nel panorama di Jacarta. La forma regolare della base, sulla quale inserisce la lavorazione della massiccia facciata, completa il disegno del coronamento dell'edificio.

Dit superblok werd door de architecten ontworpen als multifunctioneel gebouw, gelegen op een vijftien hectare groot terrein in het centrum van Jakarta. Vervolgens ontstond de kantoorkolos met 46 verdiepingen, tot op heden de hoogste van Indonesië.
Met zijn karakteristieke top met hoge mast, de buitenkant van licht graniet en de blauwe reflecterende wand vormt het gebouw het belangrijkste oriënteringspunt in de skyline van Jakarta. De regelmatige vorm van het ontwerp en de massieve buitenkant van het gebouw worden gecompleteerd door de 'kroon' op de top.

The volumetry of the building is divided into three zones; a stone base, a square tower which combines stone with glass, and a glass-covered coronation.

La struttura dell'edificio è divisa in tre blocchi; una base di pietra, una torre quadrata nella quale la pietra è combinata con il vetro ed il coronamento di vetro.

Het volume van het gebouw is opgedeeld in drie delen: een basis van steen, een vierkante toren waarin steen wordt gecombineerd met glas en een bovenkant van glas.

The use of materials and the design of the building suggest that as it gains height, the construction evolves towards lightness and freedom of form.

L'impiego dei materiali ed la linea dell'edificio suggeriscono che quanto più si eleva in altezza, tanto più la costruzione evolve verso una forma leggera e libera.

Het gebruik van materialen en het ontwerp van het gebouw wekken de indruk dat de constructie naar boven toe steeds lichter en losser van vorm wordt.

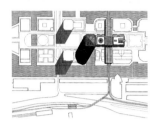

CANARY WHARF

CESAR PELLI & ASSOCIATES INC.

CLIENT / CLIENTE / OPDRACHTGEVER: OLIMPIA & YORK

1991

TOTAL AREA / SUPERFICIE / TOTALE OPPERVLAKTE: 167.200 m²

FLOORS / PIANI / VERDIEPINGEN - HEIGHT / ALTEZZA / HOOGTE: 48 fl / 236,2 m

Planned within the re-conversion of the Thames docks. The development of the project also includes the Retail and Assembly building and the light railway station; both buildings are connected by an avenue, and the station receives an average of 60,000 travelers a day. The building, technologically designed for the 21st Century, takes the shape of a great square prism with breeched corners – they give slenderness and emphasize the height – crowned by a pyramid. The surfaces of the exterior walls are covered in stainless steel, reflecting and adopting the coloring and changes in the London sky.

Progettato nell'ambito dell'operazione di ristrutturazione delle sponde del Tamigi. Il progetto comprende, inoltre, l'edificio Retail and Assembly e la stazione del treno rapido; entrambi gli edifici sono collegati da un viale ed in questa stazione transitano una media di 60.000 viaggiatori al giorno. L'edificio, che da un punto di vista tecnologico è perfettamente adeguato al xxi secolo, ha la forma di un grande prisma quadrato con gli angoli rientrati –che gli conferiscono slancio e ne accentuano l'altezza sormontato da una piramide. Le superfici esterne sono ricoperte di acciaio inossidabile, che riflette e assume i colori ed i cambiamenti del cielo londinese.

Dit gebouw maakte onderdeel uit van de reconstructie van de kade aan de Theems. Het ontwerp omvat ook het Retail and Assembly-gebouw en een station; beide gebouwen worden verbonden door een brede straat; het station verwerkt dagelijks gemiddeld 60.000 reizigers. Het gebouw is technisch uitgerust voor de 21e eeuw en heeft de vorm van een groot vierkant prisma met terugwijkende hoeken – deze verlenen rankheid en benadrukken de hoogte – en een piramide als bekroning. De vlakken van de buitenmuren zijn bedekt door roestvrij staal, die het kleurenspel van de Londense hemel overnemen en reflecteren.

The building has been designed as a strict reticle of gaps and solids, crowned with a dark pyramid deck.

L'edificio è stato ideato come un fitto reticolato di pieni e vuoti, sormontato da una copertura piramidale scura.

Het gebouw is ontworpen als een strak patroon van massa en leegte, gekroond door een donkere piramide.

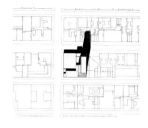

CARNEGIE HALL TOWER

CESAR PELLI & ASSOCIATES INC.

	1991
CLIENT / CLIENTE / OPDRACHTGEVER: ROCKROSE DEVELOPMENT CORPORATION	
TOTAL AREA / SUPERFICIE / TOTALE OPPERVLAKTE: 49.000 m²	
FLOORS / PIANI / VERDIEPINGEN - HEIGHT / ALTEZZA / HOOGTE: 60 fl / 230,7 m	

This slender tower is a reference point in Manhattan as it forms part of the historic Music Hall group of buildings, to which part of its surface is incorporated as an annex. It rises in a narrow lot between the Carnegie Hall building and the Russian Tea Salon. The base follows the line and height of the Music Hall cornice and above it rises the tower, only 15 meters wide, withdrawn from the façade. This works by means of two interwoven pieces of wrought iron integrating into the walls the wind resistance elements. The final design is in harmony with its surroundings.

Questa slanciata torre costituisce un punto di riferimento a Manhattan, dal momento che fa parte dello storico complesso di edifici del Music Hall, al quale annette una parte della superficie. Si innalza su un angusto terreno, tra l'edificio del Carnegie Hall e la Sala da Tè Russa. La pianta si adatta alla linea ed all'altezza del Carnegie Hall, al di sopra si erge la torre, larga solamente quindici metri, rientrata rispetto alla facciata e costituita da due solette incrociate che annettono alle pareti della facciata le componenti del meccanismo di resistenza al vento. Venne progettato in armonia con l'ambiente.

Deze slanke toren is een van de oriënteringspunten op Manhattan en vormt een onderdeel van het historische Music Hall-complex; een deel van de oppervlakte is in dit complex opgenomen. Het bouwwerk bevindt zich op een smal terrein tussen de Carnegie Hall en het Russische theehuis. De voet van het gebouw volgt de lijn en de hoogte van de deklijst van de Music Hall, daarboven verheft zich de toren, met een naar achteren geplaatste façade die slechts vijftien meter breed is. Twee verstrengelde stukken wapeningsstaal in de muren maken het gebouw windbestendig. Het uiteindelijke resultaat harmonieert met zijn omgeving.

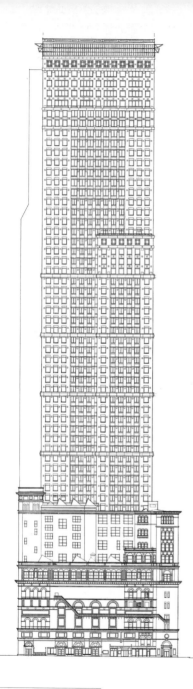

The design of the tower was supervised by the council because the Music Hall group of buildings forms part of the city's architectural heritage.

Dal momento che il complesso di edifici del Music Hall fa parte del patrimonio architettonico della città, il progetto della torre venne supervisionato dal Comune.

Er werd door de gemeenteraad toegezien op het ontwerp van de toren, omdat het Music Hall-complex deel uitmaakt van het architectonisch erfgoed van de stad.

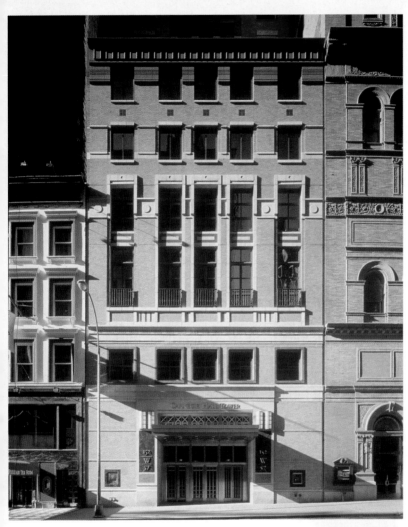

Above, main entrance to the tower. The base, six meters tall, is conditioned by the cornice of the Music Hall building situated on its left.

In alto, ingresso principale della torre. La base, alta sei metri, è limitata dalla cornice dell'edificio del Music Hall situato alla sua sinistra.

Boven: hoofdingang. De zes meter hoge toegangshal is gedefinieerd door de deklijst van de Music Hall aan de linkerkant.

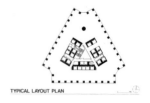

TYPICAL LAYOUT PLAN

CENTRAL PLAZA

DENNIS LAU & N.G. CHUN MAN
ARCHITECTS & ENGINEERS (H.K) LTD

CLIENT / CLIENTE / OPDRACHTGEVER: SUN HUNG KAI REAL ESTATE AGENCY. LTD. SINO LAND CO. LTD. & RYODEN (HOLDINGS) LTD.

1992

TOTAL AREA / SUPERFICIE / TOTALE OPPERVLAKTE: 130.140 m²

FLOORS / PIANI / VERDIEPINGEN - HEIGHT / ALTEZZA / HOOGTE: 78 fl / 375 m

This building is still currently the tallest in Hong Kong. When it was finished, it was the tallest of the skyscrapers of reinforced concrete structure and the tallest in the world outside the United States. Elegantly designed in the form of a triangular prism, the tower has a pyramidal deck crowned with a 60 meter mast, illuminated at night with golden neon on the glass pyramid of its base, which shines with different colors. The building gives a new dimension to the concept of high level offices, developing high quality connection areas, a swimming pool, a luxurious club and social and leisure facilities.

Questo edificio, attualmente il più alto di Hong Kong, quando venne ultimato era il più alto dei grattacieli costruiti in cemento armato ed il più alto del mondo, eccezion fatta per gli Stati Uniti. La torre, elegantemente disegnata con la forma di un prisma triangolare, presenta un tetto a forma di piramide sormontato da un'asta alta 60 metri, che di notte viene illuminata, dalla base della piramide di vetro, con una luce al neon dorata che risplende con diversi colori. L'edificio inaugura un nuovo concetto d'ufficio di alto livello, con la creazione di aree sociali di grande classe; come ad esempio una piscina un circolo per i soci ed una offerta di attività sociali e ricreative.

Dit gebouw is nog altijd het hoogste van Hongkong. Toen het werd voltooid was het de hoogste wolkenkrabber van gewapend beton en de hoogste ter wereld buiten de Verenigde Staten. De toren is elegant ontworpen in de vorm van een driehoekig prisma, een piramidevormig dak bekroond met een zestig meter hoge mast. 's Nachts wordt deze in goudkleurig neon gehuld vanaf de glazen piramide aan de voet van de mast, die zelf verschillende kleurschakeringen aanneemt. Het gebouw geeft een nieuwe dimensie aan het concept van hoge kantoorgebouwen, uitgerust met uitstekende verbindingen, een zwembad, een luxe club en sociale en vrijetijdsvoorzieningen.

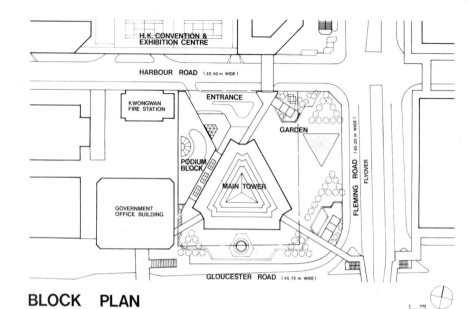

H.K. CONVENTION &
EXHIBITION CENTRE

HARBOUR ROAD (22.50 m WIDE)

KWONGWAN
FIRE STATION

ENTRANCE

GARDEN

FLEMING ROAD (45.20 m WIDE)

FLYOVER

PODIUM
BLOCK

MAIN TOWER

GOVERNMENT
OFFICE BUILDING

GLOUCESTER ROAD (45.72 m WIDE)

BLOCK PLAN

0   10M

An equilateral triangle, elegantly breeched at its vertexes, forms the plan of the building, culminating with a gradually withdrawn deck.

La struttura dell'edificio è costituita da un triangolo equilatero elegantemente rientrato ai vertici, che culmina con un tetto anch'esso leggermente rientrato.

Een gelijkzijdige driehoek, elegant voorzien van naar binnen gekeerde hoeken, vormt het basisontwerp van het gebouw, gekroond door een geleidelijk terugwijkende top.

Its size and purity of form confer on the building an ample capacity for domination of the built-up surroundings.

La grandezza e la purezza delle forme dell'edificio determinano un impatto notevole nell'ambito del panorama urbanistico.

Het gebouw domineert de bebouwde omgeving sterk door de omvang en de zuivere vormgeving.

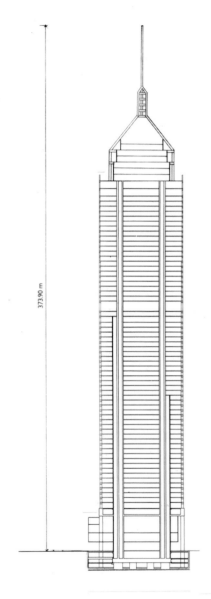

373.90 m

0   10M

The curtain wall of the façade of the skyscraper combines white, black and golden tonalities of reflective glass.

La parete a cortina della facciata del grattacielo è realizzata con vetro riflettente dai toni bianchi, neri e dorati.

Het reflecterende glas van de façade van de wolkenkrabber combineert witte, zwarte en goudkleurige tinten.

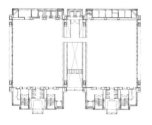

CENTURY TOWER
FOSTER & PARTNERS
1991

CLIENT / CLIENTE / OPDRACHTGEVER: OBUNSHA CORPORATION

TOTAL AREA / SUPERFICIE / TOTALE OPPERVLAKTE: 26.590 m²

FLOORS / PIANI / VERDIEPINGEN - HEIGHT / ALTEZZA / HOOGTE: 21 fl / 104 m

This office building continues developing the ideas of the Hong Kong and Shanghai Bank. It responds to the necessities of the client, who wants the greatest economic performance from the building, and the architect's necessities with a quality design. Located in the city center, the volume of the building is divided into two bodies united by the lower floor, so that by having narrower spaces, a greater quantity of light penetrates. If, in addition, the structural and communications core is moved towards the façades, the plan is freed from obstacles, which allows any kind of layout.

Questo edificio di uffici prosegue lo sviluppo delle idee della Hong Kong & Shanghai Bank. Il progetto soddisfa i bisogni del cliente che cerca di ricavare il maggior profitto economico dall'edificio– e dell'architetto, con un design notevole. Situato al centro della città, il volume dell'edificio è diviso in due corpi uniti al pianterreno; le intercapedini (passaggi) più strette lasciano penetrare una maggior quantità di luce; inoltre il nucleo strutturale e di comunicazione, spostato verso le facciate laterali, lascia libera la superficie da ostacoli e permette qualsiasi tipo di distribuzione.

Dit kantoorgebouw vormt de belichaming van de ideeën van de Hongkong & Shanghai Bank. Het beantwoordt aan de eisen van de opdrachtgever om het gebouw een zo groot mogelijk economisch nut te verlenen en de wens van de architect om een ontwerp van hoge kwaliteit te presenteren. Het bouwwerk staat in het stadscentrum; het volume wordt opgedeeld in twee delen, die door de begane grond worden verenigd. De breedte van de verdiepingen werd smal gehouden, zodat er meer licht kan binnenvallen. Bovendien werd de structurele kern met de liften aan de zijkant van het gebouw geplaatst, zodat er een oppervlak zonder obstakels ontstond die alle mogelijke ruimtelijke indelingen toelaat.

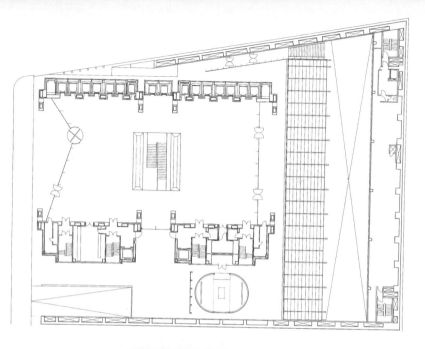

Above, the lower floor of the building where the glass-covered lobby is found, in the central area a vacuum is generated because the building is divided into two parallel bodies. This vacuum is shown in the picture on the right.

In alto, il pianterreno dell'edificio, dove si trova l'atrio di vetro; essendo l'edificio diviso in due corpi paralleli, tra di essi rimane uno spazio vuoto (foto a destra).

Boven: de begane grond van het gebouw, waar zich de met glas overdekte lobby bevindt. Doordat de constructie uit twee parallel aangelegde delen bestaat, ontstond in het midden een grote open ruimte. Deze is ook op de rechterbladzijde te zien.

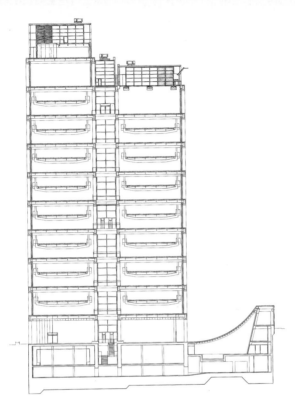

In addition to the offices, the building is equipped with several rest areas, a gymnasium, a swimming pool, a restaurant and a museum. The upper picture shows the swimming pool. The sloping roof, which filters light, and the vegetation create a special atmosphere. It is a place to relax.

Oltre agli uffici, l'edificio dispone di varie dotazioni, come ad esempio aree di riposo, una palestra, una piscina, un ristorante ed un museo. La foto mostra la piscina; il soffitto spiovente, che lascia trapelare la luce, e la vegetazione creano un'atmosfera particolare che lo rende un luogo estremamente adatto al relax.

Naast kantoren is het gebouw uitgerust met verscheidene ontspanningsgebieden, een fitnessruimte, een zwembad, een restaurant en een museum. Bovenstaande foto toont het zwembad. Het aflopende dak dat het licht filtert en de vegetatie creëren een bijzondere sfeer. Het is een ruimte om te relaxen.

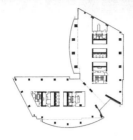

CITYBANK PLAZA

ROCCO SEN KEE YIM

CLIENT / CLIENTE / OPDRACHTGEVER: CITYBANK

1992

FLOORS / PIANI / VERDIEPINGEN - HEIGHT / ALTEZZA / HOOGTE: 40 - 50 fl / 120 - 150 m

Located in the center of Hong Kong, it is situated next to the Bank of China, by I.M. Pei, one of the city's most emblematic constructions. Far from competing with it, the new building seeks differentiation. Fruit of the intersection of two towers of different heights that combine straight and curved façades, contrasting with the straight volume of the Bank of China. The towers go straight into the ground, without any base body, and the curtain wall of the façades withdraws to leave the structure bare and provoke the entrance to the building, letting it flow towards the garden and the square which accompany the building.

Situato nel cuore di Hong Kong, si trova accanto alla Banca della Cina, dell'I.M. Pei, uno degli edifici più rappresentativi della città, con il quale non vuole competere, ma differenziarsi. L'edificio è costituito dall'intersezione di due torri di differente altezza dalle facciate combinate, sia rette che curve, contrastano con la forma retta della Banca della Cina. Le torri, prive di basamento, poggiano direttamente sul terreno; la parete a cortina delle facciate indietreggia per lasciare la struttura libera e permettere l'accesso all'edificio, in modo che la circolazione possa fluire verso il giardino e la piazza che fanno parte del complesso.

De Citybank Plaza ligt in het stadscentrum naast een van de meest emblematische gebouwen van de stad, de Bank of China van architect I.M. Pei. Het nieuwe gebouw probeert deze niet de loef af te steken, maar er zich van te onderscheiden. Twee torens van verschillende hoogte combineren rechte en gebogen façaden, in contrast met de rechte vorm van de Bank of China. Zonder enige basisstructuur lopen de torens direct de grond in. De buitenkant is aan de onderkant naar achteren geplaatst en vormt de ingang van het gebouw, die uitkomt op een parkeerplaats en een plein.

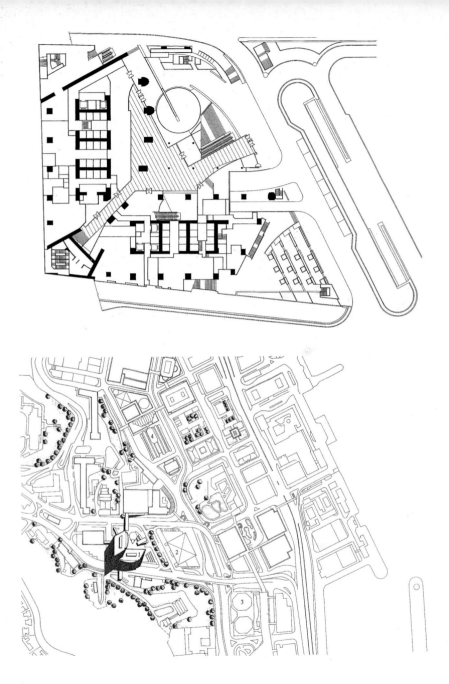

Interior and exterior views of the pedestrian entrance
from the street to the lobby, in the area of intersection
of the two towers.

*Veduta interna ed esterna dell'ingresso pedonale dalla
strada all'atrio, nel punto di intersezione delle due torri.*

Binnen- en buitenaanzicht van de voetgangersingang van
de straat naar de lobby, op de plaats waar beide torens
elkaar ontmoeten.

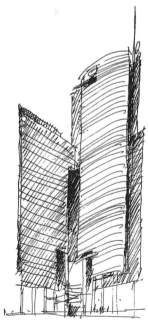

Interior escalators between the entrance at street
level and the raised square which is developed in
the lobby.

*Veduta delle scale e dei corridoi di distribuzione
dei piani di uffici dell'edificio.*

Roltrappen verbinden binnen de ingang aan de
straat met de hoger gelegen toegangshal.

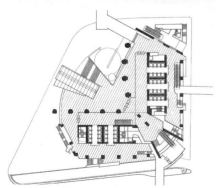

Picture of the view pedestrians have when entering the lobby and looking upwards.

Veduta che si può ammirare entrando nell'atrio e rivolgendo lo sguardo verso l'alto.

Beeld van het uitzicht dat voetgangers hebben als ze de lobby betreden en omhoogkijken.

Views of the stairs and distribution hallways of the building's office floors.

Veduta delle scale e dei corridoi di distribuzione dei piani di uffici dell'edificio.

Blik op het trappenhuis en de gang op de verdiepingen met kantoren.

COMMERZBANK HQTRS.

FOSTER & PARTNERS

1997

CLIENT / CLIENTE / OPDRACHTGEVER: COMMERZBANK	
TOTAL AREA / SUPERFICIE / TOTALE OPPERVLAKTE: 100.000 m²	
FLOORS / PIANI / VERDIEPINGEN - HEIGHT / ALTEZZA / HOOGTE: 53 fl / 259 m	

This is the first green skyscraper in Europe. A building that tries to be respectful with the city and the environment. The central concept is based on the natural system of illumination and ventilation instead of the usual mechanical systems in office buildings. Each office allows its user to adjust the environmental conditions, which means a reduction in the energy consumption of the building. The triangular plan allows a central space which illuminates and ventilates the grouped floors, interspersing gardens between them. In addition to the psychological effect created by looking at them, they function as rest areas.

Si tratta del primo grattacielo "verde" d'Europa, un edificio che rispetta la città e l'ambiente. L'idea principale su cui si basa è un sistema naturale di illuminazione e di ventilazione che sostituisce l'abituale sistema artificiale degli edifici. In questo modo ogni ufficio permette, a chi ne fa uso, di regolarne le condizioni ambientali, e ciò comporta inoltre la riduzione del consumo di energia dell'edificio. La struttura triangolare lascia al centro uno spazio che illumina e arieggia i piani. Questi sono sistemati in gruppi, e tra di essi si trovano dei giardini che producono un gradevole effetto alla vista e che vengono utilizzati come area di riposo.

Dit is de eerste zogenaamde 'groene' wolkenkrabber van Europa, die zowel de stad en ook het milieu met respect bejegent. De kerngedachte bestaat eruit natuurlijk daglicht en ventilatie te gebruiken in plaats van de gebruikelijke mechanische systemen in kantoorgebouwen. In elk kantoor kunnen de gebruikers de klimatologische omstandigheden aanpassen, hetgeen resulteert in een reductie van het energieverbruik van het gebouw. Het driehoekige ontwerp biedt een open binnenruimte die de gegroepeerde verdiepingen verlicht en ventileert. Daartussen zijn tuinen aangelegd, die niet alleen een positief psychologisch effect geven, maar ook dienen als ontspanningsgebieden.

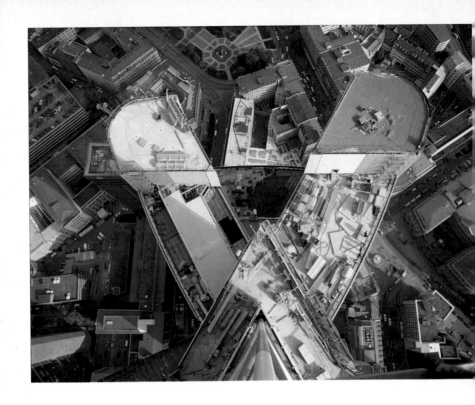

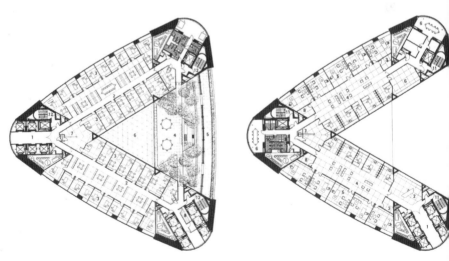

Above, view of the building from the opposite river bank. The interspersed gardens break the continuity of the façade, offering a modern image of transparency and luminosity.

In alto, veduta dell'edificio dall'altra sponda dal fiume. I giardini interrompono la continuità della facciata ed offrono un'immagine moderna di trasparenza e luminosità

Boven: uitzicht op het gebouw vanaf de andere oever. De tussenliggende groenvoorzieningen breken de continuïteit van de façade en bieden een modern uiterlijk van transparantie en lichtheid.

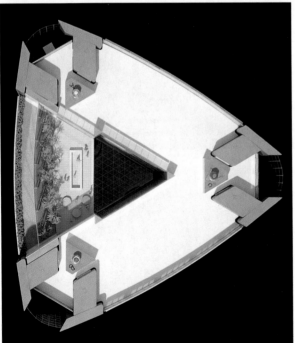

Above, different mock-ups of the phases of the project. On the left, mock-up of the plan which is clearly organized with the structural communications cores in the vertexes of the triangle.

In alto, alcuni plastici delle varie fasi del progetto. A sinistra, modellino della struttura costituita dai nuclei delle comunicazionistrutturali ai vertici del triangolo.

Boven: verschillende modellen van afzonderlijke bouwfasen. Links: model van het ontwerp met een duidelijke indeling; de liften zijn ondergebracht in de hoeken van de driehoek.

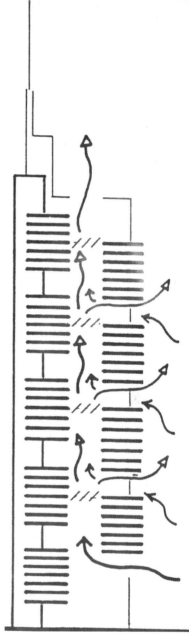

Details of the façade and diagram of the building, where the gardens can be seen interspersed between the floors, and the natural ventilation.

Particolari della facciata e schema dell'edificionei quali è possibile osservare i giardini situati tra i piani e il sistema di ventilazione naturale.

Details van de façade en een schema van het gebouw, waarin de tussengeplaatste tuinen en de natuurlijke ventilatie worden weergegeven.

CONDÉ NAST

FOX & FOWLE

1999

CLIENT / CLIENTE / OPDRACHTGEVER: THE DURST ORGANIZATION	
TOTAL AREA / SUPERFICIE / TOTALE OPPERVLAKTE: 154.218 m²	
FLOORS / PIANI / VERDIEPINGEN - HEIGHT / ALTEZZA / HOOGTE: 48 fl / 247 m	

Located on a corner of Times Square, at the junction between Broadway and 42nd Street and Bryant Park, rises the first building born of a public and private consortium which promotes the development of the traditional center of Manhattan. Its image starts out for tow differentiated readings reflected in the facades. The north and west assume the boisterous character of Times Square, made of metal and glass. The south and east reflect a personality made up of the texture and scale of the treatment of the most appropriate masonry for the midtown Manhattan urban context and the refined style of Bryant Park. The building is born with the vocation to be a new standard of the Manhattan of the 21st Century, capturing the essence of the commercial city and proposing a contemporary corporate image.

Situato in un angolo di Times Square, all'incrocio di Brodway con la 42esima strada e il "Bryant Park", si eleva il primo edificio nato da un consorzio pubblico e privato che promuove lo sviluppo del tradizionale centro di Manhattan. La sua immagine parte da due letture differenziate, riflesse nella facciata. Quella nord e quella ovest assumono il carattere vivace di Times Square e sono di metallo e cristallo. Quella sud e quella est riflettono una personalità composita attraverso la trama e le proporzioni nel trattamento del rivestimento in pietra più appropriata al contesto urbano del "midtown" di Manhattan e al raffinato stile del "Bryant Park". L'edificio nasce con la vocazione di essere un nuovo stendardo della Manhattan del XXI secolo, catturando l'essenza della città commerciale e proponendo un'immagine corporativa contemporanea.

Op de kruising tussen Broadway en 42nd Street en Bryant Park, gelegen op een hoek van Times Square, verheft zich het eerste gebouw van een publiek en particulier consortium dat de ontwikkeling van het traditionele centrum van Manhattan promoot. De façaden wekken twee uiteenlopende indrukken. De noord- en westkant van staal en glas dragen het levendige karakter van Times Square. De zuid- en oostkant van het gebouw weerspiegelen door textuur en schaal de stedelijke omgeving van Midtown Manhattan en de elegantie van Bryant Park. Het gebouw ontstond met de bedoeling een nieuwe standaard te worden voor het Manhattan van de 21e eeuw, welke de essentie van een zakenstad behelst en een beeld geeft van een moderne onderneming.

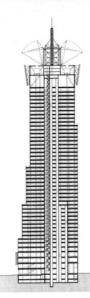

The north-west corner of the building, which houses the Nasdaq headquarters, is joined with an eleven-storey high semi-cylinder whose exterior panel emits current stock market quotations for passers-by to observe.

L'angolo nordest dell'edificio si chiude mediante un semicilindro di undici piani di altezza dove alberga la sede del Nasdaq, il cui rivestimento è uno schermo che raccoglie gli indici borsari in modo che i passanti possano essere informati degli ultimi movimenti.

De noordwestkant van het gebouw, waarin het hoofdkantoor van de Nasdaq is ondergebracht, versmelt met een halve cilinder van elf verdiepingen. Het buitenpaneel toont de voorbijgangers de actuele beurskoersen.

Environment-conscious architects planned a building with an integral energy concept, using recycled waste material in the construction process.

Gli architetti sensibili ai fattori medioambientali progettarono un edificio con un concetto energetico integrale e fin dal processo costruttivo furono riciclati materiali di scarto.

Milieubewuste architecten ontwierpen een gebouw met een integraal energieconcept, waarbij al tijdens de constructie gebruik werd gemaakt van gerecycled materiaal.

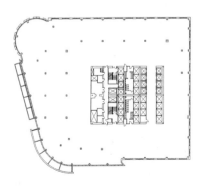

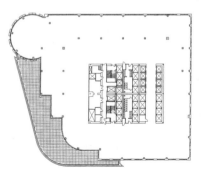

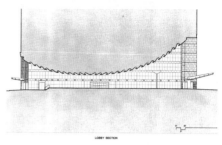

LOBBY SECTION

The multi-level concourse is a walkway that joins 42nd and 43rd street. It is covered by a double ceiling in the shape of an inverted parabola that heightens the feeling of depth of field, which is pierced by two elevator shafts.

Le hall, sur plusieurs hauteurs, joint les rues 42 et 43, il joue le rôle d'un passage. Il est recouvert d'un faux toit en parabole inversée, ce qui accentue la sensation de profondeur du parcours qui est coupé par deux batteries d'ascenseurs.

De hoge hal doet dienst als voetgangersverbinding tussen de 42nd en 43rd Street, overdekt door een dubbel plafond in de vorm van een omgekeerde parabool, dat de passage diepte verleent. Twee liftschachten kruisen het geheel.

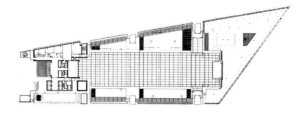

DEBIS HAUS

RENZO PIANO BUILDING WORKSHOP
+ CHRISTOPH KOHLBECKER

1999

CLIENT / CLIENTE / OPDRACHTGEVER: DAIMLER-CHRYSLER AG	
TOTAL AREA / SUPERFICIE / TOTALE OPPERVLAKTE: 45.100 m²	
FLOORS / PIANI / VERDIEPINGEN - HEIGHT / ALTEZZA / HOOGTE: 21 fl / 106 m	

This is the first skyscraper in Postdammer Platz, which has radically altered the city's skyline. This square, where a railway station was built in 1840, was the biggest in Berlin until the Second World War. Due to the heavy traffic flow, in 1920 a set of traffic lights was installed, the first in Europe. After being sectioned by the construction of a wall in 1961, it became an immense barren lot. After its fall, it was the object in 1992 of an urban planning competition which has returned the place to its condition of urban and social center. The Debis Haus complex is located in the lots which were occupied by the Daimler-Benz factory and comprises several office buildings which form a triangular base topped by a tower.

Questo è il primo grattacielo de la Postdamer Platz che ha alterato radicalmente lo skyline della città. Questa piazza, dove nel 1840 si costruì una stazione ferroviaria fu la più importante di Berlino fino alla seconda guerra mondiale. A causa dell'elevato flusso di traffico, nel 1920 si installò un semaforo, il primo d'Europa. Dopo la divisione per la costruzione nel 1961 del muro si trasformò in un'immensa area trascurata. Dopo la caduta del muro, fu oggetto nel 1992 di un piano urbanistico messo a concorso che ha restituito al sito la condizione di centro urbano e sociale. Il complesso della Debis Haus si colloca nei terreni che occupava la fabbrica Daimler-Benz e include vari edifici di uffici che formano una base triangolare rifinita con una torre.

Dit is de eerste wolkenkrabber aan de Potdamer Platz, die de skyline van de stad radicaal heeft veranderd. Op dit plein werd in 1840 een station aangelegd, dat tot aan de Tweede Wereldoorlog het grootste van Berlijn was. Door de enorme toename van het verkeer werd in 1920 een verkeerslicht geplaatst – de eerste van Europa. Na de opdeling van de stad door de bouw van de Muur in 1961 werd dit een braakliggend terrein. Na de val van de Muur werd anno 1992 een competitie voor stadsplanning uitgeschreven, die dit gebied weer tot een stedelijk en sociaal middelpunt maakte. Het Debis Haus-complex bevindt zich op het terrein van Daimler-Benz AG en bestaat uit verscheidene kantoorgebouwen die een driehoekige basis vormen waarop een toren rust.

148 | DEBIS HAUS

The materials chosen are ceramics, steel and glass. The tower dedicates equal attention to office space and functional aspects (elevators and stairwells), so the façade features stairwells and ventilation ducts.

I materiale scelti sono la ceramica, l'acciaio e il vetro. La torre combina gli spazi di uffici con quelli più funzionali (ascensori e scale) trattandoli con la stessa attenzione, così appaiono sulla facciata vani di scala e condotti di ventilazione.

Het gekozen materiaal bestaat uit keramiek, staal en glas. Er wordt evenveel aandacht besteed aan kantoorruimte als aan functionele aspecten (liften en trappenhuizen). De trappenhuizen en het ventilatiesysteem zijn zo van buiten af te zien.

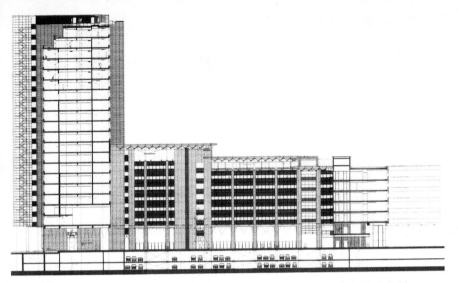

Debis Haus is included in a triangular block 163 metres in length that respects the even height of other historic buildings, except the tower that signals the entrance to the Tiergarten tunnel.

La Debis Haus comprende un isolato triangolare di 163 m. di lunghezza che mantiene l'altezza regolare degli edifici storici ad eccezione della torre che segna l'entrata del tunnel Tiergarten.

Het Debis Haus bevindt zich op een driehoekig terrein met een lengte van 163 meter en is qua hoogte aangepast aan de historische gebouwen in de omgeving, met uitzondering van de toren, die de tunnelingang naar de Tiergarten markeert.

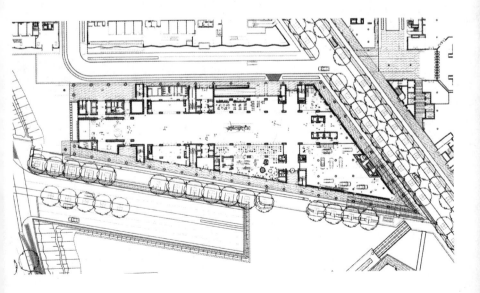

Incoming daylight is controlled by sophisticated filtering systems. The same happens with the building's heating control, which gives energy savings by automatically regulating the interior/exterior temperature and the angle of sunlight using glass panels.

Il controllo della luce solare si ottiene mediante sofisticati sistemi che la filtrano la stessa cosa succede con il controllo termico dell'edificio con il quale si ottiene un risparmio energetico mediante la regolazione automatica della temperatura interna/esterna e l'angolo di incidenza dei raggi solari mediante pannelli di vetro.

Het binnenvallende daglicht wordt geregeld door geavanceerde filtersystemen. Ditzelfde geldt voor de regulatie van de temperatuur. Er wordt aanzienlijk op de kosten van energieverbruik bespaard door de automatische afstemming van binnen- en buitentemperatuur en door verstelbare glaspanelen die de invalshoek van het zonlicht kunnen aanpassen.

There are magnificent views from the tower in the former Mitte district city centre of west Berlin and the Kurfürstendamm. Likewise, the new Potsdamer Platz looks radically different from the rest of the city and is injected with new life.

Dalla torre si può godere di magnifiche vedute dal vecchio centro della cittpà nel distretto Mitte fino alla zona ovest di Berlino e al suo Kurfürstendamm. A sua volta, dalla città la nuova Postdamer Platz ha cambiato radicalmente immagine e inizia una nuova vita.

De toren biedt een fantastisch uitzicht over het oude deel van de stad, de wijk 'Mitte' tot aan West-Berlijn met de Kurfürstendamm. Ook ziet de weer levendig gemaakte Potsdamer Platz er vanuit de rest van de stad nu totaal anders uit.

DEUTSCHE POST AG

MURPHY / JAHN INC. ARCHITECTS

CLIENT / CLIENTE/ OPDRACHTGEVER: DEUTSCHE POST

1999

FLOORS / PIANI / VERDIEPINGEN - HEIGHT / ALTEZZA / HOOGTE: 44 fl / 162 m

The building is a mixed-use complex of offices, catering area, bars, restaurants, bookstores, conference halls and multi-use halls. Together with the Deutsche Welle and Langer Eugen buildings, it makes up the strip of the city towards the Rheinauenpark. The platform of the tower completes the upper terrace of the park, connected with ramps and stairs towards the lower terraces near to the River Rhine. The oval-shaped plan, separated, is positioned in the direction of the Rhine, opening itself to the city, facilitating its views and minimizing the negative effects of the wind by means of its aerodynamic shape.

Questo edificio è un complesso adibito a vari usi,con uffici, servizi di ristorazione (bar, ristoranti), librerie, sale per conferenze e sale polivalenti. Costituisce, con gli edifici del Deutsche Welle ed il Langer Eugen, la zona della città limitrofa al Rheinauenpark. La piattaforma della torre è unita alla terrazza superiore del parco, collegata con rampe e scale alle terrazze inferiori vicine al fiume Reno. La costruzione, ovale e divisa,collocata in direzione del fiume Reno, si apre verso la città, della quale offre un bel panorama e neutralizza gli effetti negativi del vento grazie alla sua forma aerodinamica.

Een multifunctioneel gebouw met kantoren, bars en restaurants, boekwinkels, congreszalen en multifunctionele ruimten. Samen met de gebouwen van de Deutsche Welle en Langer Eugen geeft het vorm aan het stadsdeel bij het aangrenzende Rheinauenpark. De toren staat op het hoogste terras van het park en is door looppassages en trappen verbonden met de lager gelegen terrassen aan de Rijn. Het ovale ontwerp van het gebouw is gericht op de Rijn en is naar de stad toe geopend. Op deze wijze is een vrij uitzicht mogelijk en worden de negatieve effecten van de wind door de aërodynamische vorm geminimaliseerd.

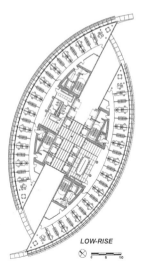

The project reflects on the tall building through its function, technology and the users' comfort.

Il progetto riflettel'edificio di grande altezza attraverso la funzionalità, la tecnologia ed il comfort di chi ne usufruisce.

Bij het ontwerp werden functie, technologie en gebruikersvriendelijkheid meegewogen.

LOW-RISE

HIGH-RISE

DEUTSCHE POST   Plan   DP/Drawings/HiRes/DP_PLAN_HR

DG BANK HQTRS.

KOHN PEDERSEN FOX ASSOCIATES PC (KPF)

CLIENT / CLIENTE / OPDRACHTGEVER: AGIMA	**1993**

TOTAL AREA / SUPERFICIE / TOTALE OPPERVLAKTE: 85.000 m²

FLOORS / PIANI / VERDIEPINGEN - HEIGHT / ALTEZZA / HOOGTE: 54 fl / 208 m

DG's program includes, in addition to its offices, shopping areas, residential areas, parking and public spaces. It is found in an important shopping avenue near the historical center. The building must create a relationship between these areas. This was the starting point for the architects, against the big two which would have difficulty creating a relationship with the city. The program is organized by levels which respond to volumes and heights, the central offices of the bank in the tower and the other uses in buildings. Also, the entrances and movement had to be separate because of the security measures that the bank required without losing the original idea of a nexus.

Il progetto del DG comprende, oltre agli uffici, anche zone commerciali, residenziali, un parcheggio ed uno spazio pubblico. Si trova in un'importante zona commerciale vicina al centro storico. Lo scopo era collegare queste aree. Il punto di partenza, contrari alla grande torre, che difficilmente si sarebbe potuta integrare nella città, era un progetto organizzato su diversi livelli corrispondenti ai volumi ed alle altezze, gli uffici centrali della banca sarebbero stati situati nella torre, mentre ed il resto negli edifici noltre, si sarebbero dovuti costruire separatamente gli ingressi e le zone di passaggio a causa dei motivi di sicurezza della banca, senza però sacrificare l'idea originale.

Het DG-gebouw herbergt naast de bankkantoren ook winkels, woningen, parkeerplaatsen en openbare ruimten. Het bevindt zich aan een belangrijke winkelstraat nabij het historische centrum. Het gebouw dient tussen deze gebieden een relatie tot stand te brengen. Aanvankelijk betwijfelden de architecten of hoogbouw deze relatie met de stad wel zou kunnen creëren. Het gebouw is samengesteld uit delen die elk een eigen hoogte en volume hebben. In de toren bevindt zich het hoofdkantoor van de bank, de overige delen worden voor andere doeleinden gebruikt. Ook moesten vanwege de vereiste veiligheidsmaatregelen van de bank de ingangen en doorgangen worden gescheiden, zonder daarbij het oorspronkelijke concept van samenhang te verliezen.

In Frankfurt, the tall towers stand out from the traditional city. They form part of a concentration of office buildings which exemplify the financial hegemony of the city. On the right, section of the tower through the façade. Technically, its double wall and triple-glazed windows system is the most advanced in the city. It means a saving on energy and responds to the restrictive government ruling on environmental concerns.

Francoforte. Le alte torri spiccano sul resto della città. Fanno parte dell'insieme di edifici di uffici che simboleggiano la supremazia finanziaria della città. A destra, sezione della torre dalla facciata. Da un punto di vista tecnico, il sistema del doppio muro e delle finestre dal triplo vetro è il più moderno della città. Comporta il risparmio di energia ed è conforme alla rigida normativa ambientale del governo.

In Frankfurt rijzen de torens hoog boven de traditionele stad uit. De concentratie van kantoorgebouwen benadrukt de betekenis van de stad als financieel centrum. Rechts: doorsnede van de buitenfaçade van de toren. De dubbele muur en de driedubbele beglazing zijn het meest geavanceerd van de stad. Het geeft energiebesparing en beantwoordt aan de strenge wettelijke milieueisen.

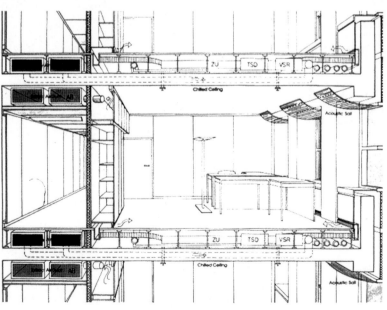

The cornice of the building is a crown, a symbol which identifies the complex from anywhere in the city.

La cimasa dell'edificio, una corona, un simbolo che rende visibile il complesso da qualsiasi punto della città.

De top van de toren is uitgerust met een kroon, die overal in de stad te herkennen is.

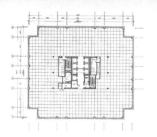
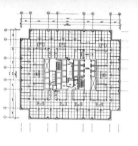

DONNELLEY BUILDING

RICARD BOFILL TALLER D'ARQUITECTURA

CLIENT / CLIENTE / OPDRACHTGEVER: THE PRIME GROUP & KEMPER INSURANCE COMPANY	**1992**

TOTAL AREA / SUPERFICIE / TOTALE OPPERVLAKTE: 110.000 m²

FLOORS / PIANI / VERDIEPINGEN - HEIGHT / ALTEZZA / HOOGTE: 50 fl / 247 m

In the project for this office tower, the possibility of a panoramic view over the city was desired, which means that glass is predominant in the façade. In the context of American skyscrapers, especially attractive in Chicago, thought was given to the need to reestablish a dialogue between the classicism of stone (white granite) and the high technology of glass. The façade presents a design of classical proportions with divisions on several levels, united among themselves by columns. The upper part, in the form of a pediment which stands out against the sky, is the distinctive sign of the building in the skyline of Chicago.

Questa torre di uffici cerca, con l'uso predominante del vetro per la facciata, la vista panoramica della città. Nel panorama dei grattacieli americani, particolarmente affascinante a Chicago, sorse l'esigenzadi ristabilire un dialogo tra il classicismo della pietra (il granito bianco) e l'alta tecnologia del vetro. La facciata mostra un disegno di proporzioni classiche e zone divise, a diversi livelli, collegate tra di loro da colonne. La parte superiore che, a mó di frontone, si staglia contro il cielo, distingue l'edificio nel panorama di Chicago

Voor het ontwerp voor deze kantoorkolos bestond de wens naar een panoramisch uitzicht over de stad. Om deze reden bestaat de façade hoofdzakelijk uit glas. In de context van Amerikaanse wolkenkrabbers, die vooral in Chicago zeer mooi zijn vormgegeven, wilde men weer een dialoog tussen het classicisme van steen (wit graniet) en geavanceerde beglazing bereiken. De façade toont een ontwerp van klassieke verhoudingen met op verschillende niveaus opdelingen, die onderling door zuilen zijn verbonden. Boven eindigt het gebouw met een geveldriehoek die scherp aftekent tegen de hemel, waardoor het gebouw goed te herkennen is in de skyline van Chicago.

The ground floor lobby is 18 meters tall. It is made of gray and white marble. In addition, it is adorned with four sculptures and a mural by the catalan artists Xavier Corberó and Antoni Tàpies.

L'atrio del pianterreno ha un'altezza di 18 metri e venne eseguito in marmo bianco e grigio. È decorato da quattro statue ed un mural degli artisti catalani Xavier Corberó e Antoni Tàpies.

De lobby op de begane grond is achttien meter hoog en vervaardigd uit grijs en wit marmer. Daarnaast is de lobby gedecoreerd met vier sculpturen en een wandschildering van de Catalaanse kunstenaars Xavier Corberó en Antoni Tàpies.

The building as a whole expresses the will to make an impact on the city's skyline.

L'edificio, nell'insieme, esprime il desiderio di inserirsi nell'orizzonte della città.

Het gebouw drukt in zijn totaliteit de wens uit om in de skyline van de stad op te vallen.

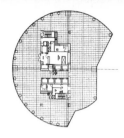

FIRST BANK PLACE

PEI COBB FREED & PARTNERS

CLIENT / CLIENTE / OPDRACHTGEVER: IBM ASSOCIATES LTD PARTNERSHIP & THE OPUS CORPORATION	**1992**

TOTAL AREA / SUPERFICIE / TOTALE OPPERVLAKTE: 140.000 m²

FLOORS / PIANI / VERDIEPINGEN - HEIGHT / ALTEZZA / HOOGTE: 58 fl / 236,2 m

This building, located in central commercial area of the city, was projected attending to three urban conditioners: large skyscrapers, historical buildings of medium height, and a much-loved green space in the congested city center. Thus, the building, which does not occupy the entire lot, rises on an L-shaped plan, in three volumes generated from squares and cylinders in a harmonic succession of materials and heights. Finally, a tower sticks out and is crowned with a semi-circular steel structure.

Questo edificio, situato in un quartiere nel centro commerciale della città, venne progettato tenendo in conto tre fattori urbanistici: la notevole altezza dei grattacieli, l'altezza media degli edifici storici e una deliziosa area verde nel centro congestionato della città. In questo modo l'edificio, che non occupa la superficie edificabile complessiva, sorge su una base a forma di elle, con tre strutture costituite da quadrati e cilindri collocati sulla base di una successione armonica di materiali ed altezze. Per ultimo, emerge la torre, sormontata da una struttura semicircolare di acciaio.

Dit gebouw staat in de centrale zakenwijk van de stad en werd zo ontworpen dat het rekening hield met drie stedelijke gegevens: hoge wolkenkrabbers, historische gebouwen van gemiddelde hoogte en een zeer populaire groene ruimte in het hectische stadscentrum. Zo beslaat het gebouw niet het hele terrein en verrijst het in de vorm van een L, opgebouwd uit drie volumes van rechthoeken en cilinders in een harmonische opeenvolging van materialen en hoogten. Tot slot stijgt boven alles een toren uit, gekroond door een stalen structuur in de vorm van een halve cirkel.

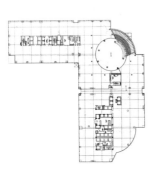

Exterior views of the building, the crown which finishes off the tower characterizes it, making it recognizable from different points of the city.

Veduta esterna dell'edificio, caratterizzato dal coronamento che lo sormonta e lo distingue da ogni punto della città.

Uitzichten op het gebouw. De toren wordt gekarakteriseerd door de kroon op de top, waardoor hij op veel punten in de stad te herkennen is.

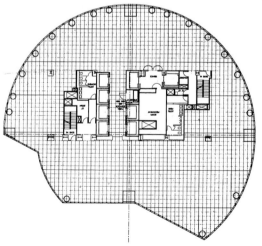

Glass-covered atrium at the corner of the building which opens onto the garden, creating a square at the entrance to the commercial area.

Atrio di vetro dello spigolo dell'edificio che da sul giardino e che crea una piazza presso l'entrata della zona commerciale.

Het met glas bedekte atrium in de hoek van het gebouw dat uitkomt op de tuin en een binnenplein vormt voor de toegang tot het winkelcentrum.

Inside, a conical rotunda opens out, surrounded by restaurants and commercial spaces.

All'interno, si apre una rotonda conica circondata da ristoranti e spazi commerciali.

Binnen bevindt zich een conische rotonde, omringd door restaurants en winkels.

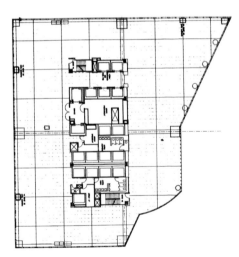

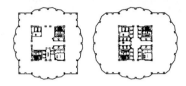

FIRST INTERSTATE WORLD CENTER

PEI COBB FREED & PARTNERS

1990

CLIENT / CLIENTE / OPDRACHTGEVER: MAGUIRE THOMAS PARTNERS	
TOTAL AREA / SUPERFICIE / TOTALE OPPERVLAKTE: 139.000 m²	
FLOORS / PIANI / VERDIEPINGEN - HEIGHT / ALTEZZA / HOOGTE: 75 fl / 310,3 m	

The design of this tower was inspired by the old Los Angeles Central Library by the architect B. Goodhue. It has light features except for the base and the multiple-faced glass apex. The design of the plan and volumetry divide the articulation between a circle and a square surreptitiously, where the circle ends up dominating the geometric form. The structure of the building is prepared to receive an earthquake of 8·3 on the Richter scale as well as resisting the gusts of wind that a 75 floor tall building suffers.

Il design, del First ispirato all'antica Biblioteca Centrale di Los Angeles dell'architetto B. Goodhue, presenta linee nitide, eccezion fatta per la base e la cuspide di vetro dalle molteplici facce. Il design della pianta e della volumetria si basa sull'articolazione tra un cerchio ed un quadrato sovrapposti, nel quale il cerchio finisce per dominare la forma geometrica. La struttura dell'edificio è stata progettata per sopportare un terremoto del 8,3° della scala Richter e per resistere alle spinte del vento a cui è soggetta normalmente una torre di 75 piani.

Het ontwerp van deze toren werd geïnspireerd door de oude hoofdbibliotheek van Los Angeles van de architect B. Goodhue. Afgezien van de basis en de polygonale glazen top overheersen lichte heldere lijnen. Het ontwerp en de omvang ontstaan door een vierkant en een overlappende cirkel, waarbij de cirkel uiteindelijk als geometrische vorm domineert. De structuur van het gebouw is uitgerust om aardbevingen van 8,3 op de schaal van Richter te doorstaan en kan bovendien de windstoten aan die een gebouw van 75 verdiepingen doorgaans kent.

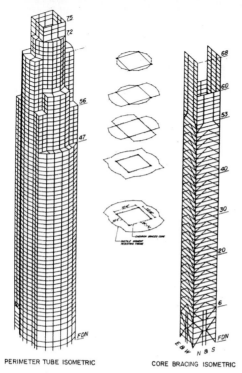

On the left, section, structural
diagrams and development of the plan
of the tower from the geometric figures
of the square and the circle.

*A sinistra, una sezione, schemi
strutturali e sviluppo della pianta della
torre costituita dalle figure geometriche
del cerchio e del quadrato.*

Links: doorsnede, structuurschema's
en de opbouw van de toren uit de
geometrische figuren vierkant en cirkel.

PERIMETER TUBE ISOMETRIC   CORE BRACING ISOMETRIC

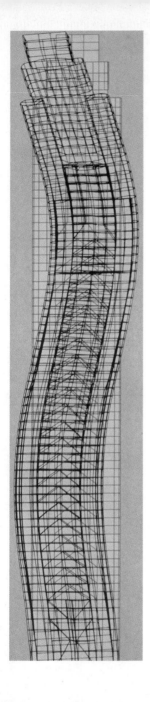

The tower, which is located 42 km away from the San
Andrés fault, is currently the tallest building in the world in
a seismic zone 4. On the left, the building's response to an
earthquake.

*La torre, ubicata a quarantadue chilometri dalla faglia di
sant'Andrea, è attualmente l'edificio più alto del mondo
in una zona sismica 4. A sinistra, reazione dell'edificio
ad un terremoto.*

De toren bevindt zich op 42 kilometer van de San Andreas-
breuk en is momenteel het hoogste gebouw ter wereld in een
seismische zone van niveau 4. Links: de reactie van het
gebouw op een aardbeving.

On the next page, views of the monumental colonnade of ground floor pillars, coated with translucent glass dyed green. On this page, different details of the interior of the lobby, the plan of the siting and different plan types.

Nell'altra pagina, veduta del monumentale colonnato del pianterreno, ricoperto con vetro traslucido di color verde. In questa pagina, alcuni particolari degli interni dell'atrio, la piantina dell'ubicazione e varie piante-tipo.

Op de andere bladzijde: doorkijk op de begane grond met monumentale zuilen van groen gekleurd, licht doorschijnend glas. Op deze bladzijde: verschillende uitzichten op de toegangshal, plattegronden van de locatie en van uiteenlopende soorten verdiepingen.

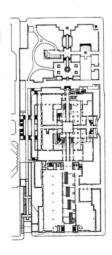

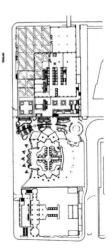

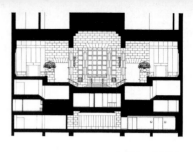

FOUR SEASONS HOTEL

PEI COBB FREED & PARTNERS + FRANK WILLIAMS

CLIENT / CLIENTE / OPDRACHTGEVER: EIE REGENT AVENUE	**1993**
TOTAL AREA / SUPERFICIE / TOTALE OPPERVLAKTE: 46.450 m²	
FLOORS / PIANI / VERDIEPINGEN - HEIGHT / ALTEZZA / HOOGTE: 54 fl / 167,65 m.	

This building, designed as a hotel, is sited in one of the most exclusive areas of New York, designed with a classical elegance which transcends time and fashions. The building's program develops beneath street level a gymnasium and meeting halls, the entrance, lobby and public areas in the base, and 372 rooms in the tower. The façade, with plates of high quality limestone, frames large glass windows. The volumetry is defined from a cruciform prism which gradually loses section as it gains great height.

Albergo, si trova in una delle zone più esclusive di New York. È stato progettato con un'eleganza classica che va al di là dell'epoca e delle mode. Il progetto dell'edificio prevede al di sotto del livello della strada, una palestra e sale riunioni; l'ingresso, l'atrio e le zone di passaggio al pianoterra ed i 372 appartamento-monolocale della torre. La facciata è ricoperta di pietra calcarea di ottima qualità che incornicia le grandi finestre di vetro, e la sua forma è costituita da un prisma cruciforme che perde superficie gradualmente con l'altezza.

Dit hotelgebouw ligt in een van de meest exclusieve wijken van New York. Het is ontworpen met een klassieke elegantie die uitstijgt boven tijd en mode. Onder de grond bevinden zich een fitnessruimte en vergaderzalen, op de begane grond de ingang, vestibule en ontvangstruimte en de toren herbergt 372 kamers. De met kalksteen uitgeruste façade wordt onderbroken door grote ramen. De omvang van het gebouw is gebaseerd op een cirkelvormig prisma dat kleiner wordt naarmate de hoogte toeneemt.

The tower maintains the domestic scale of the façade by means of the reticle of windows an entire floor high

La torre conserva un aspetto domestic nella facciata graz al reticolato di finestre su tutta l'altezza dell'edificio.

De façade van de toren behoudt een menselijke schaal door een patroon van ramen die een hele etage hoog zijn.

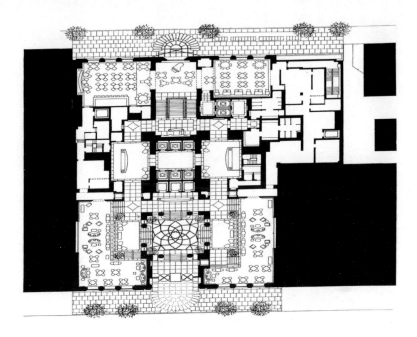

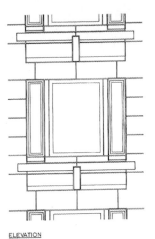

ELEVATION

SECTION

The ground floor is devoted to the public areas of the hotel, regulated by means of a representative luxury entrance.

Il pianoterra è destinato alle aree comuni dell'albergo, alle quali si accede grazie ad un'entrata lussuosa e rappresentativa.

De begane grond is gewijd aan de openbare ruimten van het hotel, te bereiken via een representatieve ingang.

The sumptuous interior decoration in
the public areas is designed as part
of the luxury set design which the
hotel represents.

*La sfarzosa decorazione degli interni
nelle zone comuni è stata ideata
come parte della scenografia di lusso
dell'hotel.*

De weelderige interieurdecoratie in de
publieke ruimte geeft uitdrukking aan
het luxeueze karakter van het hotel.

GAS NATURAL

ENRIC MIRALLES & BENEDETTA TAGLIABUE ARQ. ASSOCIATS

CLIENT / CLIENTE / OPDRACHTGEVER: GAS NATURAL SDG	**1999**
TOTAL AREA / SUPERFICIE / TOTALE OPPERVLAKTE: 22.000 m²	
FLOORS / PIANI / VERDIEPINGEN - HEIGHT / ALTEZZA / HOOGTE: 21 fl / 86 m	

This new head office will be situated between the Coastal Ring Road and the old fishermen's quarters of Barceloneta. The architects have described it as a building with a very clear will to be compatible with its urban environment, composed from the small scale of the housing blocks, a park and tall buildings soon to be built. The building responds with the verticality of an office tower at the same time as it is fragmented in smaller scale bodies, which give rise to a projection, which forms a singular public space through an urban landscape of different dimensions, which forms a great bridge towards Barceloneta.

Questo nuovo edificio di uffici sarà costruito tra la zona del Litorale e l'antico quartiere di pescatori di Barceloneta. Gli architetti lo hanno presentato come "un edificio il cui chiaro proposito è la compatabilità con il resto del panorama urbanistico, formato da case di piccole dimensioni, da un giardino pubblico e da alti edifici che verranno costruiti nei prossimi anni. L'edificio è verticale, come una torre di uffici, anche se, allo stesso tempo, è frammentato in volumi di dimensioni inferiori, che originano un corpo sporgente e costituiscono un peculiare spazio pubblico nell'ambito di un paesaggio urbanistico dalle dimensioni differenti e che rappresenta una grande porta su Barceloneta".

Dit nieuwe hoofdkantoor zal worden gesitueerd tussen de zogenaamde Cinturó del Litoral en de oude visserswijk Barceloneta. De architecten hebben het omschreven als een gebouw met een zeer duidelijke wens om te passen in de stedelijke omgeving, die gekenmerkt wordt door lage woonhuizen, een park en spoedig verrijzende hoogbouw. Het ontwerp is daarom opgebouwd uit de verticale kantoortoren en tegelijk opgedeeld in volumes van kleinere afmetingen, die zich als vleugels over een enkele open ruimte zullen spannen om in het stadsbeeld de poort naar Barcelona te verbeelden.

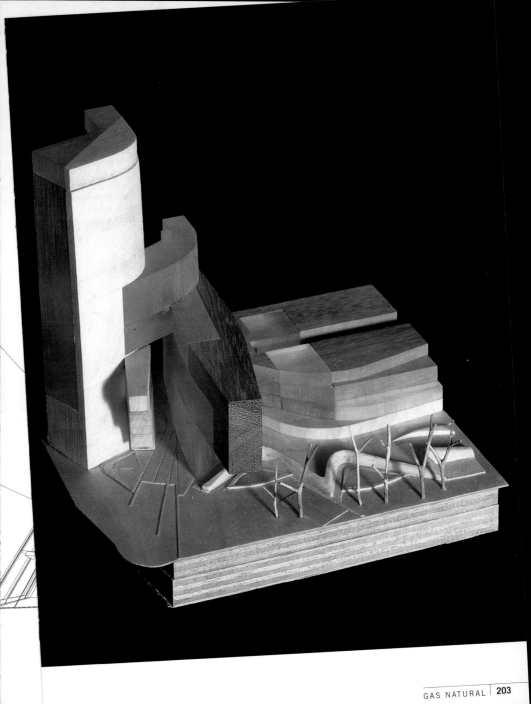

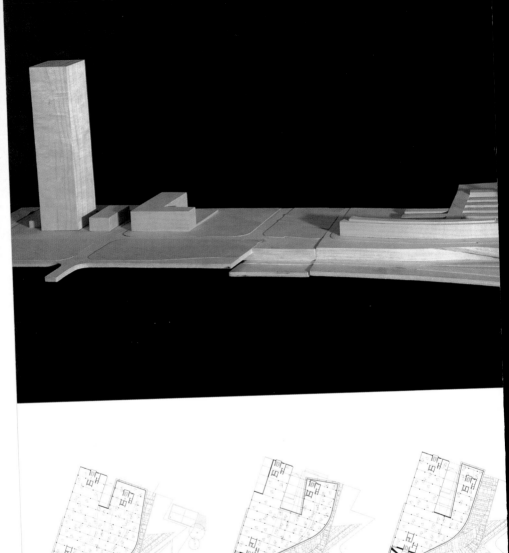

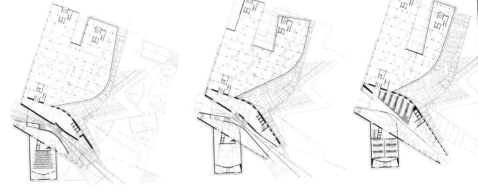

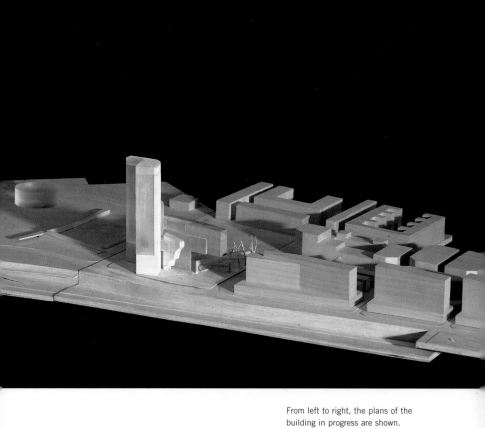

From left to right, the plans of the building in progress are shown.

Da sinistra a destra, è possibile vedere la progressione dei piani dell'edificio.

Van links naar rechts: de plattegronden van elke afzonderlijke bouwfase.

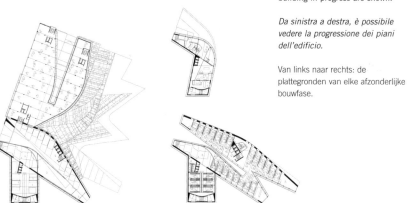

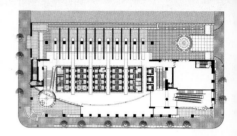

GAS COMPANY TOWER

SKIDMORE, OWINGS & MERILL LLP (SOM)

CLIENT / CLIENTE / OPDRACHTGEVER: MAGUIRE THOMAS PARTNERS	**1991**

TOTAL AREA / SUPERFICIE / TOTALE OPPERVLAKTE: 130.000 m²

FLOORS / PIANI / VERDIEPINGEN - HEIGHT / ALTEZZA / HOOGTE: 55 fl / 228,3 m

Central element of the rehabilitation of a downtown area together with the First Interstate World Center, it responds in terms of urban planning and composition as a ball and socket joint between public spaces, historical buildings and modern skyscrapers. It incorporates the volumes and materials that surround it while still representing a corporate image. Its design responds to the neighboring buildings. Starting out from a base which takes its height from the Baltimore Hotel next door, a central trunk of blueish granite rises (like the neighboring Arco Tower) and the sides are wrapped in a metallic cladding (like the First Interstate). A volume of eliptical blue glass which penetrates the granite of the trunk symbolizes a gas flame. As it rises, the trunk shrinks until only the blue glass and the infinite sky are left.

Elemento centrale del recupero di una zona del downtown insieme al First Interstate World Center, risponde urbanisticamente e strutturalmente come una rotula tra spazi pubblici, edifici storici e moderni grattacieli. Incorpora i volumi e i materiali che lo circondano senza con questo smettere di rappresentare un'immagine corporativa. Il suo disegno risponde al vocabolario degli edifici vicini. A partire da uno zoccolo che prende come altezza di riferimento quella del vicino Baltimore Hotel, si eleva con un tronco centrale di granito azzurrato (come il vicino Arco Tower) e i lati sono avvolti da un rivestimento metallico (come il First Iterstate). Un volume di vetro azzurro ellittico che penetra nel granito del tronco simboleggia una fiamma di gas, a misura che aumenta in altezza, il tronco si riduce fino a restare soltanto il vetro azzurro e il cielo infinito.

Samen met de First Interstate World Center vormt dit gebouw een kernelement in de sanering van een deel van het centrum, qua stadsplanning en compositie een draaischijf tussen de openbare ruimten, historische gebouwen en moderne wolkenkrabbers. De toren weerspiegelt de bouwstijlen en materialen uit zijn omgeving, maar er wordt niet vergeten het bedrijf te representeren. Het ontwerp is afgestemd op de naburige gebouwen. De hoogte van de basis is afgeleid van het aangrenzende Baltimore Hotel, waarboven zich de centrale toren verheft in blauwachtig graniet (als de naburige Arco Tower) terwijl de zijkanten zijn bedekt met metaal (als de First Interstate). Het elliptische volume van blauw glas rijst op uit de basis van graniet en symboliseert een gasvlam. Het granieten deel versmalt naar boven toe tot alleen het blauwe glas en de eindeloze horizon overblijven.

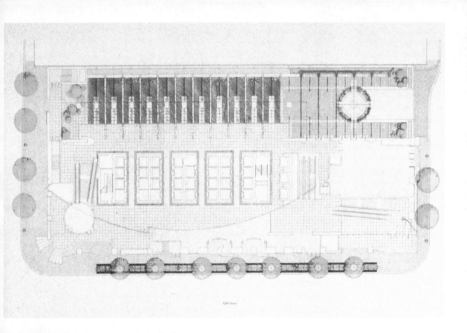

The base of the building, which contains three foyers joined by stairs and elevators, walkways and hanging gardens, is a link between two refurbished public spaces – the Central Library building and Pershing Square. Access to the square is gained from the park and the historic Baltimore Hotel in a sweeping curve.

La base dell'edificio che contiene tre ingressi uniti mediante scale e ascensori, corridoi interni e giardini pensili, è un collegamento tra due spazi pubblici riabilitati: l'edificio della Central Library e la piazza Pershing. L'accesso verso la piazza si apre in direzione del parco e dello storico Baltimore Hotel con un gesto curvo.

Drie verschillende foyers op de begane grond worden door trappen, liften, passages en hangende tuinen met elkaar verenigd en vormen een verbinding met twee heringerichte openbare ruimten: het gebouw van de Central Library en Pershing Square. Men komt in een wijde boog via het park en het historische Baltimore Hotel uit op het plein.

The structure is a combination of steel elements that provide the necessary lateral resistance to wind and seismic forces, and carry the vertical gravitational burden.

La structure est une combinaison d'éléments en acier, ce qui garantit la résistance latérale nécessaire face aux forces sismiques et éoliques, elle supporte aussi les charges verticales gravitatoires.

De structuur bestaat uit een combinatie van staalelementen, die de noodzakelijke laterale weerstand bieden tegen wind en seismische krachten; tegelijkertijd dragen deze het verticale gewicht van de gravitatie.

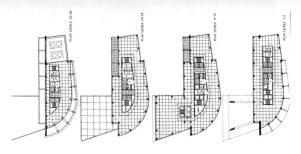

GENERAL BANK TOWER

MURPHY / JAHN INC. ARCHITECTS

CLIENT / CLIENTE / OPDRACHTGEVER: GENERAL BANK

1996

FLOORS / PIANI / VERDIEPINGEN - HEIGHT / ALTEZZA / HOOGTE: 30fl/ 104 m

This building is found in an office area. It has the will to respond to the urban context. With a corner lot the encounter and continuity between streets with different buildings had to be resolved. The architects decided to search for partial solutions and instead of projecting a single building they split it up into parts, unifying them with a uniform treatment of the façades. From the location of the bank's offices on the corner, with a curved tower, the lateral encounters are resolved with volumes of forms and heights which adapt to the neighboring buildings. Thus, the building offers three different images.

Questo edificio, che si trova in una zona di uffici, riflette l'intenzione di inserirsi nel panorama urbano. Dal momento che fa angolo, avrebbe dovuto risolvere l'incontro e la continuità tra le strade ed i diversi edifici. Gli architetti decisero di ricorrere a soluzioni parziali ed invece di progettare un unico edificio, lo scomposero in diverse parti, che omogeneizzarono lavorando in modo simile le facciate. Grazie alla collocazione degli uffici della banca ad angolo, e alla torre incurvata, vengono risolti gli incontri laterali con gli edifici con una struttura ed un'altezza che si adattano alle costruzioni attigue. In questo modo l'edificio offre diverse immagini.

Dit gebouw bevindt zich in een kantoorwijk en is goed aan de stedelijke omgeving aangepast. Aangezien het op een hoek staat, moest er een oplossing worden gevonden voor de samenkomende straten met verschillende gebouwen. De architecten besloten te zoeken naar deeloplossingen en in plaats van een enkel gebouw te ontwerpen deelden ze het op in verschillend hoge gedeelten, waarbij de façaden overigens wel een zelfde uiterlijk kregen. In de richting van de kruising is het bankgebouw een afgebogen toren, terwijl het achterste deel van het gebouw zich in volumes qua vorm en hoogte aanpast aan de aangrenzende bebouwing. Op deze wijze biedt het gebouw drie verschillende aangezichten.

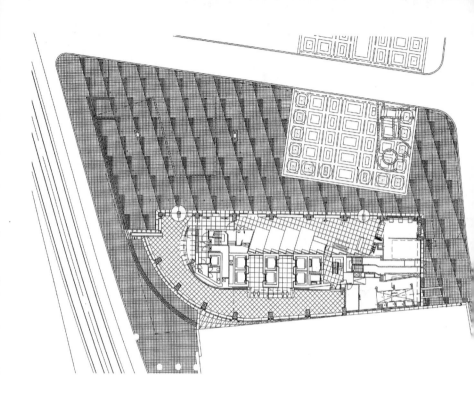

Looking at the building from different angles and positions, the images and perceptions we have of it are not the same.

Se osserviamo l'edificio da diversi punti di vista, l'immagine e la percezione che ne abbiamo non sono mai le stesse.

Als men vanuit verschillende hoeken en posities naar het gebouw kijkt, ontstaat er steeds een ander beeld.

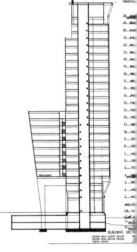

Above, the tower leaves part of the ground floor free,
thus offering a view of the Maritime Museum
as well as creating a square.

*In alto, la torre lascia parte del pianoterra libero,
in questo modo offre una bella vista del Museo
Marittimo ed allo stesso tempo forma una piazza.*

Boven: de toren laat een deel van de begane grond open,
zodat een plein ontstaat en een uitzicht op het Maritiem
Museum wordt geboden.

GOLDEN CENTER

DENNIS LAU & N.G. CHUN MAN ARCHITECTS & ENGINEERS (H.K) LTD

CLIENT / CLIENTE / OPDRACHTGEVER: HANG LUNG DEVELOPMENT COMPANY LIMITED

1991

TOTAL AREA / SUPERFICIE / TOTALE OPPERVLAKTE: 14.535 m²

FLOORS / PIANI / VERDIEPINGEN - HEIGHT / ALTEZZA / HOOGTE: 31 fl / 112 m

Commercial building constructed by a private agent over a metropolitan railway station, it is made up of a four-floor base which contains the most public usages – shops, restaurants- above which a 25 floor office tower rises. In spite of the form and the size of the siting – a triangle of only 800 m2 – which the base occupies totally, the tower is breeched from the most acute angle of the lot and obtains a fairly regular prismatic form. The façade is resolved with a reflective glass curtain wall of golden tones, which together with similar tones in the interior decoration, gives the building its name.

Edificio ad uso commerciale costruito per un'azienda privata su una stazione della metropolitana, è costituito da una base alta quattro piani per usi pubblici –negozi e ristoranti– e sulla quale si innalza una torre di uffici alta 25 piani. Nonostante la forma e l'estensione del terreno –un triangolo di 800 m² solamente– che occupa tutta la base, la torre presenta una rientranza dall'angolo più acuto del terreno ed assume una forma prismatica abbastanza regolare. La facciata è costituita da una parete a cortina di vetro riflettente dalle sfumature dorateche, anche per i toni simili della decorazione interna, dà il nome all'edificio.

Een particuliere onderneming liet dit bedrijvenpand oprichten boven een metrostation. Het bestaat uit een basis van vier verdiepingen waar de meeste publieke functies zijn ondergebracht – winkels, restaurants – met daarboven een kantoortoren van 25 verdiepingen. Ondanks de vorm en de afmetingen van het perceel – een driehoek van slechts 800 m² – dat volledig door de basis in beslag wordt genomen, staat de toren naar achteren op de basis die de scherpe hoek langs de straten volgt, met een vrij regelmatige prismavorm. De façade bestaat uit reflecterend glas in gouden tinten, die in combinatie met soortgelijke kleuren in de decoratie van het interieur het gebouw zijn naam verleent.

The base is adapted to the lot, while the tower rises more freely, adopting irregular forms. The golden tone of the reflective glass dominates the building.

Mentre la base si adatta all'edificio, la torre si innalza più liberamente, assumendo una forma regolare. Il tono dorato dei vetri riflettenti domina l'edificio.

De voet richt zich naar de hoekvorm van het perceel, terwijl de toren zich vrijer verheft en onregelmatige vormen aanneemt. De gouden kleur van het reflectieve glas domineert het gebouw.

HONG KONG & SHANGHAI BANK HQTRS.

FOSTER & PARTNERS

1986

CLIENT / CLIENTE / OPDRACHTGEVER: HONG KONG & SHANGHAI
BANKING CORPORATION

TOTAL AREA / SUPERFICIE / TOTALE OPPERVLAKTE: 99.000 m²

FLOORS / PIANI / VERDIEPINGEN - HEIGHT / ALTEZZA / HOOGTE: 44 fl / 180 m

This building was projected between 1979 and 1983, when Hong Kong was still under British government. Sited in a narrow plot, it was designed considering the local tradition of Feng Shui, which seeks cosmic equilibrium. It wanted to define the financial character of the city, seeking a new concept of the office building. The decision to move the structure and the vertical communications from the center of the plan breaks with the traditional diagram of skyscrapers with a central core. The exterior treatment is also different, foregrounding the structure instead of hiding it behind a curtain wall.

Questo edificio venne progettato tra il 1979 ed il 1983, quando Hong Kong era ancora sotto il governo inglese. Costruito su un angusto terreno, fu disegnato tenendo in considerazione la tradizione locale del Feng Shui, il cui fine è il raggiungimento dell'armonia cosmica. La volontà di rappresentare il carattere finanziario della città, e come questo avrebbe dovuto materializzarsi in una costruzione, spinse rol'architetto a cercare un nuovo concetto per l'edificio di uffici. La decisione di dislocare la struttura e le comunicazioni verticali dal centro del piano rompe lo schema tradizionale del grattacielo dal nucleo centrale. La lavorazione esterna, inoltre, è differente, presenta infatti in primo piano la struttura invece di occultarla dietro una parete-cortina.

Dit gebouw werd ontworpen tussen 1979 en 1983, toen Hongkong nog onder Brits bestuur stond. Het ligt op een smal terrein en werd uitgewerkt volgens de plaatselijke traditie van feng shui, een leer die zoekt naar kosmisch evenwicht. Het gebouw moest het financiële karakter van de stad benadrukken door een nieuw concept van kantoorgebouw. Het besluit om de verticale staalstructuur en de liften uit het midden te halen en aan de zijkant te plaatsen, breekt met het traditionele ontwerp van een wolkenkrabber met een centrale kern. Ook de buitenkant is afwijkend, door de structuur zichtbaar te laten en niet zoals gebruikelijk achter een façade te verstoppen.

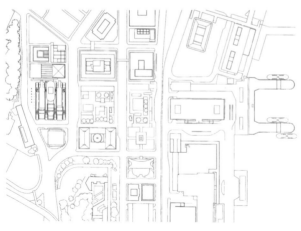

Different views of the building highlight the nocturnal view, where the transparency of the building is highlighted and the skeleton effect that the structure gives in the treatment of the façade.

Alcune vedute dell'edificio; tra tutte spicca quella notturna, nella quale è maggiormente visibile la trasparenza dell'edificio e l'aspetto dello scheletro che la struttura presenta sulla facciata.

Verschillende uitzichten op het gebouw. 's Nachts is de transparantie goed zichtbaar en komt het skelet van het gebouw duidelijk naar voren.

The plan is subdivided into
three rectangular bodies of 28,
45 and 41 floors respectively.
The interior of the building
is very luminous because
by moving the technical core
towards the perimeter,
it permits free floors.

*La struttura è divisa in tre corpi
rettangolari di–rispettivamente–
ventotto, quarantacinque e
quarantuno piani. L'interno
dell'edificio è molto luminoso,
dal momento che la
disposizione dell'area tecnica
lungo il perimetro lascia i piani
liberi.*

Het complex is onderverdeeld in
drie rechthoekige volumes met
respectievelijk 28, 45 en 41
verdiepingen. Het interieur van
het gebouw is zeer licht doordat
de technische kern naar de
zijkant is verplaatst, zodat veel
meer open ruimte werd
verkregen.

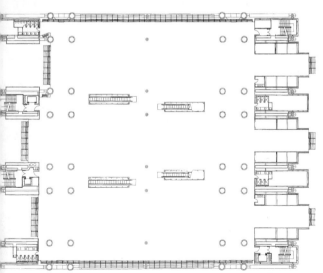

HOTEL ARTS

SKIDMORE OWINGS & MERRILL LLP (SOM)

TOTAL AREA / SUPERFICIE / TOTALE OPPERVLAKTE: 70.000 m²

1992

FLOORS / PIANI / VERDIEPINGEN - HEIGHT / ALTEZZA / HOOGTE: 47 fl / 152 m

In 1985, Barcelona City Council began an ambitious project which would transform the maritime front and part of the gothic quarter. The Olympic Games 1992 nomination made them come true. The new residential neighborhood of the Olympic Village links the gothic city and the sea. Two towers will symbolize this urban transformation and signal the new Olympic Port and its surrounding area. Commercial areas, restaurants, cafés, offices and the Hotel de les Arts. It is characterized by the exterior view of its metallic structure, which is submerged in a pond where it reaches the ground. Thus, the whole building seems to emerge from the water.

Il Comune di Barcellona intraprese, nel 1985, un progetto ambizioso che avrebbe trasformato la zona marittima e parte della città gotica. La designazione come sede dei Giochi Olimpici del 1992 convertirono questo progetto in realtà. Il nuovo quartiere residenziale della Villa Olímpica unisce la città gotica al mare. Due torri simboleggeranno questa trasformazione urbanistica e indicheranno il nuovo Port Olímpic e la zona contigua. Aree commerciali, ristoranti, caffè, uffici e l'Hotel de les Arts, caratterizzato dalla struttura metallica bianca sommersa alla base, che dà l'impressione che l'intero edificio emerga dalle acque.

In 1985 startte het gemeentebestuur van Barcelona een ambitieus project om de wijk aan de zee en een deel van de gotische wijk te renoveren. De nominatie voor de Olympische Spelen van 1992 verwezenlijkte dit project. De nieuwe woonwijk 'Vila Olímpica' verbindt het gotische deel van de stad met de zee. Twee torens zullen deze stedelijke vernieuwing symboliseren en staan voor de nieuwe Port Olímpic en omgeving. Er zijn winkelcentra, restaurants, cafés, kantoren en het Hotel de les Arts opgericht. De alles overstijgende witte stalen structuur van het hotel eindigt op de grond in een vijver. Zo lijkt het hele gebouw uit het water te komen.

Aerial view from the summit of the tower, the sculpture of a fish with golden scales was designed by the American architect Frank Gehry.

Veduta aerea dall'alto della torre, la statua di un pesce con squame dorate venne eseguita dal-l'architetto americano Frank Gehry.

Uitzicht vanaf de top van de toren op de sculptuur van de goudgeschubde vis, die door de Amerikaanse architect Frank Gehry werd ontworpen.

The hotel and the base of the tower are connected by means of terraces which offer intermediate spaces between the exterior and the public spaces of the interior.

L'albergo è collegato alla base grazie alle terrazze che costituiscono uno spazio intermedio tra l'esterno e gli spazi pubblici dell'interno.

Het hotel en de voet van de toren zijn verbonden door middel van terrassen die een overgang vormen tussen het exterieur en de openbare ruimten binnen.

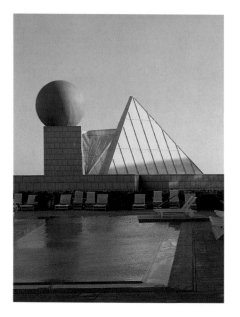

Both the Hotel Arts and the Mapfre Tower are currently the tallest buildings in the city of Barcelona.

Sia l'Hotel de les Arts, che la Torre Mapfre sono attualmente gli edifici più alti della città di Barcellona.

Zowel het Hotel Arts als de Torre Mapfre zijn momenteel de hoogste gebouwen van Barcelona.

BARCELONA

HOTEL ATTRACTION

ANTONI GAUDÍ

CLIENT / CLIENTE / OPDRACHTGEVER: UNKNOWN / SCONOSCIUTO/ ONBEKEND	**1908**
FLOORS / PIANI / VERDIEPINGEN - HEIGHT / ALTEZZA / HOOGTE: 120 fl - 360 m	

The Hotel Attraction began as five sketches drawn by Gaudí at the beginning of the 20th century as part of a project for a hotel in a skyscraper in New York. The sheer magnitude of the project was considerable for the time since there were no buildings of similar dimensions in the city. The design features a large central tower (like the Sagrada Família in Barcelona) flanked by smaller towers where the guestrooms were to be located. This project by Gaudí, whose promoter is unknown, was recuperated by one of his disciples, Joan Matamala. He analysed the original sketches in the late 1950s and tried to imagine what the cross section would be like. The Catalan artist Marc Mascort i Boix took up where Matamala left off, and his research into the final volumetric aspect of the building is shown in the digital mockups on these pages.

L'Hotel Attraction ha la sua origine in cinque bozzetti che Gaudí tracciò all'inizio del secolo XIX da un progetto per un grattacielo che doveva ospitare un hotel nella città di New York. La grandezza del progetto era già importante a quell'epoca perché non c'era nessun edificio delle stesse dimensioni nella città. Il disegno consiste in una grande torre centrale (come quella della Sagrada Família di Barcellona) che è circondata da altre di minore dimensione in cui si ubicano le abitazioni. Questo progetto di Gaudí, del quale non si conosce il promotore, venne recuperato da uno dei suoi discepoli, Joan Matamala, che alla fine degli anni cinquanta analizzando i bozzetti originali immaginò come sarebbe potuta essere la sezione dell'edificio. L'artista catalano Marc Mascort i Boix riprese le ricerche di Matamala e dopo diversi lavori circa la volumetria finale dell'edificio, ha presentato la ricostruzione digitale che mostriamo in queste pagine.

Hotel Attraction begon als vijf schetsen die aan het begin van de 20e eeuw door Gaudí werden gemaakt als onderdeel van een project voor een hotel in een wolkenkrabber te New York. De afmetingen van het gebouw waren destijds enorm, want er bestonden geen gebouwen van dergelijke dimensies. Het ontwerp is opgebouwd uit een grote centrale toren (zoals de Sagrada Familia in Barcelona), geflankeerd door kleinere torens waar de hotelkamers zouden komen. De opdrachtgever van dit project van Gaudí is onbekend gebleven. Het ontwerp werd door een van zijn aanhangers, Joan Matamala, herontdekt; hij analyseerde de oorspronkelijke schetsen eind jaren 1950 en probeerde zich voor te stellen hoe de doorsnede eruit zou zien. De Catalaanse kunstenaar Marc Mascort i Boix ging verder waar Matamala was gestopt en zijn onderzoek naar de uiteindelijke volumeverhoudingen van het gebouw is te zien in de digitale modellen op de volgende bladzijden.

All the rooms are located in the perimeter of the façade, leaving the spacious central area free for an immense hall. There would be five in the entire building and each one would reflect the culture of each of the five continents.

Tutte le abitazioni si collocano sul perimetro della facciata, collocando nell'ampio spazio centrale un immenso salone. In tutto l'edificio ce ne sarebbero stati cinque ognuno dei quali avrebbe mostrato la cultura dei cinque continenti.

Alle kamers bevinden zich aan de rand rond een enorme centraal gelegen hal. In het totale bouwwerk zouden er vijf van deze komen, waarbij elke hal de cultuur van elk van de vijf continenten zou weerspiegelen.

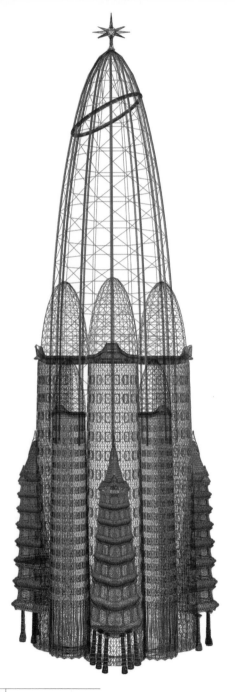

Besides accommodating the lobby, the ground floor could also be used for religious purposes such as a Catholic church or a Protestant or Buddhist temple.

Il piano terra oltre ad ospitare un ingresso poteva essere riservato a diversi fini religiosi come una chiesa cattolica, un tempio protestante o buddista.

De begane grond zou naast de functie als toegangshal ook gebruikt kunnen worden voor religieuze doeleinden, bijvoorbeeld een katholieke of protestantse kerk of boeddhistische tempel.

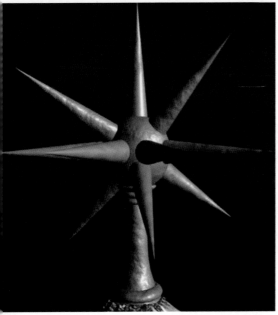

This project shows that the vision of
the genius Catalan architect
coincided at a specific, fleeting
moment with the metropolitan energy
of turn-of-the-century New York, a
city which he himself never visited.

*Questo progetto dimostra la visione
del genio catalano che coincise in un
concreto ed effimero momento con
l'energia metropolitana della città di
New York d'inizio secolo, che mai
arrivò a visitare.*

Dit ontwerp laat zien dat de visie van
het Catalaanse genie op een bepaald,
vluchtig moment samenviel met de
bruisende metropool New York aan het
begin van de 20e eeuw, een stad die
hij zelf nooit bezocht.

gaudí 2002

HOTEL DIAGONAL 1

OSCAR TUSQUETS BLANCA ARQUITECTURAS

CLIENT / CLIENTE / OPDRACHTGEVER: ESPAIS, APEX & LANDSCAPE S.L.	**2004**
TOTAL AREA / SUPERFICIE / TOTALE OPPERVLAKTE: 20.000 m²	
FLOORS / PIANI / VERDIEPINGEN - HEIGHT / ALTEZZA / HOOGTE: 26 fl - 92 m	

The Hotel Diagonal 1 is located in an exceptional spot of the city. This location will lend uniqueness to the building, which will be strengthened by municipal willingness to erect a tower and the geometry of the building site, a triangle with a sharp corner like the prow of a ship facing the immense square of the "Fòrum 2004". Initial response by architects was a double tower, but since the projection for the building was a hotel, it was not possible, so the original idea was maintained by projecting two towers linked by a glass walkway. The view of the hotel from Diagonal against the light will be the most frequent and characteristic, since the sunlight shining through the glass bridge will project a spectacular wake of light onto the pavement of l'Avinguda Diagonal.

L'Hotel Diagonal 1 si colloca in unpunto eccezionale della città, Questa collocazione imprimerà un carattere di singolarità all'edificio che si vedrà rafforzato dalla volontà municipale di elevare una torre e la geometria dell'area. Di firma triangolare e con un angolo molto pronunciato come una prua che punta verso la grande piazza del "Forum 2004" La proposta degli architetti fu inizialmente una torre doppia, ma dal momento che il programma dell'edificio – un hotel – non lo permetteva, si progettarono due torri comunicanti mediante un ponte di vetro, mantenendo così l'idea originale. Dalla Diagonal la visione in controluce dell'edificio sarà la più frequente e allo stesso tempo la più caratteristica giacché quando i raggi del sole colpiranno e attraverseranno l'apertura vetrata (il ponte) se proietterà una spettacolare frangia di luce sul pavimento della Avenida.

Het Hotel Diagonal 1 zal op een bijzondere locatie in de stad komen te staan, daar waar de 'Eixample' en de Avenida Diagonal ontspringen. Deze plaats zal het gebouw uniciteit verlenen. Daarbij komt de gemeentelijke wens om een toren op te richten en de geometrie van het perceel, een driehoek met een scherpe hoek, die als een scheepsboeg in de richting van het plein 'Forum 2004' wijst. Het oorspronkelijke ontwerp van de architecten voorzag in een tweetal torens, maar dit past niet bij de functie van het bouwwerk, te weten een hotel. Het aangepaste ontwerp handhaaft het oorspronkelijke idee door de oprichting van twee torens die door glazen loopbruggen zijn verbonden. Het uitzicht op het hotel vanaf Diagonal zal gewoonlijk tegen het licht in zijn, want het zonlicht schijnt door de glazen brug en werpt zo spectaculair licht op het trottoir.

Access to the Hotel at ground level on the façade facing Diagonal via a downward extension of the glimmering walkway. In contrast with the south facing façade, this one is opaque and abstract, with a wide strip of polished granite running the length of the entire ground floor.

L'accesso dell'Hotel si realizza per l'ampliamento a piano terra della facciata dal lato della Diagonal della fenditura luminosa. In contrapposizione con la facciata sud questa è opaca e astratta laddove uno zoccolo di granito lucido corre lungo tutto il piano terra.

De ingang van het hotel op de begane grond tegenover de Avenida Diagonal door een neerwaartse extensie van de lichte loopbrug. In contrast met de façade op het zuiden is deze ondoorzichtig en abstract, met een brede strook gepolijst graniet dat door de hele begane grond loopt.

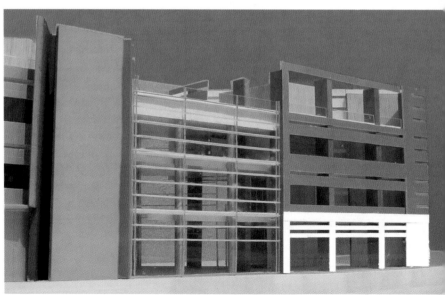

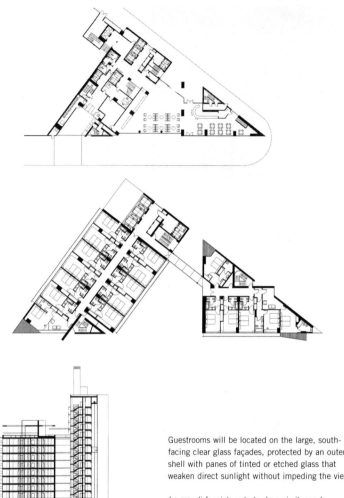

Guestrooms will be located on the large, south-facing clear glass façades, protected by an outer shell with panes of tinted or etched glass that weaken direct sunlight without impeding the view.

Le grandi facciate vetrate dove si situano le abitazioni, si aprono verso il sud, di vetro trasparente ricoperto da una pelle esterna con frange di vetro colorato o serigrafato che senza interrompere la vista protegge dalla radiazione diretta del sole.

De enorme glazen façaden, waar zich de hotelkamers bevinden, liggen op het zuiden. De transparante dubbele beglazing zal worden uitgerust met een buitenlaag van gekleurd of bedrukt glas, die het directe zonlicht afzwakken zonder het uitzicht te belemmeren.

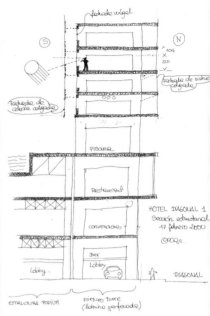

The idea of projecting a double tower stems from the desire to achieve a slim building. The building site is fractioned in two parts, increasing the sensation of height and visually strengthening the idea of a tower.

L'idea di progettare una torre doppia è frutto della volontà di ottenere un edificio snello, e se si fraziona così l'isolato in due volumi la sensazione di altezza aumenta e l'idea di torre resta visibilmente rafforzata.

Het concept van een dubbele toren ontstond uit de wens om een slank gebouw op te richten. Op deze wijze wordt het gebouwencomplex in twee delen opgesplitst, de indruk van hoogte wordt versterkt en het idee van een toren wordt visueel benadrukt.

HOTEL HESPERIA

RICHARD ROGERS PARTNERSHIP & ALONSO - BALAGUER ARQ. ASSOCIATS

CLIENT / CLIENTE / OPDRACHTGEVER: HESPERIA

2002

TOTAL AREA / SUPERFICIE / TOTALE OPPERVLAKTE: 27.000 m²

FLOORS / PIANI / VERDIEPINGEN - HEIGHT / ALTEZZA / HOOGTE: 32 fl / 105 m

Located in a new urban park of 2,5 hectares, the building is framed within a greater mixed-use operation and services package. Planned as an entrance gate to Barcelona on the edge of L'Hospitalet – the second highest populated city in Catalonia – it develops a hotel program of 304 rooms, a congress center with capacity for 4,500 people, an auditorium for 450 persons and a sports club. The building is crowned with a panoramic restaurant under a glass dome.
In the development of the program, sophisticated state of the art technology has been used for the structure and the electrical and water systems.

Situato in un nuovo giardino pubblico di 2,5 ettari, l'edificio faceva parte di un progetto più grande adibito ad usi, dotazioni e servizi vari. Concepito come una porta d'accesso a Barcellona nella zona limitrofa dell'Hospitalet –la seconda città della Catalogna per numero di abitanti– comprende il progetto di un albergo di trecentoquattro stanze, un centro congressi con una capienza di 4.500 persone, un auditorium con 450 posti ed un circolo sportivo. L'edificio è sormontato da un ristorante panoramico con una cupola di vetro. Per la costruzione della struttura e degli impianti vennero utilizzate le più sofisticate tecnologie.

Het gebouw staat in een nieuw stadspark van 2,5 hectare en maakt deel uit van een groter multifunctioneel geheel. Het dient de toegangspoort tot Barcelona te worden aan de rand van L'Hospitalet, qua inwonertal de op een na grootste stad van Catalonië. Er is een hotel met 304 kamers, een congrescentrum met plaats voor 4.500 personen, een auditorium voor 450 personen en een sportclub. Het gebouw wordt bekroond door een panoramisch restaurant in een glazen koepel. De meest geavanceerde technologie is gebruikt voor de constructie en de elektrische en watersystemen.

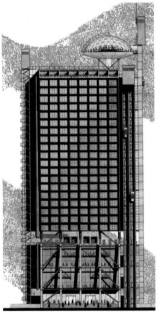

A rectangular prism is situated next to the cylindrical communication an electrical and water systems core, giving the whole a futuristic look.

Un prisma rettangolare, situato accanto al nucleo di comunicazione impianti di forma cilindrica, da al complesso un aspetto futurista.

Naast de cilinder met het trappenhui en de elektrische en watersystemen bevindt zich een rechthoekig prisma, hetgeen zorgt voor een zeer futuristische aanblik.

HOTEL NOVA DIAGONAL

DOMINIQUE PERRAULT & VIRGÍNIA FIGUERAS

CLIENT / CLIENTE / OPDRACHTGEVER: GRUP RIUSEC	**2004**
TOTAL AREA / SUPERFICIE / TOTALE OPPERVLAKTE: 28.000 m²	
FLOORS / PIANI / VERDIEPINGEN - HEIGHT / ALTEZZA / HOOGTE: 27 pl / 112,8 m	

This building forms part of a series of skyscrapers that will be constructed during the next few years in Barcelona. The lack of a tradition of tall buildings means that the architects must find the means of relating the city (of constant height) and the skyscrapers which will automatically become an outstanding element from many points of the city. Dominique Perrault analyzes Barcelona as a horizontal city, that of the Eixample, and another vertical city, that of the towers of the Sagrada Família and the Olympic Village. The Hotel will respond to this reading with a building whose base is inserted in the horizontal city and whose body will be in the vertical city.

Questo edificio è uno dei grattacieli che saranno costruiti a Barcellona nei prossimi anni. Dal momento che non esiste una tradizione edilizia di edifici di grande altezza, gli architetti dovranno trovare il modo di armonizzare gli edifici di uguale altezza ed il grattacielo, che diventerà immediatamente un punto di riferimento da molti luoghi della città. D. Perrault analizza Barcellona come una città orizzontale, la città dell'Eixample, e verticale, come città delle torri della Sagrada Família e della Villa Olimpica. L'albergo risponderà a questa lettura con un edificio la cui base sarà inserita nella città orizzontale ed il cui corpo in quella verticale.

Dit gebouw is een van de wolkenkrabbers die de komende jaren in Barcelona zal worden gebouwd. Aangezien de stad tot dusverre amper hoogbouw kende, moesten de architecten een manier vinden om deze wolkenkrabbers in het stadsbeeld (met gelijkmatige bouwhoogte) op te nemen, zodat ze automatisch uitstekende elementen vormen die op vele plaatsen in de stad te herkennen zullen zijn. Dominique Perrault analyseerde Barcelona en nam de Eixample als horizontaal en de torens van de Sagrada Familia en van het olympische dorp als verticaal. Het hotel beantwoordt aan dit inzicht en richt zich in de basis naar de horizontale stad en met de toren naar de verticale stad.

The morphology of the building creates a set of volumes, a cube (the base) which acts as a counterpoint to a parallelepiped (the body of the tower).

La morfologia dell'edificio crea un gioco di volumi, un cubo (la base) in cui si inserisce il parallelepipedo

De morfologie van het gebouw schept een reeks volumes, een kubus (de basis) die als tegenwicht dient van een parallellepipedum (de toren).

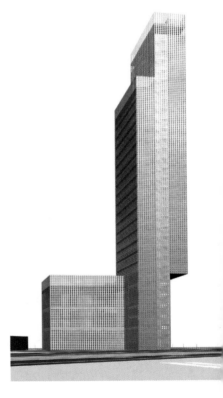

The building will house a five-star hotel and conference center, with gymnasium, restaurants, swimming pool and bar on the terrace of the cube-building.

L'edificio ospiterà un hotel di cinque stelle e un centro congressi, con una palestra, ristoranti, una piscina ed un bar sulla terrazza dell'edificio-cubo.

Het gebouw zal een vijfsterrenhotel en een congrescentrum herbergen, met fitnessruimte, restaurants, een zwembad en een bar op het terras van de kubus.

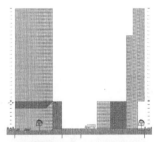

Each room will have exterior views as if the façade were a great screen made up of small apertures. These work like television sets constructing the wall of the façade through images.

Ogni stanza goderà di una vista panoramica all'esterno come se la facciata fosse un grande schermo costituito da piccole aperture.Queste, quasi fossero televisioni, costruiscono la superficie della facciata con immagini.

Elke kamer zal door openingen in de façade uitzicht bieden. Deze openingen wekken de indruk van televisietoestellen die de muur van de façade middels beelden samenstellen.

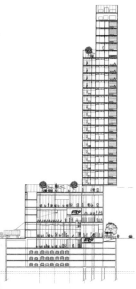

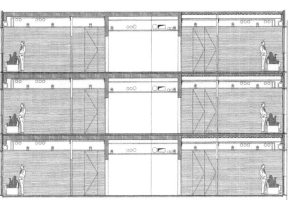

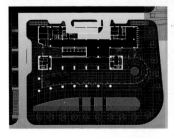

I&C BANK OF CHINA

FOX & FOWLE ARCHITECTS + FFGL PARTNERSHIP

CLIENT / CLIENTE / OPDRACHTGEVER: THE INDUSTRIAL AND COMERCIAL BANK OF CHINA	**2000**
TOTAL AREA / SUPERFICIE / TOTALE OPPERVLAKTE: 58.000 m²	
FLOORS / PIANI / VERDIEPINGEN - HEIGHT / ALTEZZA / HOOGTE: 28 fl / 114 m	

This is the first of five towers planned for the financial district of Pudong. To respond to the place, orientation and the program, the building is organized between three blocks (masses) which are interwoven parallel to the Pudong Avenue. Two frontal masses form the tower containing the private spaces and the third (not as tall) takes the traditional urban scale back up. It contains the public functions and shared private functions like rest areas and conference rooms. The access square to the building acts as an oasis in the middle of the urban boisterousness and the use of the traditional Chinese language, by means of bridges and artificial ponds, gives it a tempo that turns the transit towards the interior into an experience.

Questa è la prima di cinque torri previste per il distretto finanziario di Pudong. Per rispettare il luogo, l'orientamento e il progetto, l'edificio si struttura in tre blocchi (masse) intrecciati, paralleli a Corso Pudong. Due masse frontali formano la torre contenendo gli spazi privati e la terza (di altezza inferiore) riprende la scala urbana tradizionale. Contiene le funzioni pubbliche e le private comuni come zone di riposo e sale per conferenze. La piazza di accesso all'edificio funge da oasi in pieno fermento urbano e la utilizzazione del linguaggio architettonico tradizionale cinese, con ponti e stagni artificiali, offre una spazio temporale che trasforma in un'esperienza perticolare il transito verso l'interno.

Dit is de eerste van vijf torens c gepland zijn voor de zakenw Pudong. Het gebouw bestaat drie parallel aan Pudong Aven lopende blokken (massa's) a aanpassing aan de wijk, de loc tie en het bouwprogramma. Tw van de gebouwen vormen toren, waarin bedrijven z ondergebracht en het der gebouw heeft de hoogte van omringende traditionele bebo wing. Laatstgenoemd gebou biedt publieke functies, maar o gedeelde particuliere functies ontspanningsruimten en co gresruimten. Het toegangsple naar het gebouw vormt een oa in de hectische stad, dat m bruggen, kunstmatige vijvers tempels de Chinese tradi belichaamt, zodat de toegang het gebouw een ware belever wordt.

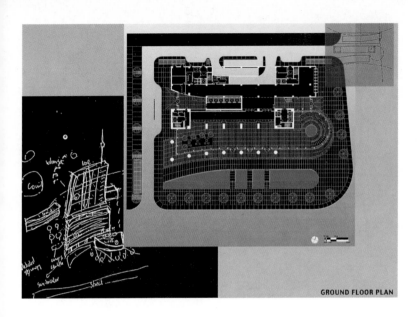

GROUND FLOOR PLAN

LONGITUDINAL SECTION

Rationality in the design of areas destined to work space contrasts with the gestural flexibility of public spaces.

La razionalità del design degli spazi dedicati al lavoro contrasta con la flessibilità gestuale degli spazi pubblici.

Het rationele ontwerp van de werkomgeving contrasteert met het royale gebaar van de openbare ruimten.

The approach of the building is perceptible in the composition of its façades; the opaque north contrasts with the south, which is completely open to the exterior. Protected by a "brise-soleil" and crowned by a sunshade, glass combines with stainless steel and granite.

L'orientamento dell'edificio è percepibile nella composizione delle facciate, quella nord opaca in comparazione con quella sud che si apre completamente verso l'esterno. Protetta da un "bris-soleil" e cinta da un parasole, il vetro si combina con l'acciaio inossidabile e il granito.

De oriëntatie van het gebouw is herkenbaar in de compositie van de façaden: de ondoorzichtige noordkant contrasteert met de zuidkant, die naar buiten toe volledig open is. Het gebouw wordt beschermd door een zogenaamde 'brise-soleil' en gekroond door een zonnescherm. Aan de buitenkant wordt het glas gecombineerd met roestvrij staal en graniet.

The base of the tower is a volume which is characterised by the curved, inclined forms of the north side that swirl around the corner behind the pillars on the ground floor on the south-facing façade, which provides access to the large foyer that connects the public and the private areas.

La base della torre è un volume che si caratterizza per le forme curve e inclinate del lato nord che volta l'angolo passando dietro ai pilastri a piano terra della facciata sud da dove si accede alla grande sala d'ingresso che unisce lo spazio pubblico con quello privato.

De voet van de toren is een volume dat wordt gekenmerkt door de ronde vormen van de noordkant, die de hoek omgaan en achter de zuilen op de begane grond aan de zuidkant langslopen. Hier bevindt zich de grote toegangshal, waar de openbare en particuliere ruimten met elkaar worden verbonden.

TRANSVERSE SECTION

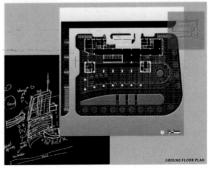

GROUND FLOOR PLAN

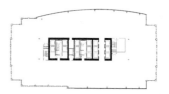

IDX TOWER

ZIMMER GUNSUL FRASCA PARTNERSHIP (ZGF)

CLIENT / CLIENTE / OPDRACHTGEVER: HINES INTERESTS LIMITED PARTNERSHIP

2002

TOTAL AREA / SUPERFICIE / TOTALE OPPERVLAKTE: 97.800 m²

FLOORS / PIANI / VERDIEPINGEN - HEIGHT / ALTEZZA / HOOGTE: 38 fl / 134 m

Conceived by private promoters as the biggest building constructed in Seattle in the last decade, its program includes an underground car park with 637 spaces, a three-floor base which includes shopping and public areas and two juxtaposed towers of offices of 38 and 32 floors. The architectural expression of the building seeks to distinguish itself from other nearby financial districts through the creation of a slender tower covered in lightly colored metal and a glass-covered curtain wall. The building incorporates high level technological features, ready to enter the 21st Century.

Concepito dallo sponsor privato come l'edificio più alto costruito a Seattle negli ultimi dieci anni, il progetto prevede un parcheggio sotterraneo con 637 posti, una base alta tre piani con zone commerciali e di passaggio e due torri giustapposte di uffici rispettivamente di 38 e 32 piani. L'espressione architettonica di questo edificio vorrebbe differenziarsi dalle altre aree d'affari vicine con una torre slanciata ricoperta di metallo leggermente colorato, e con una parete a cortina di vetro. L'edificio è dotato di dispositivi tecnologici di alto livello che lo adeguano al nuovo millennio.

Ontworpen als het grootste gebouw dat het afgelopen decennium in Seattle werd opgericht. Het project omvat een ondergrondse parkeerplaats met 637 plaatsen, een basis van drie verdiepingen met winkels en openbare ruimte en twee naast elkaar geplaatste kantoortorens met 38 en 32 verdiepingen. De architectuur van dit elegante gebouw wil zich van andere bouwwerken in de zakenwijk onderscheiden door het ontwerp van een ranke toren met een façade van licht gekleurd metaal en glas. Het gebouw voldoet aan de hoogste technologische eisen en is daarmee klaar voor de 21e eeuw.

The project, on a site occupying three corners of a block at a different levels, takes advantage of this to generate a base with multiple entrances.

Il progetto, che occupa tre angoli di un isolato su vari livelli, presenta una base con numerosi accessi.

Het bouwwerk ligt op verschillende niveaus aan drie straathoeken, waardoor er meerdere toegangsmogelijkheden zijn.

The façade will be formed by a curtain wall which has the particular feature of being sustained by structural glass and lightly colored metal.

La facciata sarà costituita da una parete a cortina che presenterà una particolare composizione di vetro strutturale e metallo leggermente colorato.

De façade is bijzonder vanwege de glasstructuur en het licht gekleurde metaal.

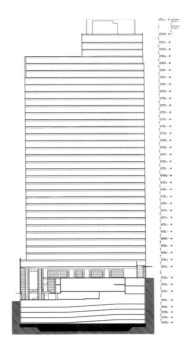

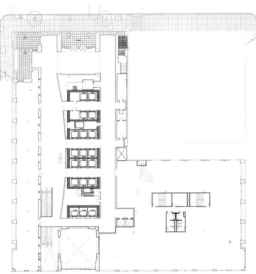

The entrance floor allows crossed traffic and distribution, avoiding communication cores in the relation areas in the lower body.

Il piano dell'ingresso permette la circolazione in vari sensi e la distribuzione delle zone di passaggio nel corpo inferiore, evitando i nuclei di comunicazione.

De verdieping met de toegang maakt een vrije doorgang in alle richtingen mogelijk, zonder te stuiten op de liften in het lagere deel van het gebouw.

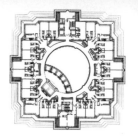

JIN MAO TOWER

SKIDMORE, OWINGS & MERRILL LLP SOM

CLIENT / CLIENTE / OPDRACHTGEVER: CHINA SHANGHAI FOREIGN TRADE CO. LTD.

1988

TOTAL AREA / SUPERFICIE / TOTALE OPPERVLAKTE: 279.000 m²

FLOORS / PIANI / VERDIEPINGEN - HEIGHT / ALTEZZA / HOOGTE: 88 fl / 420,6 m

This building, which is currently the tallest in China, is sited in the commercial and financial district of Pudong. It is a multi-use complex (offices, hotel, shopping center, conference halls, exhibitions and cinema) distributed between the tower and a six-floor podium building. The base of the tower is surrounded by a garden courtyard with a pond. The entrance lobby is a glass shopping atrium with wavy forms which give the visitor a lively spatial experience. The architecture of Jin Mao is reminiscent of the forms of Chinese pagodas, based on multiples of eight (traditonally a lucky number in China). Its metallic profile takes on different color ranges as the sun slides over its articulated surfaces, to become a lighthouse of the Shanghai sky when night falls.

Questo edificio che attualmente è il più alto della Cina è situato nel distretto commerciale e finanziario di Pudong. Si tratta di un complesso dai molteplici usi (uffici, hotel, centro commerciale, sale per conferenze, esposizioni e cinema) distribuiti tra la torre e un edificio-podio di sei piani di altezza. La base della torre è circondata da una zona verde con uno stagno. Il vestibolo di accesso, un atrio commerciale rivestito di vetrate in forma ondulata, offre un'intensa esperienza spaziale al visitatore. L'architettura del Jin Mao ricorda le forme delle pagode cinesi, basata sui multipli di otto (il numero della fortuna nella tradizione cinese). Il suo profilo metallico acquista differenti gamme cromatiche man mano che il sole scivola sulle sua superfici articolate fino a trasformarsi in un faro nel cielo di Shanghai quando giunge la notte.

Dit is momenteel het hoogste gebouw van China. Het bevindt zich in de commerciële en financiële wijk Pudong. Het multifunctionele complex (met kantoren, hotel, winkelcentrum, congreszalen, tentoonstellingsruimten en bioscoop) is verdeeld over een toren en een podiumvormig gebouw van zes verdiepingen. De toren wordt omringd door groenvoorzieningen met een vijver. De toegangshal is een golvend aangelegd atrium van glas, dat de bezoeker een gevoel geeft van een levendige ruimte. De architectuur van de Jin Mao doet denken aan Chinese pagodes, die zijn gebaseerd op veelvouden van acht (traditioneel een geluksgetal in China). Het metalen profiel neemt verschillende kleuren aan met de stand van de zon. Bij het vallen van de avond lijkt de Jin Mao op een vuurtoren in de skyline van Shanghai.

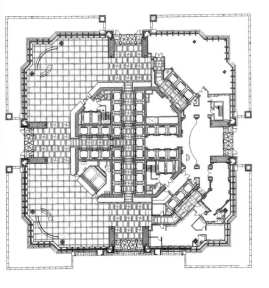

The base of the tower holds a shopping area, an auditorium and spaces connected with the five-star Grand Hyatt Hotel. Offices take up the next 47 floors and the following 38 floors contain the hotel, with spectacular view from its more than 500 rooms.

La base della torre ospita una zona commerciale, un auditorium e spazi relazionati con il Grand Hotel Hyatt di cinque stelle. Gli uffici occupano i primi 47 piani e nei restanti 38 si trova l'hotel con spettacolari vedute dalle sue oltre 500 camere.

In de voet van de toren is een winkelcentrum ondergebracht, een auditorium en ruimten die zijn verbonden met het vijfsterrenhotel Grand Hyatt. Kantoren nemen de volgende 47 verdiepingen in beslag, en de daaropvolgende 38 verdiepingen behoren tot het hotel. De meer dan vijfhonderd kamers bieden een spectaculair uitzicht.

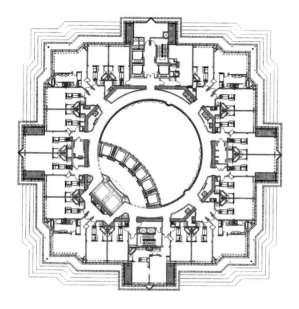

Beneath the ground floor there are three underground parking levels, hotel facilities, a shopping area, a courtyard, a foyer and areas set aside for electrical, water and waste treatment installations, as well as central heating and airconditioning units.

Sotto il livello del suolo si trovano tre piani di parcheggio, installazioni dell'hotel, uno spazio commerciale, un patio, una sala d'ingresso ed aree per installazioni elettriche, acqua, trattamento di residui, impianti di riscaldamento e refrigerazione.

Ondergronds bevinden zich een parkeergarage van drie verdiepingen, hotelvoorzieningen, een winkelgebied, een binnenplein, een foyer en gebieden die zijn voorbehouden aan installaties voor elektriciteit, water en afvalverwerking, centrale verwarming en airconditioning.

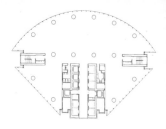

JIUSHI CORP. HQTRS.

FOSTER & PARTNERS

CLIENT / CLIENTE / OPDRACHTGEVER: JIUSHI CORPORATION

TOTAL AREA / SUPERFICIE / TOTALE OPPERVLAKTE: 62.000 m²

FLOORS / PIANI / VERDIEPINGEN - HEIGHT / ALTEZZA / HOOGTE: 40 fl / 168 m

2000

The Chinese city of Shanghai has experienced a drastic transformation caused by the emergence of tall office buildings. The location of this building, half way between the river and the traditional neighborhoods, conditions its structure (form and layout). Thus, a semi-circular glass-covered façade opens towards the river and two sloping planes towards the city. The building tries to propose a respectful architecture to the city and people, proposing novel mechanisms like the triple ventilated façade system which allows natural light to enter without altering the energetic behavior of the interior of the building, or the incorporation of gardens in the interior of the building.

La città cinese di Shangai ha subito, negli ultimi dieci anni, una trasformazione drastica che ha determinato la costruzione indiscriminata di alti edifici di uffici tra gli edifici di case tipiche, che hanno cambiato il volto di alcuni quartieri. L'ubicazione del terreno, a cavallo tra il fiume e due rioni tradizionali, determina la struttura –sia la forma che la disposizione– dell'edificio. La facciata di vetro semicircolare è rivolta verso il fiume e le due pareti inclinate verso la città. L'edificio propone un tipo di architettura rispettosa della città e delle persone grazie a dispositivi innovativi come il sistema della tripla facciata ventilata che lascia trapelare la luce naturale senza modificare l'equilibrio energetico dell'edificio o l'incorporazione di giardini al suo interno.

De Chinese stad Shanghai heeft een drastische verandering ondergaan door de komst van hoge kantoorgebouwen. De ligging van dit gebouw halverwege de rivier en de traditionele wijken heeft de structuur gedefinieerd (vorm en verdeling). Een glazen façade in de vorm van een halve cirkel staat gericht op de rivier en twee schuin aflopende delen zijn georiënteerd op de stad. De architectuur van het gebouw wil de stad en de inwoners met respect tegemoet treden en biedt voordelen als natuurlijke ventilatie van de driezijdige façade, waarbij natuurlijk licht kan binnenvallen zonder het energetisch gedrag van het interieur te beïnvloeden, en de toevoeging van tuinen in het interieur van het gebouw.

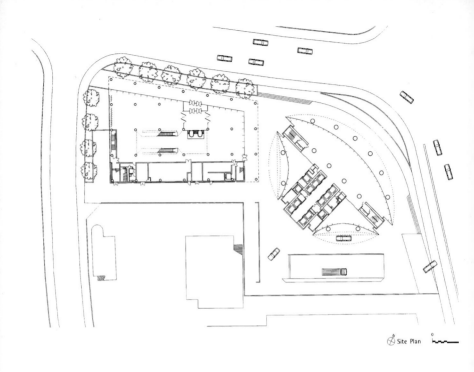

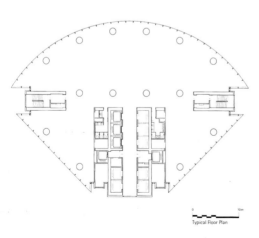

Typical Floor Plan

The tower is located on the corner of a lot with a gentle gesture, next to the base, a six-floor building with shops, restaurants and bars follows the line of the street, a porch with arcades is situated on the ground floor, reminiscent of the city's traditional shops.

La torre è situata in un angolo del terreno; accanto, un edificio di sei piani con negozi, bar e ristoranti segue l'allineamento della strada, al pianterreno un sottoportico con arcate si richiama alle tradizionali arcate dei negozi della città.

De toren bevindt zich op de hoek van een perceel met een lichte curve. Naast de basis volgt een gebouw van zes verdiepingen met winkels, restaurants en bars de loop van de straat. Op de begane grond zijn doorgangen met arcaden gesitueerd die herinneren aan de karakteristieke winkels in de stad.

The tower occupies a very significant neighborhood in the city which has been turned into a new financial area. Jiushi Corporation's investments have helped in the development of the South Bund and its building wishes to be a positive symbol of the new economic and town planning development of the city.

La torre sorge in un quartiere estremamente rappresentativo della città, diventato un moderno centro d'affari. Gli investimenti della Jiushi Corporation hanno contribuito allo sviluppo del South Bund ed il loro edificio aspira ad essere il simbolo dell'attuale sviluppo economico ed urbanistico della città.

De toren ligt in een zeer belangrijke buurt van de stad die is omgetoverd tot een nieuwe zakenwijk. De investeringen van Jiushi Corporation hebben de ontwikkeling van de South Bund bevorderd en het gebouw van het bedrijf wil een positief symbool van de nieuwe economische en stedenbouwkundige ontwikkeling van de stad zijn.

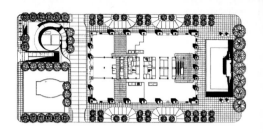

JOHN HANCOCK CENTER

SKIDMORE, OWINGS & MERILL LLP (SOM)

CLIENT / CLIENTE / OPDRACHTGEVER: JOHN HANCOCK MUTUAL LIFE INSURANCE CO.

1969

TOTAL AREA / SUPERFICIE / TOTALE OPPERVLAKTE: 260.000 m²

FLOORS / PIANI / VERDIEPINGEN - HEIGHT / ALTEZZA / HOOGTE: 100 fl / 344 m

Popularly known as Big John, it occupies a dominant place in the city's skyline. The complexity of the program (offices, shopping areas, leisure and residential zones) reflects the multiple activities of the luxurious district where it is located. The tower, whose surface area shrinks from the ground floor to the top floor, contains a chunk of the city. The base contains the shopping and leisure areas together with the lobbies of the office floors immediately above. Half way up are the 711 apartments of different typologies which have their own lobbies and parking spaces. The metallic structural system is the material of the façade, which acts as a corset, strengthening the building along with the structural floors.

Popolarmente conosciuto come Big John, occupa un luogo dominante nella linea dell'orizzonte della città. La complessità del programma (uffici, zone commerciali, ozio e abitazioni) rispecchia la molteplice attività del lussuoso distretto in cui si colloca. La torre che diminuisce di superficie dal piano terra fino all'ultimo piano, contiene un pezzo della città. Alla base si trovano le zone commerciali e di ozio insieme ai vestiboli dei piani destinati agli uffici immediatamente superiori; a mezza altezza si dispongono i 711 appartamenti di differenti tipologie che hanno ingressi propri e parcheggi. Il sistema strutturale metallico è il materiale della facciata, che agisce come un corsetto, irrigidendo l'edificio insieme ai piani strutturali.

Dit gebouw, dat in de volksmond ook wel Big John wordt genoemd, neemt een dominante plaats in de skyline van de stad. Het multifunctioneel karakter (kantoren, winkelcentra, vrijetijdsruimte en woningen) weerspiegelt de levendigheid van de luxe wijk waarin het gebouw staat. De toren wordt naar boven toe steeds smaller en vormt een stad op zich. In de voet bevinden zich de winkel- en vrijetijdsruimten met de toegangshallen naar de kantooretages direct erboven. Halverwege bevinden zich de 711 verschillende appartementen, die over eigen toegangshallen en parkeerplaatsen beschikken. De façade bestaat uit een korsetachtige metalen structuur die het gebouw verstevigt.

Due to the considerable functional approach required by the John Hancock Center, a 70-storey office block and a 45-storey apartment block, the building site was too small. The problem was resolved by building a sole, 100-storey tower that freed a large portion of the ground floor.

A causa dell'importante programma funzionale che richiedeva il Centro John Hancock, una torre di uffici di 70 piani e un'altra di appartamenti di 45, risultava un'occupazione superiore a quanto permesso dall'area edificabile. Si risolse il problema costruendo un'unica torre di 100 piani, liberando gran parte del piano terra.

Vanwege het aanzienlijke functionele programma zou het John Hancock Center worden uitgerust met een kantoortoren van 70 verdiepingen en daarnaast een toren met 45 verdiepingen voor appartementen. Deze omvang ging de capaciteit van het perceel echter te boven. Het probleem werd opgelost door de bouw van een enkele toren van honderd verdiepingen.

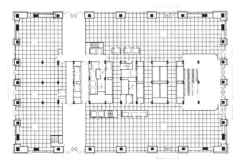

The core of the tapered tower lends structural stability to the whole and resolves the functional requirements at the same time. The tower gradually tapers from the ground floor to the top, with offices on the lower floors and apartments on the upper floors.

Il tronco della torre di forma affusolata conferisce stabilità strutturale all'insieme e ad un tempo rispetta i requisiti funzionali, in modo che la torre diminuisce di superficie dal piano terra all'ultimo piano ospitando uffici nel piano terra e appartamenti in quelli superiori.

De kern van de taps toelopende toren biedt het geheel structurele stabiliteit en voldoet tegelijkertijd aan functionele eisen. De toren versmalt geleidelijk naar boven toe. Op de lagere verdiepingen bevinden zich kantoren, op de hogere verdiepingen appartementen.

The tower's rigidity is achieved through diagonal elements on the façade together with the structural floors, which are determined by the intersection of diagonal elements and corner pillars. In its time, this great tubular structure was both innovative and economical.

La rigidit`a della torre si ottiene mediante elementi diagonali nella facciata insieme ai piani strutturali che si determinano grazie all'intersezione degli elementi diagonali e dei pilastri negli angoli. Questa grande struttura tubolare fu nel suo momento innovatrice ed economica.

De stevigheid van de toren wordt bewerkstelligd door diagonale elementen op de façade en de structurele verdiepingen, die worden bepaald door de kruising van diagonale elementen en hoekpilaren. Deze fantastische buisvormige structuur was op het moment van bouw zowel vernieuwend als kostenbesparend.

The steel structure that makes up the façade is covered with black aluminium and anti-dazzle glass with bronze coloured window frames. Both the base of the building and its several foyers are walled with travertine marble.

La facciata che è la struttura di acciaio è ricoperta di alluminio nero e vetri antiriflesso con stipiti di alluminio in color bronzo alle finestre. Tanto la base dell'edificio così come i differenti ingressi sono ricoperti con mermo travertino.

De stalen structuur van de façade is bedekt door zwart aluminium en niet-reflecterend glas met bronsgekleurde raamlijsten. Zowel de basis als de verschillende toegangshallen zijn bekleed met travertijn.

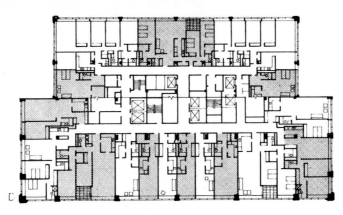

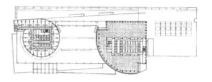

JR CENTRAL TOWER & STATION

KOHN PEDERSEN FOX ASSOCIATES PC (KPF)

CLIENT / CLIENTE / OPDRACHTGEVER: JR TOKAI

2000

TOTAL AREA / SUPERFICIE / TOTALE OPPERVLAKTE: 409.000 m²

FLOORS / PIANI / VERDIEPINGEN - HEIGHT / ALTEZZA / HOOGTE: 59 fl / 250 m

The JR Central is a complex for different uses like shops, hotel, cultural center, offices, car park and a train station. It is a complex work of architecture and engineering because apart from the metro, there are other trains circulating and it is ready to welcome the magnetic train in the future (which is in the development phase). The structural solution plays a very important role in the design of the building because it conditions it, allowing a large and complex mixed-use building with the great flows of people an intermodal station implies. The JR Central works as a door to the 21st Century.

Il JR Central è un complesso con varie funzioni, vi si trovano infatti dei negozi, un hotel, un centro culturale, degli uffici, un parcheggio ed una stazione ferroviaria. Si tratta di una complessa opera architettonica ed ingenieristica. Oltre alla metropolitana, passano qui altri treni; la stazione inoltre è pronta per accogliere in futuro il treno "magnetico" che attualmente è in fase di progetto. La soluzione strutturale gioca un ruolo importante nel progetto dell'edificio dal momento che lo condiziona e rende possibile un edificio grande e complesso con differenti funzioni e un notevole traffico, dovuto alla stazione intermodale. Il JR Central rappresenta una porta sul XXI secolo.

JR Central is een multifunctioneel complex met winkels, hotel, cultuurcentrum, kantoren, parkeerplaats en station. Het is een uitzonderlijk staaltje architectuur en bouwkunst, die naast de metro en andere treinverbindingen ook voorzien zal worden van een magneetzweefbaan (in ontwikkeling). De structurele oplossing speelt een zeer belangrijke rol in het ontwerp van dit gebouw, aangezien deze oplossing het ontwerp bepaalt. Zo kan een groot complex en multifunctioneel gebouw gecreëerd worden, wat in is staat de grote menigten te verwerken die van en naar het station gaan. Het JR Central geldt als een poort naar de 21e eeuw.

The vertical elements intersect with horizontal volume. The composition of all the façades is based on the rhythm of stripes.

Le elementi verticali si intersecano su una struttura orizzontale. La composizione delle facciate si basa su una successione di fasce.

De verticale elementen kruisen het horizontale volume. De samenstelling van alle façaden is gebaseerd op het ritme van de 'strepen'.

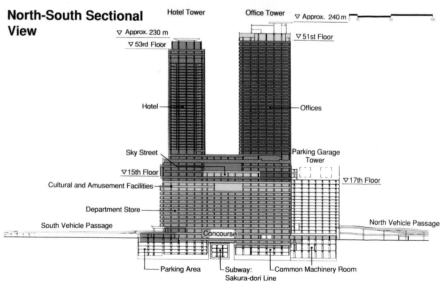

North-South Sectional View

Hotel Tower

Office Tower ▽ Approx. 240 m

▽ Approx. 230 m

▽ 53rd Floor

▽ 51st Floor

Hotel

Offices

Sky Street

Parking Garage Tower

▽ 15th Floor

▽ 17th Floor

Cultural and Amusement Facilities

Department Store

South Vehicle Passage

North Vehicle Passage

Concourse

Parking Area

Subway: Sakura-dori Line

Common Machinery Room

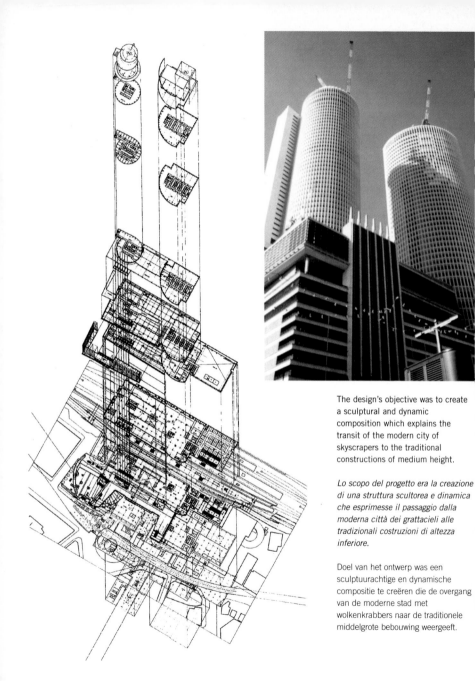

The design's objective was to create a sculptural and dynamic composition which explains the transit of the modern city of skyscrapers to the traditional constructions of medium height.

Lo scopo del progetto era la creazione di una struttura scultorea e dinamica che esprimesse il passaggio dalla moderna città dei grattacieli alle tradizionali costruzioni di altezza inferiore.

Doel van het ontwerp was een sculptuurachtige en dynamische compositie te creëren die de overgang van de moderne stad met wolkenkrabbers naar de traditionele middelgrote bebouwing weergeeft.

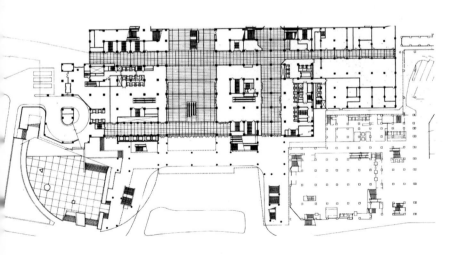

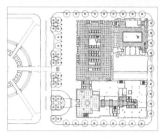

KEY TOWER

CESAR PELLI & ASSOCIATES INC.

1991

CLIENT / CLIENTE / OPDRACHTGEVER: RICHARD & DAVID JACOBS GROUP

TOTAL AREA / SUPERFICIE / TOTALE OPPERVLAKTE: 116.200 m²

FLOORS / PIANI / VERDIEPINGEN - HEIGHT / ALTEZZA / HOOGTE: 57 fl / 289,6 m

This office tower, also known as Society Center, is found between the two main public spaces of the city center, the Mall and the Public Square. It is situated next to the Society for Savings Bank (1890, Burnham y Root). The base follows the basic lines of the Society from the stone cladding, the changes of material and the treatment of the façade plan which moves towards the interior for the tower to rise gently without absorbing the building, which is much less tall. Both buildings form part of the same financial entity, which is why they are connected internally, although this is not reflected in the exterior treatment.

Questa torre di uffici, nota anche con il nome di Society Center, si trova tra due delle aree pubbliche più importanti del centro della città, il Mall e la Public Square. Si trova accanto alla Society for Savings Bank, (1890, Burnham e Root). La base si attiene ai dettami fondamentali della Society sia per l'incamiciatura di pietra che per i cambiamenti dei materiali e la lavorazione della superficie della facciata, che si ritrae mano a mano verso l'interno per lasciare spazio alla torre che si innalza senza assorbire l'edificio, di altezza inferiore. Entrambi gli edifici sono di proprietà dello stesso ente finanziario e sono messi in comunicazione da un passaggio che non è visibile dall'esterno.

De kantoorkolos staat ook bekend als Society Center en bevindt zich tussen twee grote pleinen, de Mall en de Public Square. Het gebouw staat naast de Society for Savings Bank (1890, Burnham en Root) De voet volgt de basislijnen van de stenen façade van de Society. Na verandering van materiaal en vervolgens het trapsgewijze terugwijken van de façade verheft zich de toren geleidelijk en voorkomt zo dat het veel kleinere aangrenzende gebouw wordt 'opgeslokt'. Beide bouwwerken behoren tot dezelfde bank en zijn van binnen met elkaar verbonden, iets wat aan de buitenkant niet te zien is.

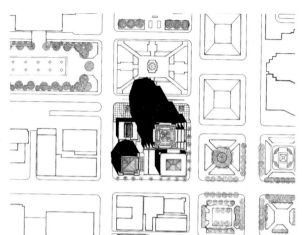

Siting plan of the tower which is situated in the northern corner of the Public Square, where the BP America Tower and the Terminal Towers are also located.

Pianta dell'ubicazione della torre, che si trova nell'angolo nord della Public Square, dove si trovano anche la BP America Tower e le torri Terminal.

Plattegrond van de toren, die zich in de noordelijke hoek van de Public Square bevindt, waar eveneens de BP America Tower en de Terminal Towers staan.

The tower gradually loses mass as it rises, starting out from the base which is at the same height as the Society, an example of the classical American skyscraper of the end of the 19th Century.

La torre, un classico esempio di grattacielo americano della fine del XIX secolo, situato all'altezza della Society, perde volume mano a mano che guadagna in altezza.

De toren verliest naar de top toe geleidelijk aan massa, te beginnen bij de voet, die dezelfde hoogte heeft als de Society, een voorbeeld van de klassieke Amerikaanse wolkenkrabber aan het eind van de 19e eeuw.

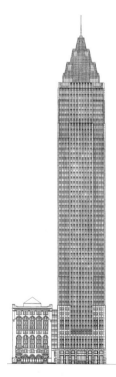

LEE THEATRE PLAZA

DENNIS LAU & NG CHUN MAN
ARCHITECTS & ENGINEERS (H.K) LTD

CLIENT / CLIENTE / OPDRACHTGEVER: HYSAN DEVELOPMENT COMPANY LIMITED

1994

TOTAL AREA / SUPERFICIE / TOTALE OPPERVLAKTE: 29.300 m²

FLOORS / PIANI / VERDIEPINGEN - HEIGHT / ALTEZZA / HOOGTE: 24 fl / 99 m

The building is a high-rise shopping center, its classical style is a reference to the large department stores of the past. The project has 22 commercial floors in a tower, which contain shops, stores, restaurants and a cinema, which rise above two more floors, defined by the base of the building, where the projects are developed for access, relationship with the city and the most public activities of the complex. Formally, the tower is a series of prisms which combine with a glass-covered cylinder topped with a dome which contains viewing platform spaces related to the patio.

L'edificio è un centro commerciale sviluppato in altezza di stile classico che si rifà alla gloria ereditata dai grandi magazzini commerciali di epoche passate. Il progetto è costituito da una torre di ventidue piani con negozi, magazzini, ristoranti ed un cinema che sorgono su due piani della base dell'edificio, nei quali si trovano l'ingresso, il punto d'incontro con la città e le attività pubbliche del complesso. Da un punto di vista strutturale, la torre è costituita da una serie di prismi combinati con un cilindro di vetro sormontato da una cupola nella quale si trova un belvedere collegato con il patio.

Het gebouw doet dienst als winkelcentrum, opgetrokken in de klassieke stijl van de grote warenhuizen van vroeger. Er zijn 22 etages met winkels, boetieks, warenhuizen, restaurants en een bioscoop boven een basis, die wordt gebruikt voor de toegang, de relatie tot de stad en de meeste publieke activiteiten van het complex. Qua vorm bestaat de toren uit een reeks prisma's, gekroond door een met glas bedekte cilinder met koepel, met uitzicht op het open binnenplein.

The design of the main staircase aims for continuity from the lobby to the dome by means of an interior patio.

Il disegno della scala principale cerca la continuità, dall'atrio alla cupola, per mezzo di un patio interno.

Het ontwerp van het trappenhuis streeft naar continuïteit van de lobby tot aan de koepel door middel van een open binnenplein.

The public areas of the building aim to express their social vocation by means of the use of triple spaces and viewing platforms.

Le zone di collegamento dell'edificio vogliono esprimere la loro finalità sociale per mezzo dell'uso di spazi e belvederi tripli.

De openbare ruimten van het gebouw zijn zo ingericht dat ze hun sociale functie uitdrukken door middel van het gebruik van drie etages en uitkijkplatformen.

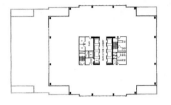

LIBERTY PLACE

MURPHY / JAHN INC. ARCHITECTS + ZEIDER ROBERTS

CLIENT / CLIENTE / OPDRACHTGEVER: ROUSE & ASSOCIATES

1990

TOTAL AREA / SUPERFICIE / TOTALE OPPERVLAKTE: 112.000 m² (I) + 111.600 m² (II)

FLOORS / PIANI / VERDIEPINGEN : 61 fl / 58 fl
HEIGHT / ALTEZZA / HOOGTE: 288 m (I) / 258,5 m (II)

The Liberty Place complex was the first to rise above the height limit of 150 meters, defined by the upper part of the William Penn (the founder of the city) statute in the City Hall. In 1983, a promoter presented a plan to build two office buildings, the Liberty Place towers, several blocks from City Hall, in Market Street. Following its approval, the plan radically altered the city's silhouette, because the municipal council established a special corridor of high-rise buildings along this street. With the construction of Two Liberty Place, a shopping complex and a hotel were incorporated into the program.

Il complesso Liberty Place è stato il primo a superare il limite di 150 metri segnatodalla parte superiore della statua di William Penn (il fondatore della città) nel City Hall. Nel 1983, un imprenditore presentò un progetto per la costruzione di due edifici di uffici, le Torri Liberty Place a vari isolati dal City Hall, a Market Street. Una volta approvato,il progetto cambiò drasticamente il volto della città dal momento che la giunta municipale decise di assegnare un corridoio speciale per gli edifici alti lungo Market Street. Con la costruzione delle Two Liberty Place vennero aggiunti al progetto un centro commerciale ed un albergo.

Liberty Place was het eerste complex dat uitsteeg boven de hoogtegrens van 150 m van het William Penn-standbeeld (de stichter van de stad) in de City Hall. In 1983 presenteerde een promotor het ontwerp voor de bouw van twee kantoortorens, de Liberty Place-torens in Market Street, op enkele huizenblokken van de City Hall verwijderd. Na inwilliging van het project werd het ontwerp drastisch gewijzigd, want de gemeenteraad besloot in deze straat een speciaal deel te bestemmen voor hoge gebouwen. Met de bouw van de twee torens van Liberty Place werden er nog een winkelcomplex en een hotel opgenomen in het bestemmingsplan.

Above, panoramic view of
Philadelphia before the construction
of Two Liberty Place. On the right,
interiors of the elegant split-level
lobby of One Liberty Place.

*In alto, panorama di Filadelfia prima
della costruzione delle Two Liberty
Place. A distra, interno dell'elegante
atrio su diversi livelli del-l' One
Liberty Place.*

Boven: een panorama op Philadelphia
vóór de bouw van Two Liberty Place.
Rechts: het elegante interieur van de
toegangshal van One Liberty Place,
dat meerdere verdiepingen beslaat.

The two towers hold a formal dialog. Thus the use of materials and the form of the coverings serve to link them both together.

Tra le due torri esisteun dialogo formale. L'impiego dei materiali e la forma dei tetti fungono da legame tra loro.

De beide torens zijn qua vorm in samenspraak. Het gebruik van dezelfde materialen en een gelijke vorm van het dak dient ertoe ze met elkaar te verbinden.

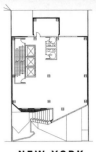

LVMH TOWER

CHRISTIAN DE PORTZAMPARC

CLIENT / CLIENTE / OPDRACHTGEVER: LVMH

1999

TOTAL AREA / SUPERFICIE / TOTALE OPPERVLAKTE: 8.683 m²

FLOORS / PIANI / VERDIEPINGEN - HEIGHT / ALTEZZA / HOOGTE: 24 fl -100 m

The building, headquarters of the French firm of luxury goods Louis Vuitton Moët Hennessy, is located on a narrow site with very little façade, flanked by the grey granite Chanel building and the brick Chemical Bank and facing the green granite IBM prism at the landmark corner of Madison Avenue with 57th street. With all these premises, the architect was faced with the dilemma of how to resolve a façade that was supposed to be representative without getting absorbed by the surroundings and without reflecting it as a mirror by using a conventional curtain wall. Christian de Portzamparc skilfully resolved the problem by designing a translucent curtain wall that folds back at several levels creating a stepped effect as it gains height.

L'edificio è situato in un area stretta con pochissima facciata; è la sede corporativa di una firma francese di articoli di lusso (Louis Vitton e Moët Hennessy); è circondato dall'edificio di granito grigio di Chanel e da quello di mattoni del Chemical Bank e dirimpetto al prisma di granito verde di IBM, alla confluenza della Madison Avenue con la 57° Strada, un luogo emblematico. Con tutte queste premesse l'architetto si misurò con il problema di una facciata che doveva essere rappresentativa senza essere assorbita dall'ambiente circostante e senza rifletterlo come una specchio utilizzando un muro cortina convenzionale. Christian de Portzamparc ha risolto con maestria questo esercizio disegnando un muro cortina traslucido di frange orizzontali che si ripiega su diversi livelli e si allinea man mano che acquista altezza.

Het gebouw bevindt zich op een smal stuk grond met een zeer kleine façade. Het is het hoofdkantoor van de Franse producent van luxeartikelen (Louis Vuitton Moët Hennesy) op de hoek van Madison Avenue en 57th Street. Aangrenzende gebouwen zijn het Chanelgebouw uit grijs graniet en de bakstenen Chemical Bank. Tegenover staat het IBM-prisma van groen graniet. Door al deze omstandigheden zag de architect zich voor de taak gesteld om voor dit gebouw een representatieve façade te creëren die niet door de omgeving zou worden geabsorbeerd, zonder gebruik te maken van een conventionele spiegelfaçade. Christian de Portzamparc loste het probleem vaardig op door een doorzichtige façade te ontwerpen die op meerdere niveaus op verschillende wijze naar achteren wordt 'gevouwen' en steeds verder terugwijkt naarmate de hoogte toeneemt.

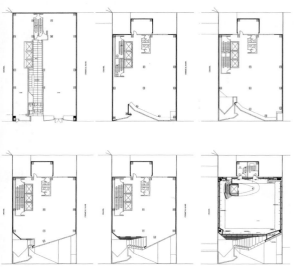

Floors of different levels of the tower where the lower floors have a greater surface area since an adjoining, narrow, four-storey building was bought by the owners.

Pianta dei diversi livelli della torre in cui i primi alloggi hanno più superficie sul piano dal momento che addossato all'area della torre c'era un edificio di poco spessore e di quattro piani di altezza che venne acquistato dalla proprietà.

Verschillende verdiepingen van de toren, waarbij de lagere verdiepingen een grotere oppervlakte bezitten, omdat ze zich uitstrekken over het terrein waar eerder een aangrenzend smal gebouw van vier verdiepingen stond, dat de eigenaren hebben opgekocht.

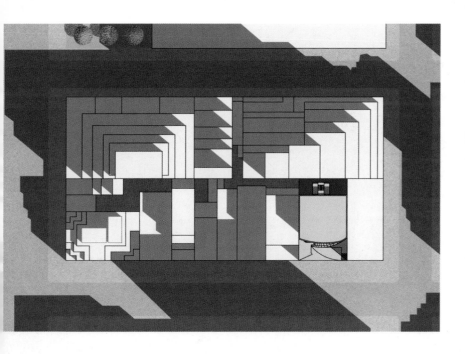

The wall curtain on the façade is the result of a well-thought design that creates a quality atmosphere in which to work and through which the city can be observed through a screen with different degrees of transparency.

Il muro cortina della facciata è frutto di un meditato disegno che crea un ambiente circostante caldo nei posti di lavoro dai quali la città è percepita attraverso una trama con differenti gradi di trasparenza.

De façade is het resultaat van een zeer goed uitgedacht ontwerp, dat een uitstekende sfeer heeft geschapen om in te werken. De stad kan worden geobserveerd door een scherm met verschillende graden van transparantie.

MAX BUILDING

MURPHY / JAHN INC. ARCHITECTS

CLIENT / CLIENTE / OPDRACHTGEVER: DEUTSCHE GRUNDBESITZ MANAGEMENT GMBH	**1999**

TOTAL AREA / SUPERFICIE / TOTALE OPPERVLAKTE: 111.334 m²

FLOORS / PIANI / VERDIEPINGEN - HEIGHT / ALTEZZA / HOOGTE: 63 fl / 228 m

This office tower seeks its space among the forest of buildings which surround it, its own merits shining forth like a torch which finally melts with the sky. How did this idea come about? By means of the use of a few strategies; for example, treating the volume of the building as an ascending figure. At the same time, the design of the plan and the choice of materials create a sense of lightness. The building gradually loses mass as it ascends, the floor surface gradually diminishes and the façade gradually gains more glass and leaves steel behind in the race to the summit of the city.

Questa torre di uffici cerca spazio tra la selva di edificiche la circondano, brilla di luce propria come una fiaccola, per poi fondersi con il cielo. Come si è materializzata quest'idea? Grazie all'uso di alcune tattiche. Per esempio, la lavorazione del volume dell'edificio come un corpo ascendente. A sua volta, la forma della base, come la scelta e l'impiego dei materiali, danno una sensazione di leggerezza. L'edificio innalzandosi perde volume, la superficie diminuisce gradualmente e la facciata guadagna in vetro mentre si spoglia dell'acciaio nella corsa alle vette della città.

Deze kantoorkolos zoekt zijn plek te midden van een zee van omringende gebouwen. Zijn eigen licht schijnt als een fakkel om ten slotte in de hemel te verdwijnen. Hoe is dit concept ontstaan? Door verscheidene strategieën toe te passen, bijvoorbeeld door het gebouw te beschouwen als een opstijgende figuur. Tegelijkertijd scheppen het ontwerp en de gekozen bouwmaterialen een gevoel van lichtheid. Het gebouw verliest geleidelijk aan massa bij toenemende hoogte, terwijl de beglazing van de façade steeds nadrukkelijker wordt en het staal achter zich laat in de race naar de top van de stad.

The Max Building is found in the financial center of Frankfurt, where the majority of the skyscrapers rise, very close to the Commerzbank by N. Foster and the new Rhein-Main Tower.

Il Max Building si trova nella zona degli affari di Francoforte, dove si innalzano la maggior parte dei grattacieli, vicinissimo al Commerzbank di N. Foster e la nuova Rhein-Main Tower.

Het Max Building ligt in het financiële hart van Frankfurt, waar zich de meeste wolkenkrabbers bevinden, vlak bij de Commerzbank van N. Foster en de nieuwe Rhein-Main Tower.

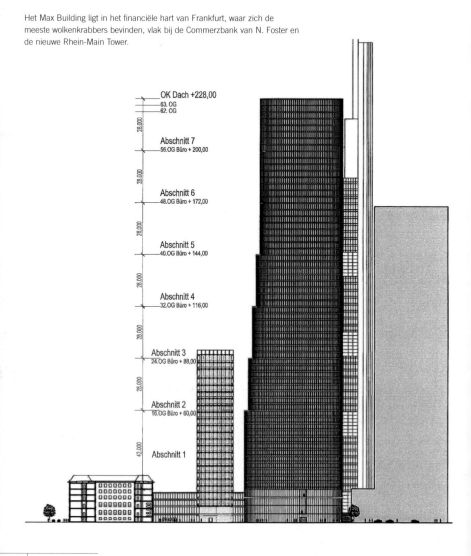

OK Dach +228,00
63. OG
62. OG

Abschnitt 7
56.OG Büro + 200,00

Abschnitt 6
48.OG Büro + 172,00

Abschnitt 5
40.OG Büro + 144,00

Abschnitt 4
32.OG Büro + 116,00

Abschnitt 3
24.OG Büro + 88,00

Abschnitt 2
16.OG Büro + 60,00

Abschnitt 1

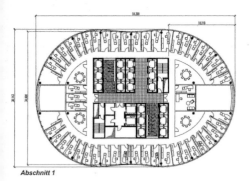

Abschnitt 1

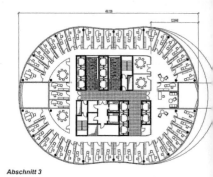

Abschnitt 3

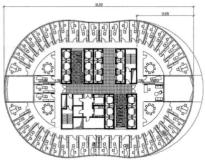

Abschnitt 2

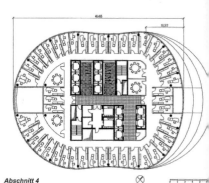

Abschnitt 4

The project was the winner of a competition to build on a block with existing mixed-use buildings.

Il progetto vinse un concorso per la costruzione in un isolato con edifici già esistenti adibiti a varie funzioni.

Het ontwerp kreeg de eerste prijs in een wedstrijd om een hoekperceel te bebouwen in een blok met al bestaande multifunctionele gebouwen.

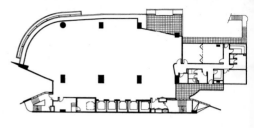

MENARA-UMNO

T.R. HAMZAH & YEANG SDN BHD

CLIENT / CLIENTE / OPDRACHTGEVER: SOUTH EAST ASIA DEVELOPMENT CORPO-
RATION BREAD KOMPLEK KEWANGAN, JALAN RAJA CHULAN, KUALA LUMPOUR

TOTAL AREA / SUPERFICIE / TOTALE OPPERVLAKTE: 19.091 m²

FLOORS / PIANI / VERDIEPINGEN - HEIGHT / ALTEZZA / HOOGTE: 21 fl / 94 m

1998

This office building incorporates an auditorium with its own entrance from the exterior, as well as locating on the ground floor the different lobby spaces of a bank. The design of the office floors responds to the following requirements: To use as far as possible natural ventilation (although the building has an air conditioning system as a reinforcement) and that no work space is more than 6·5 m from a window to receive illumination and renew the natural air. This was the first high-rise building in Malaysia to use the wind as a ventilation system to create interior conditions of comfort instead of using mechanical systems.

Questo edificio di uffici incorpora un auditorium con accesso indipendente dall'esterno, oltre all'ubicazione a piano terra dei differenti spazi dell'ingresso di una banca. Il disegno dei piani per gli uffici risponde ai seguenti requisiti: utilizzare al massimo la ventilazione naturale (sebbene l'edificio abbia tuttavia installazioni di aria condizionata come rinforzo), e che nessuno spazio di lavoro sia a più di 6,5 m. da una finestra per ricevere illuminazione e rinnovamento d'aria naturali. Questo fu il primo edificio di grande elevazione in Malesia a utilizzare il vento come sistema di ventilazione per creare condizioni interne di comfort invece di utilizzare sistemi meccanici.

In dit kantoorgebouw is een auditorium opgenomen met een eigen ingang; daarnaast bevinden zich op de begane grond de verscheidene lobby's van een bank. Het ontwerp van de kantoorverdiepingen is afgestemd op de volgende eisen: maximaal gebruik van natuurlijke ventilatie (hoewel het gebouw ook extra is voorzien van airconditioning) en geen enkele werkplek mag meer dan 6,5 meter van een raam zijn verwijderd, om gebruik te kunnen maken van natuurlijk licht en de ventilatie. Dit is de eerste hoogbouw in Maleisië waarin wind als ventilatiesysteem wordt gebruikt in plaats van mechanische systemen.

Air walls, an experimental element designed by the architects, besides forming part of the energy system, also serve the purpose of a powerful aesthetic element. The building rises as an urban sculpture, trimmed off by the sky over the city.

Les murs à chambre à air, un élément expérimental conçu par les architectes, outre leur appartenance au système d'énergie, ils représentent un élément esthétique puissant. Le bâtiment s'élève comme une sculpture urbaine qui est coupée contre le ciel de la ville.

De luchtmuren vormen een experimenteel element van de architecten. Ze maken niet alleen deel uit van het energiesysteem, maar dienen ook als een sterk esthetisch element. Het gebouw verrijst als een stedelijke sculptuur, die zich aftekent tegen de hemel.

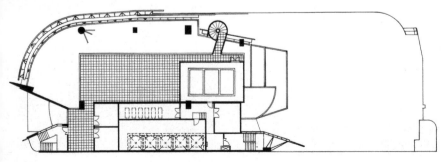

The relationship between the
building and the exterior is constant,
incorporating terraces and balconies,
which is unusual in a traditional
office block, usually characterised by
a closed space which is isolated from
the exterior.

*Il rapporto dell'edificio con l'esterno
è costante, incorporando terrazze e
balconi inusuali in un edificio di
uffici tradizionale che è invece per lo
più un ambiente chiuso e isolato
dall'esterno.*

Het gebouw is door middel van
terrassen en balkons overal verbonden
met het exterieur, iets wat
ongebruikelijk is in een traditioneel
kantoorgebouw, dat zich gewoonlijk
kenmerkt als een gesloten ruimte,
geïsoleerd van het exterieur.

The tower is full of elements that
serve both functional and aesthetic
purposes, where looks is not the at
the centre of its architectural
planning. The end result is a
personal, innovative and
revolutionary language.

*La torre è piena di elementi che
rispettano tanto i requisiti funzionali
quanto quelli estetici, senza essere
quest'ultima premessa il punto di
partenza dell'architettura, il
risultato finale è un linguaggio
personale, innovatore e ....
rivoluzionario.*

De toren kent talloze elementen die
zowel functionele als esthetische doe-
len dienen, terwijl het uiterlijk niet het
uitgangspunt was in de architectonische planning. Het eindresultaat is een
persoonlijk, vernieuwende en revolu-
tionaire wijze van uitdrukken.

MESSETURM

MURPHY / JAHN INC. ARCHITECTS

1990

CLIENT / CLIENTE / OPDRACHTGEVER: MESSE FRANKFURT

TOTAL AREA / SUPERFICIE / TOTALE OPPERVLAKTE: 85.200 m²

FLOORS / PIANI / VERDIEPINGEN - HEIGHT / ALTEZZA / HOOGTE: 63 fl / 251 m

The Messe Tower or Messeturm is located in the Messe Frankfurt complex, a large exhibition center where the historical buildings, the Festhalle of 1909 and the Kongresshalle, from after the Second World War, are found. The tower is like a bell tower functioning as the main gate to the site and was at one time the tallest building in Europe. Its design should symbolize the commercial power of Frankfurt. The architects were inspired by those American skyscrapers of the twenties and thirties. The result is a classical building which aims to stand out from the anonymous container buildings of the contemporary city.

La Messe Tower, altrimenti-detta Messeturm, si trova nel Complesso Messe Frankfurt, un grande centro di esposizioni in cui si trovano due edifici storici, il Festhalle del 1909 ed il Kongresshalle, costruito dopo la Seconda Guerra Mondiale. L'edificio assomiglia ad un campanile che funge da porta principale del recinto. Fu, all'epoca, l'edificio più alto d'Europa. Sarebbe dovuto essere il simbolo della potenza economica di Francoforte. Gli architetti si ispirarono ai grattacieli americani degli anni venti e trenta. Il risultato è un edificio classico che vorrebbe distinguersi dagli edifici anonimi "contenitori" della città moderna.

De Messeturm bevindt zich op het grote Messe-complex in Frankfurt, waarop ook twee historische gebouwen staan, te weten de Festhalle uit 1909 en de Kongreßhalle, die na de Tweede Wereldoorlog werd gebouwd. Het gebouw heeft veel weg van een klokkentoren, doet tegelijkertijd dienst als de hoofdpoort naar het terrein van de Messe en was na voltooiing het hoogste gebouw van Europa. De Messeturm belichaamde de financiële macht van Frankfurt. De architecten lieten zich inspireren door de Amerikaanse wolkenkrabbers uit de jaren 1920 en 1930. Het resultaat is een klassiek bouwwerk, dat zich onderscheidt van de anonieme bouwblokken in de moderne stad.

The building has a square base from which the tower emerges. The tower is also square, and a glass cylinder emerges from the tower and is finally crowned with a pyramid.

L'edificio ha base quadrata sulla quale si innalza la torre, anch'essa quadrata, da questa, a sua volta, emerge un cilindro di vetro sormontato da una piramide.

Het gebouw heeft een vierkante voet, waarop de eveneens vierkante toren zich verheft. In het hogere gedeelte volgt een glazen cilinder die uiteindelijk wordt bekroond door een piramide.

The materials used are glass and red granite. The way they combine makes the changes of volume of its tripartite design stand out.

I materiali impiegati sono il vetro ed il granito rosso. Il modo in cui sono combinati evidenzia i differenti volumi della forma tripartita.

De gebruikte materialen zijn glas en rood graniet. De wijze waarop ze zijn gecombineerd zorgt ervoor dat de veranderingen in volume van het drieledige ontwerp opvallen.

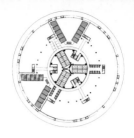

MILLENNIUM TOWER

FOSTER & PARTNERS

1989

CLIENT / CLIENTE / OPDRACHTGEVER: OBAYASHI CORPORATION

TOTAL AREA / SUPERFICIE / TOTALE OPPERVLAKTE: 1.040.000 m²

FLOORS / PIANI / VERDIEPINGEN - HEIGHT / ALTEZZA / HOOGTE: 170 fl / 840 m

Growth predictions for Tokyo predict that it will outstrip fifteen million inhabitants in 2020. The Millennium Tower approaches the growth of the city of the future proposing solutions to the social challenges that urban expansion generates and particularly, in the case of Tokyo, where the lack of land will impede continued construction in the city. The project was commissioned by a Japanese corporation to promote housing, offices and shopping areas on land reclaimed from the sea A conical tower was proposed, the tallest in the world, where a community of 60,000 people could be self-sufficient, generating their own resources.

Secondo le previsioni, nel 2020 la popolazione di Tokyo supererà i quindici milioni di abitanti. La Millenium Tower si pone il problema della crescita della città del futuro ed offre soluzioni ai problemi causati dall'espansione urbanistica, particolarmente importanti nel caso di Tokyo, dove la mancanza di aree edificabili impedisce l'ulteriore crescita della città. Il progetto è stato commissionato da una corporazione giapponese con il fine di incentivare la costruzione di abitazioni, uffici e zone commerciali in terreni sottratti al mare. Venne avanzata la proposta di una torre conica, la più alta del mondo, nella quale una comunità di 60.000 persone potesse produrre le sue proprie fonti d'energia ed essere autosufficiente.

De voorspellingen ten aanzien van de bevolkingsaanwas geven aan dat Tokyo in 2020 meer dan vijftien miljoen inwoners zal hebben. De Millennium Tower is een antwoord op de verwachte groei van de stad en de sociale problematiek waarmee stedelijke expansie gepaard gaat, met name in Tokyo, waar gebrek aan grond voortzetting van verdere woningbouw zal inperken. De opdracht voor het project werd gegeven door een Japans bedrijf dat zich bezighoudt met de promotie van woon-, kantoor- en winkelruimten op land dat op de zee is gewonnen. Men ontwierp een conische toren, de hoogste van de wereld, waarin een gemeenschap van 60.000 mensen autarkisch zou kunnen leven.

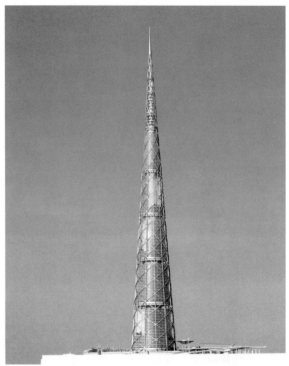

Reminiscent of Frank Lloyd Wright's one mile tower, the Millennium Tower is a vertical city where a high velocity train travels both horizontally and vertically.

La Millenium Tower, che ricorda la torre di un miglio di F.L.L. Wright, è una vera e propria città verticale nella quale un treno ad alta velocità circola sia orizzontalmente che verticalmente.

De Millennium Tower roept de 'mijltoren' van Frank Lloyd Wright in herinnering: het is een loodrechte stad waarin een hogesnelheidstrein zowel horizontaal als verticaal circuleert.

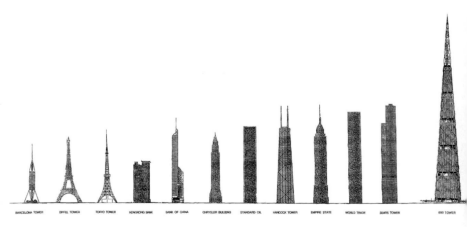

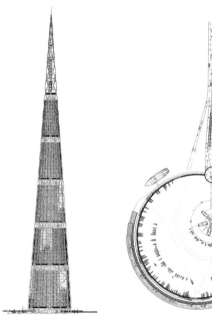

The tower groups its flats in vertical neighborhoods. Built on an artificial island and surrounded by a marina, it is connected to the coast by a bridge.

La torre riunisce i piani in quartieri verticali. Edificata su un'isola artificiale e circondata da un porto sportivo, è collegata alla terraferma da un ponte.

In de toren zijn de woningen in verticale buurten georganiseerd. Hij staat op een kunstmatig eiland, omringd door een jachthaven en is door een brug met de kust verbonden.

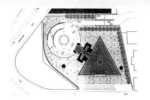

NATIONAL COMMERCIAL BANK

SKIDMORE, OWING & MERRILL LLP (SOM)

CLIENT / CLIENTE / OPDRACHTGEVER: NATIONAL REAL ESTATE COMPANY OF JEDDAH	**1984**
TOTAL AREA / SUPERFICIE / TOTALE OPPERVLAKTE: 71.160 m²	
FLOORS / PIANI / VERDIEPINGEN - HEIGHT / ALTEZZA / HOOGTE: 27 fl / 126 m	

Located on a square at the shore of the Red Sea, the project's geometry, conceived from its location and the climatology, consists of a 27-floor triangular prism of offices next to a 6-floor circular garage. The verticality of the tower is drastically interrupted by three large gaps, two of seven floors towards the city and one of nine floors towards the northwest and the sea. The windows of the offices open directly onto these courtyards, leaving the exterior volumetry of the building absolutely smooth and white, as a reference to the typical introverted orientation of the design of inner courtyards of Islamic architecture.

La struttura geometrica del progetto, situato in una piazza sulle sponde del Mar Rosso, venne ideata sulla base dell'ubicazione e del clima ed è costituita da un prisma triangolare di uffici di ventisette piani e da un garage circolare su sei livelli. La verticalità della torre è interrotta bruscamente da tre grandi spazi vuoti, due di sette piani a sud, rivolto verso la città, ed uno di nove piani a nord-est, verso il mare. Mentre le finestre degli uffici danno sui patii, la superficie esterna dell'edificio è interamente piatta e bianca, in linea con lo stile caratteristico dei patii dell'architettura islamica, rivolti verso l'interno.

De geometrie van dit gebouw is ontleend aan de locatie en de klimatologie. Het is gelegen aan een plein aan de kust van de Rode Zee en bestaat uit een driehoekig prisma van 27 verdiepingen met kantoren naast een ronde parkeergarage. Het verticale karakter van de toren wordt abrupt onderbroken door drie enorme openingen: twee aan de zuidkant naar de stad met elk zeven verdiepingen en een naar het noordwesten en de zee met negen verdiepingen. De vensters van de kantoren kijken uit op de binnenpleinen, waarbij de buitenkant van het gebouw volledig glad en wit blijft, een verwijzing naar de inwaarts gerichte oriëntatie van binnenplaatsen in de islamitische architectuur.

The interior decoration presents exquisite finishes and materials, including black granite and marble.

La decorazione degli interni presenta rifiniture e materiali raffinati, tra i quali il granito ed il marmo.

De interieurdecoratie toont schitterende bewerkingen en materialen zoals zwart graniet en marmer.

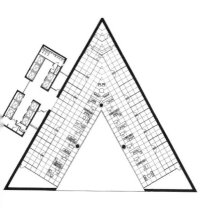

The program develops meeting spaces of a high level, a luxurious restaurant floor with mobile partitions for executives and a cafeteria full of color for employees.

Il progetto prevede spazi comuni di alto standing; un lussuoso ristorante con separé mobili per i dirigenti ed un variopinto bar per gli impiegati.

Het bouwwerk is uitgerust met ontmoetingsruimten van een hoog niveau, voor leidinggevenden een verdieping met een luxe restaurant met verplaatsbare scheidingswanden en een kleurrijke cafetaria voor de werknemers.

The building offers an introverted image towards the city, showing part of the interior through three large windows.

L'edificio, che mostra parte degli interni attraverso tre grandi finestre, offre un'immagine introversa rispetto alla città.

Het gebouw ziet er vanuit de stad gesloten uit en laat slechts een klein deel van het binnenste zien door drie grote openingen in de façade.

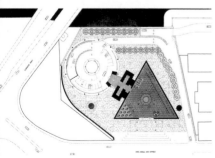

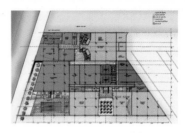

NOVA BOCANA

RICARD BOFILL TALLER D'ARQUITECTURA

CLIENT / CLIENTE / OPDRACHTGEVER: PORT DE BARCELONA

2004

FLOORS / PIANI / VERDIEPINGEN - HEIGHT / ALTEZZA / HOOGTE: 56 fl / 168

The port of Barcelona is going to be transformed over the next few years into the great port facility which symbolizes the definitive opening of the city to the sea. With the construction of the Nova Bocana, Barcelona acquires the triple vocation of capital of Catalonia, the western Mediterranean and intermodal city of the southern Mediterranean. The port enlargement project will be carried out over 15 hectares of land reclaimed from the sea, on which a new fishing port, a luxury hotel at the edge of the sea in the shape of a sail and a multimedia center for leisure and interactive activities will be built.

Il porto di Barcellona si trasformerà, nei prossimi anni, in un grande complesso portuale simboleggiante la decisiva espansione della città verso il mare. Grazie alla costruzione di Nova Bocana, Barcellona riunisce la vocazione di capuluogo della Catalogna, del Mediterraneo occidentale e di città intermodale del Mediterraneo Meridionale. Il progetto di ampliamento del porto verrà realizzato su quindici ettari di terreno sottratto al mare, sul quale verranno edificati un nuovo porto peschereccio, un albergo di lusso a forma di vela in riva al mare ed un centro multimediale per attività ricreative ed interattive.

De komende jaren wordt de haven van Barcelona grondig verbouwd en zal zo de definitieve opening van de stad naar de zee symboliseren. Met de bouw van de Nova Bocana verwerft Barcelona er een derde status bij: hoofdstad van Catalonië, van de westelijke Middellandse Zee en zuidelijke stad in het Middellandse-Zeegebied. De havenuitbreiding zal gestalte krijgen op vijftien hectare land dat op zee is gewonnen. Hier zullen een nieuwe vissershaven, een luxe hotel in de vorm van een zeil aan de kust en een vrijetijds- en multimediacentrum worden gebouwd.

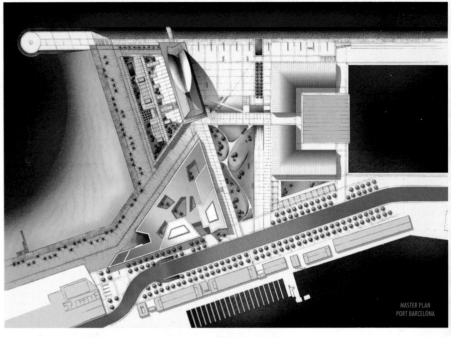

MASTER PLAN
PORT BARCELONA

N O V A   B O C A N A
P O R T   D E   B A R C E L O N A

The seashore hotel is conceived of as a signal, a sail billowing in the wind.

L'albergo in riva al mare è concepito come un segnale, una vela spiegata contro il vento.

Het hotel aan de kust is ontworpen als een zeil in de wind, een herkenningspunt in de haven.

NTT HQTRS.

CESAR PELLI & ASSOCIATES INC.

CLIENT / CLIENTE / OPDRACHTGEVER: NTT

1995

FLOORS / PIANI / VERDIEPINGEN - HEIGHT / ALTEZZA / HOOGTE: 30 fl / 127 m

The NTT was conceived as an integrated model of one of the most important commercial, corporate and cultural centers in Japan. The rectangular form of the lot is conditioned by the passage of two important streets, one of which is a transited dual carriageway raised above street level. This factor conditions the volumetric ordering of the block: a low body acts as a protective screen, closing the space devoted to a public garden and the entrance to the office tower. It also has a telecommunications center, conference hall and a bar-restaurant hall for all the staff.

L'edificio della NTT venne concepito come il modello integrato di uno dei centricommerciali, corporativi e culturali più importanti del Giappone. La forma rettangolare della costruzione si deve al passaggio di due importanti strade, una delle quali è una sopraelevata di notevole traffico. Questo fattore condiziona la disposizione dell'isolato nello spazio: un corpo inferiore,che funge da schermo, ripara e chiude l'area adibita a giardino pubblico e ad ingresso della torre di uffici. Inoltre qui si trova un centro di telecomunicazioni, una sala riunioni ed un salone con un bar ed un ristorante per il personale.

Het NTT werd ontworpen als geïntegreerd model in een van de belangrijkste winkel-, zaken- en culturele centra van Japan. Het rechthoekige perceel wordt begrensd door twee belangrijke verkeersaders. Een van deze is een hoger gelegen autoweg. Dit gegeven bepaalt de inrichting van het volume op het terrein: de basis schermt de achterliggende groenvoorzieningen af en vormt tegelijkertijd de toegang tot de kantoortoren. In het gebouw is ook een telecommunicatiecentrum, een congreszaal en een restaurant met bar voor de werknemers.

Superimposition of the tower and the base building. The chosen materials are steel, glass and Minnesota stone.

La torre e l'edificio-base sovrapposti. I materiali impiegati sono l'acciaio, il vetro e la pietra del Minnesot

De toren en de basis van het gebouw. De gekozen materialen zijn staal, glas en Minnesota-steen.

Corner of the tower with the low building, point where one of the entrances to the garden is.

Scorcio della torre con l'edificio inferiore, zona in cui si trova uno degli ingressi del giardino.

Een hoek van de toren en het lage gebouw – hier bevindt zich een van de ingangen naar de tuin.

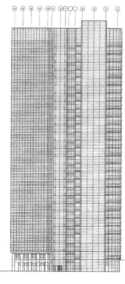

The garden is a public space where leisure and cultural acts can be held. The aim is to boost the leisure and corporate character of the building.

I giardino è uno spazio pubblico dove si possono svolgere attività ludiche e culturali.

De tuin is een openbare ruimte voor vrijetijds- en culturele activiteiten.

The connection between the two buildings is made via the square and the bridge. Interiors: lobbies of both buildings.

Il collegamento dei edifici avviene grazie alla piazza e ad un ponte. Interni: atrii dei due edifici.

Beide gebouwen zijn door een brug over een plein met elkaar verbonden. Interieurfoto's: de toegangshallen van beide gebouwen.

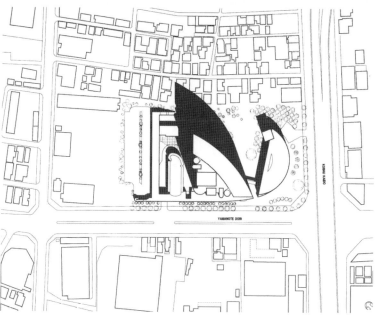

ONE CHASE MANHATTAN PLAZA

SKIDMORE, OWINGS & MERRILL LLP (SOM)

CLIENT / CLIENTE / OPDRACHTGEVER: CHASE MANHATTAN BANK

1961

TOTAL AREA / SUPERFICIE / TOTALE OPPERVLAKTE: 214.000

FLOORS / PIANI / VERDIEPINGEN - HEIGHT / ALTEZZA / HOOGTE: 60 fl / 247,8 m

This was the first great corporate skyscraper which moved from the financial center of Manhattan to be located in the area south of the Brooklyn Bridge. Its interesting design, a rectangular body of glass and aluminum with no more ornamentation than the structure, contrasts with the stone building which surround it. From the town planning point of view, it marked a new concept in 1961 by changing the zonification of the district by replacing the breeches of the first skyscrapers with the tower form, understood to mean a rectangular body, in exchange for ceding part of its surface area for a 8,300 m² public square.

È stato il primo grande grattacielo corporativo costruito fuori del centro finanziario di Manhattan e situato nella zona a sud del ponte di Brooklyn. Il suo affascinante design, un corpo rettangolare di vetro ed alluminio senza nessun'altra decorazione che la propria struttura, contrasta con gli edifici di pietra circostanti. Dal punto di vista urbanistico, l'edificio rappresentò una svolta, dal momento che diede inizio al cambiamento del quartiere, sostituendo le rientranze dei primi grattacieli con la forma della torre, concepita come un corpo rettangolare che cede una parte della sua superficie alla piazza pubblica di 8.300 m².

Dit was de eerste grote wolkenkrabber van een onderneming die niet zoals gebruikelijk in het financiële hart van Manhattan werd opgericht, maar in het deel van de stad ten zuiden van de Brooklyn Bridge. Het interessante ontwerp, een rechthoekige constructie van glas en aluminium met geen andere decoratie dan de eigen structuur, contrasteert met de omringende bakstenen gebouwen. Bezien vanuit het oogpunt van stadsplanning markeerde de toren in 1961 een nieuw bebouwingsconcept door de zone-indeling van een wijk te veranderen. De rechtlijnige massa verving de grilliger vorm van de eerste wolkenkrabbers, terwijl een deel van de oppervlakte werd vrijgemaakt voor een openbaar plein van 8.300 m².

Rising up from a glass structure
below the level of the square, a
sculptural fountain known as "the
water garden" lies in an 18 meter
diameter orientally
inspired pond.

*Su una struttura di vetro situata al di
sotto del livello della piazza, sorge
una imponente fontana nota come "Il
giardino dell'acqua", una vasca di
stile orientale con un diametro di
diciotto metri.*

Ondergronds verrijst uit een
glasstructuur een fontein met een
oosters geïnspireerde vijver van
achttien meter doorsnede, ook wel
bekend als de 'watertuin'.

Above, ground floor of the building showing part of the metallic structure. The plan, long and narrow, is fortified with three stretches of columns, a central one defining the service area, and two more defining the diaphanous office areas.

In alto, il pianterreno dell'edificio nel quale si può osservare una parte della struttura alla vista. La pianta, lunga e stretta, è dotata di tre file di colonne, una al centro che delimita l'area dei servizi e le altre due la superficie destinata all'area degli uffici a giorno.

Boven: de begane grond toont een deel van de openliggende metalen structuur. De lange en smalle bebouwing wordt versterkt door drie zuilenrijen: in het midden bevindt zich het deel met liften, terwijl links en rechts ervan de doorzichtige kantoorgedeelten liggen.

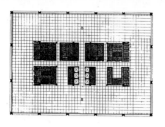

ONE LIBERTY PLAZA

SKIDOMORE, OWINGS & MERRILL LLP (SOM)

CLIENT / CLIENTE / OPDRACHTGEVER: GALBREATH-RUFFIN CORP. & U.S. STEEL CORP	**1973**

TOTAL AREA / SUPERFICIE / TOTALE OPPERVLAKTE: 200.000 m²

FLOORS / PIANI / VERDIEPINGEN - HEIGHT / ALTEZZA / HOOGTE: 54 fl / 226,5 m

Found in the heart of Wall Street, in Manhattan. The lot is divided into two different-sized blocks. And a proposal was made to use the full amount of building land in the biggest block to create a public green area in the other. The square covers the 3 meter disparity with regard to street level and concentrates part of the surface of the building in two levels below ground. When it was built, the latest structural technology advances in illumination and design were used, integrating the air conditioning systems and the vertical transport elements, thus obtaining diaphanous office floors.

Questo edificio,si trova nel cuore di Wall Street, a Manhattan. Il terreno edificabile era diviso in due isolati di dimensioni diverse. Pertanto, venne avanzata la proposta di riunire tutto il suolo edificabile nell'area più grande, per poter creare un giardino pubblico nell'altra. La piazza evita il dislivello di tre metri rispetto alla strada e accentra una parte della superficie dell'edificio su due livelli al di sotto del terreno. All'epoca, l'edificio venne dotato delle ultime innovazioni tecnologiche sia per quanto riguarda la struttura che per l'illuminazione ed il design; ottenendo superfici libere per gli uffici.

One Liberty Plaza ligt in het hart van Wall Street op Manhattan. Op het terrein stonden eerst gebouwen van verschillende hoogte. Het grootste stuk grond werd gebruikt voor de toren, het kleinere deel werd omgevormd tot een openbaar plein. Het plein kent een hoogteverschil van drie meter met het straatniveau, waardoor een deel van de bebouwde oppervlakte uit twee ondergrondse verdiepingen bestaat. Bij de constructie werd gebruik gemaakt van de nieuwste technologie in verlichting en vormgeving, waarbij de airconditioning werd geïntegreerd met de liften. Op deze wijze werden lichte kantoorverdiepingen verkregen.

The design selected in the structure of the building uses the intumescent flanges to protect the struts of the façade beams, thus notably reducing the cost of the building as well as giving character to its exterior image.

Il disegno prescelto per la struttura dell'edificio prevede ale ignifughe per proteggere l'anima dei longheroni della facciata, che diminuiscono notevolmente i costi dell'edificio e costituiscono la caratteristica del suo aspetto esterno

Het ontwerp voorzag in uitzetbare dwarsbalken van het gebouw, om de staalprofielen van de façade te beschermen. Hierdoor werden de kosten van de bouw aanmerkelijk verlaagd, terwijl het uiterlijk tegelijk aan karakter won.

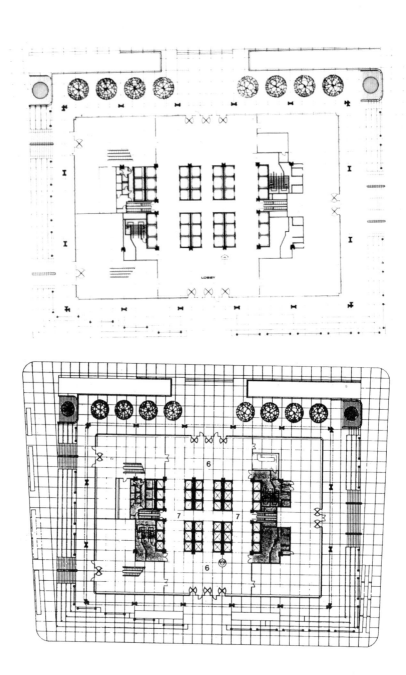

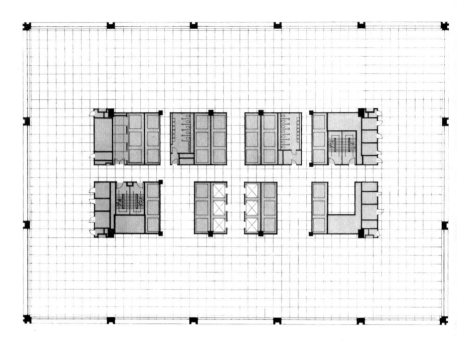

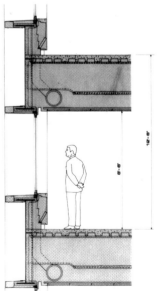

After the collapse of the Twin Towers (the result of the brutal attacks of September 11th 2001), this building has been affected in the structure and foundations.

A causa del crollo delle Torri Gemelle (provocato dal feroce attentato dell'11 settembre 2001), la struttura e le fondamenta di questo edificio sono state danneggiate e, al momento, sono pericolanti.

Door het instorten van de Twin Towers (als gevolg van de verschrikkelijke aanslag op 11 september 2001) werden de fundering en de structuur van het gebouw erg beschadigd.

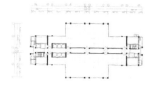

OSAKA
WORLD TRADE CENTER

NIKKEN SEKKEI

1995

TOTAL AREA / SUPERFICIE / TOTALE OPPERVLAKTE: 150,000 m²

FLOORS / PIANI / VERDIEPINGEN - HEIGHT / ALTEZZA / HOOGTE: 55 fl / 256 m

The WTCO is an office building which incorporates a series of public spaces such as shops, restaurants, bars, banquet and convention halls, the WTCO club, an auditorium and an observation platform in the form of a pyramid from which the whole bay can be seen.

The building incorporates a highly sophisticated technology which, by means of an IT system, regulates all the electricity and water systems. It is currently the tallest building on the west coast of Japan and has become a visual landmark of the coastal silhouette and the region of Kansai.

Il WTCO è un edificio da uffici, gli undici rimanenti sono destinatia varie attività comenegozi, ristoranti, bar, saloni per banchetti e convegni, il circolo WTCO, un auditorium ed un belvedere a forma di piramide dal quale si può ammirare l'intera baia. Tutti gli impianti dell'edificio, che possiede dei dispositivi tecnologici altamente sofisticati, sono regolati grazie a un sistema computerizzato. È, attualmente, l'edificio più alto della costa occidentale giapponese e fu concepito come un segno distintivo della linea costiera e della regione di Kansai.

De WTCO is een kantoorgebou met een aantal publieke functies zoals winkels, restaurants, bars feest- en vergaderruimten, d WTCO-club, een auditorium e een piramidevormig uitkijkpun met uitzicht over de hele baa In het gebouw zijn zeer geavan ceerde technologieën toegepas Zo reguleert een computersys teem alle elektrische en wate systemen.

Het is momenteel het hoogst gebouw aan de westkust va Japan en geldt als een herker ningspunt aan de kust en in d regio Kansai.

392 | OSAKA WORLD TRADE CENTER

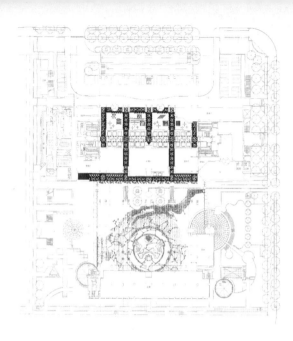

Shot of entrance to the building, ground floor. On the right, a view of an interior corridor where the choice of materials produces multiple reflections.

Piantina dell'ingresso dell'edificio, pianterreno. A destra, veduta di uno dei corridoi interni, nel quale i materiali riproducono molteplici riflessi.

Plattegrond van de ingang van het gebouw op de begane grond. Rechts een blik in een gang, waar de gebruikte materialen voor veel reflectie zorgen.

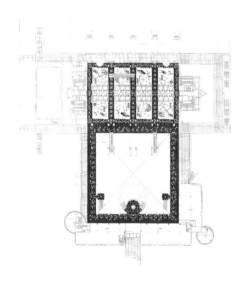

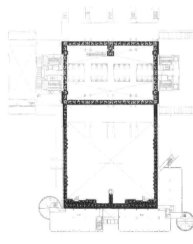

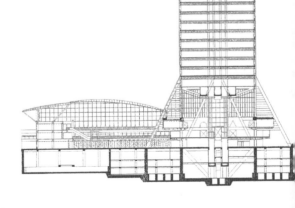

The ample 3000 m² hall also performs
the function of relating the building to
the floor, both from the functional and
volumetric point of view.

*L'ampio atrio di 3.000 m² ha la
funzione dimettere in relazione
l'edificio con il terreno sia da un
punto di vista funzionale che
dimensionale.*

De ruime 3.000 m² grote hal dient
zowel qua functie als in volume de
toren met de begane grond te
verbinden.

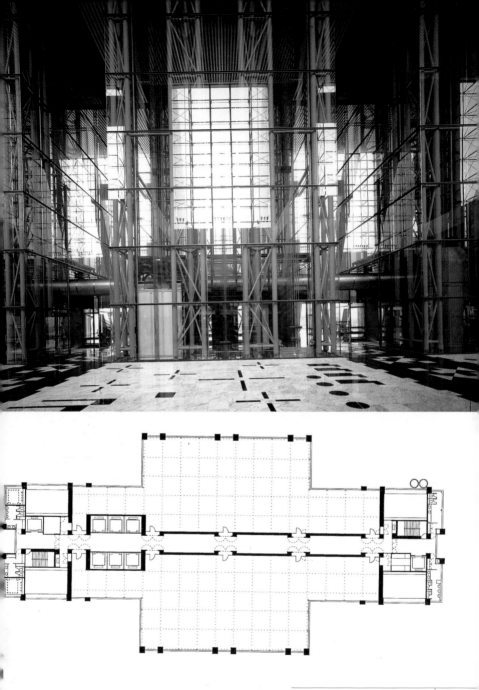

Different interior spaces, above WTCO club, the hall which is an atrium, the observation platform on the top floor and on the right, another detail of the hall.

Alcuni spazi interni, in alto, il circolo WTCO, la hall, che fa da atrio, il belvedere all'ultimo piano e, a destra, un altro particolare della hall.

Verschillende interieurs, van boven naar beneden: de WTCO-club, een atrium als toegangshal en het uitkijkpunt op de bovenste verdieping. Rechts de hal meer in detail.

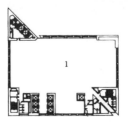

OUB CENTER

KENZO TANGE ASSOCIATES

CLIENT / CLIENTE / OPDRACHTGEVER: OVERSEAS UNION BANK

1986

TOTAL AREA / SUPERFICIE / TOTALE OPPERVLAKTE: 68.000 m²

FLOORS / PIANI / VERDIEPINGEN - HEIGHT / ALTEZZA / HOOGTE: 62 fl / 280 m

The Overseas Union Bank is one of the big Singapore banks. Its office headquarters is currently the tallest corporate building in Asia, although its battle with height hegemony is not solitary. This can be seen in the photographs taken on the banks of the Singapore River where building and financial area are perceived with all their strength. The OUB Center is found in Raffles Place where it relates to the pedestrian by means of a six-floor high base. The tower offers a double vision, rectangular from the river, triangular from the avenue.

L'Overseas Union Bankè una delle più importanti banche di Singapore. La sede dei suoi uffici è attualmente l'edificio corporativo più alto di tutta l'Asia, anche se nella competizione per la supremazia dei cieli non è solo. Ciò è particolarmente evidente nelle fotografie scattate dalle sponde del fiume Singapore, da dove sia l'edificio che l'intera zona d'affari possono essere ammirate in tutta la loromaestosità. L'Oub Center, che si trova a Raffles Place, cerca il rapporto con il cittadino con una base alta sei piani. Dalla torre si possono ammiraredue vedute, una panoramica rettangolare dal fiume, l'altra triangolare dal viale.

De Overseas Union Bank is een van de grote banken van Singapore. Het hoofdkantoor is op het ogenblik het hoogste gebouw van een onderneming in Azië, al zijn er meer gebouwen die deze titel trachten te verwerven. Dit is te zien op de foto's die werden genomen aan de oever van de Singapore River. Het financiële hart met de wolkenkrabbers laat zich nadrukkelijk gelden. Het Oub Center bevindt zich aan Raffles Place, waar de voetganger toegang heeft tot de wolkenkrabber via een voet van zes verdiepingen. De toren biedt twee verschillende aangezichten: rechthoekig vanaf de rivier en driehoekig vanaf de avenue aan de achterkant.

View of the main entrance to the
tower where the base withdraws seen
from different angles, also from the
avenue.

*Immagine dell'ingresso principale
della torre, nel punto in cui la base
indietreggia, visto da vari punti di
osservazione, tra i quali anche il
viale.*

Uitzicht op de terugwijkende
hoofdingang in de basis, gezien vanuit
verschillende hoeken en de avenue.

This broken view which the building produces from the exterior is obtained with the passage from rectangle to triangle and a subtle dodge in the design of the plan.

L'immagine frammentata che l'edificio produce ad un osservatore esterno è ottenuta con il passaggio dal rettangolo al triangolo e con una leggera torsione nelle linee del piano.

Het uiteenlopende uitzicht op de toren wordt verkregen door de overgang van rechthoek naar driehoek en een subtiele kunstgreep in het ontwerp.

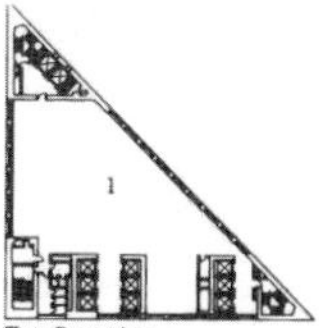

Top floor plan

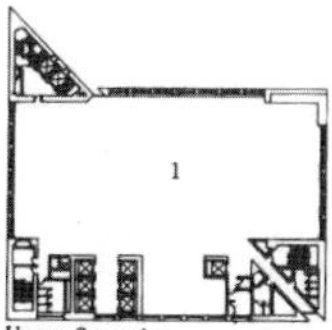

Upper floor plan

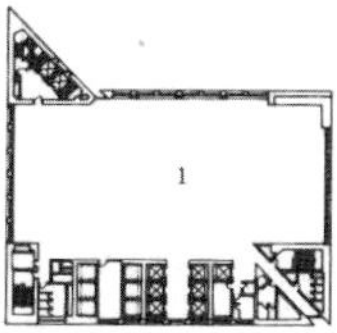

Middle floor plan

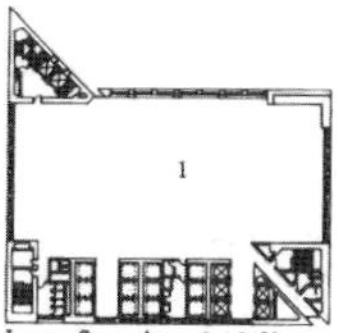

Lower floor plan 1 : 1400

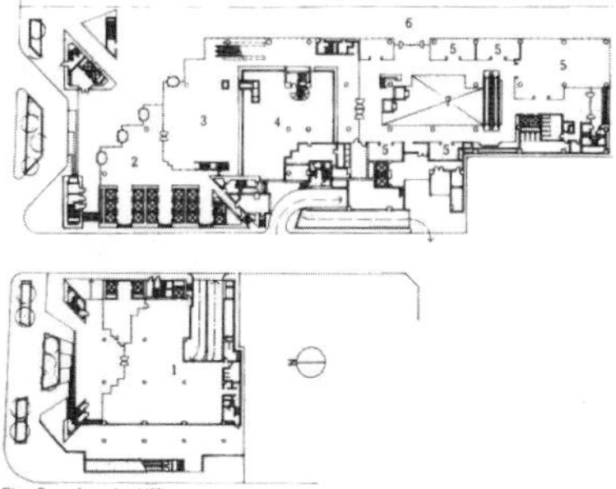

First floor plan 1 : 1400

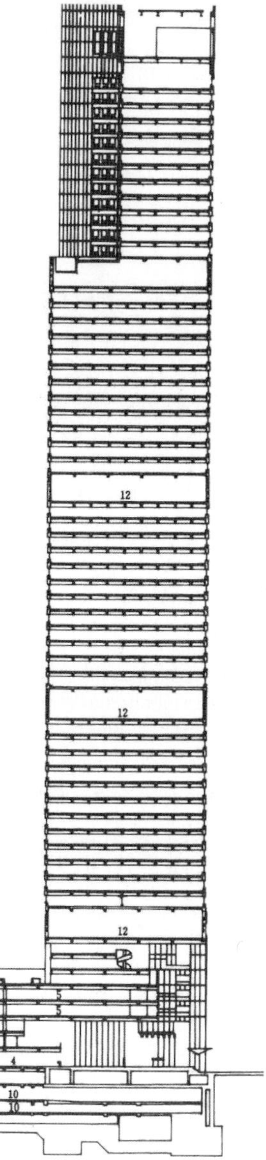

Section 1 : 1400

PETRONAS TOWERS

CESAR PELLI & ASSOCIATES INC.

CLIENT / CLIENT / OPDRACHTGEVER: KUALA LUMPUR CITY CENTER

1998

TOTAL AREA / SURFACE TOTALE / TOTALE OPPERVLAKTE: 884.000 m²

FLOORS / PLANS / VERDIEPINGEN - HEIGHT / HAUTEUR / HOOGTE: 88 fl / 452 m

The Petronas Towers, apart from being the tallest in the world at the moment, are an example of good architecture. In the rules of the competition for two towers for the city center it was requested that they have a Malaysian identity. The architects worked to define this architecture which had to reflect and resolve the physical and cultural conditions of the country: tropical climate and Islamic culture. The juxtaposition of the two squares (the most characteristic shape of Islam) gave rise to the type of plan. Meanwhile, the silhouette of the towers throws shadows reminiscent of those thrown by the traditional buildings of Malaysia.

Le Torri Petronas, oltre ad essere attualmente le più alte del mondo, sono un esempio di eccellente architettura. Le condizioni del concorso per la costruzione di due torri nel centro della città, specificavano che avrebbero dovuto possedere un forte spirito malaysiano. Gli architetti si sforzarono di creare una soluzione architettonica che rispecchiasse e risolvesse le condizioni geografiche e culturali del paese: il clima tropicale e la cultura islamica. La giustapposizione di duequadrati (la forma geometrica caratteristica dell'Islam) è alla base della tipica struttura. Inoltre, il profilo delle torri proietta un'ombra che ricordaquella degli edifici tradizionali malaysiani.

De Petronas Towers zijn op dit moment de hoogste torens van de wereld en gelden als voorbeeld van geslaagde architectuur. De voorwaarden van de competitie waren dat er twee torens in het stadscentrum moesten verrijzen, die een Maleisische identiteit moesten bezitten. De architecten kwamen met een ontwerp waarin zowel fysische als culturele kenmerken van het land waren verwerkt, zoals het tropische klimaat en de islamitische cultuur. Twee naast elkaar geplaatste vierkanten (de meest karakteristieke vorm van de islam) vormen de plattegrond. Het silhouet van de torens werpt schaduwen die herinneren aan de schaduwen van traditionele Maleisische gebouwen.

The façade is made of aluminum, glass and stainless steel. The structure is mixed: steel and concrete.

La facciata è di alluminio, vetro ed acciaio inossidabile. La struttura è mista: acciaio e cemento.

De façade bestaat uit aluminium, glas en roestvrij staal. De structuur is een mengeling van staal en beton.

At a height of 170 meters, floors 41 and 42 of the building, a panoramic bridge unites the two towers.

A 170 metri d'altezza, a livello del 41° e 42° piano del-l'edificio, un ponte panoramico unisce le due torri.

170 meter boven de grond ter hoogte van verdiepingen 41 en 42 van het gebouw verbindt een panoramische brug beide torens.

This bridge, aside from being a structural element, is symbolic at the same time, describing a gate open to the sky.

Il ponte, oltre ad essere parte della struttura, è anche un elemento simbolico dal momento che rappresenta una porta aperta verso il cielo.

Deze brug vormt niet louter een structureel element, maar staat ook symbool voor een open poort naar de hemel.

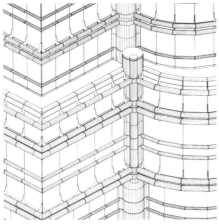

Detail of the crowning of the towers
and a stretch of the facade with the
solar protection elements.

*Particolare del coronamento delle
torri e di una parte della facciata con
gli elementi di protezione solare.*

Detail van de kroon van de torens en
een deel van de façade met
elementen ter bescherming tegen de
zon.

PLAZA 66
NANJING XI LU

KOHN PEDERSEN FOX ASSOCIATES PC

CLIENT / CLIENTE / OPDRACHTGEVER: HANG LUNG DEVELOPEMENTB CO.LTD.

2001

TOTAL AREA / SUPERFICIE / TOTALE OPPERVLAKTE: 298.000 m²

FLOORS / PIANI / VERDIEPINGEN - HEIGHT / ALTEZZA / HOOGTE: 60 fl / 288 m

This building is currently being built. It responds to a new typology of high-rise buildings. It consists of two towers connected by means of a structural bridge. The building rises along the most commercial street in the center of Shanghai. The program is a mixture of offices and shops. At street level a base of five floors with large interior public spaces houses the shops.

This atrium maintains the height of the traditional Chinese city, while the office towers maintain themselves at another level of the city.

Questo edificio, attualmenteancora in costruzione, risponde ad una nuova tipologia dell'edificiodi grande altezza. Si tratta di due torri collegate tra loro grazie ad un ponte. L'edificio si innalza in una delle strade più commerciali del centro di Shanghai. Il progetto, misto, comprende uffici e negozi; a livello della strada, uno zoccolo con un'altezza di cinque piani e con grandi spazi pubblici al suo interno ospita i negozi Questo ingresso conserva L'altezza della città cinese tradizionale, mentre le torri di uffici si trovano ad un altro livello della città.

Dit gebouw wordt momenteel opgericht en vormt een nieuw type hoogbouw – twee torens die door een brug worden verbonden. Het gebouw verrijst aan de belangrijkste handelsstraat in het centrum van Shanghai. Het project bestaat uit een mengeling van kantoren en winkels. Op straatniveau herbergt een basis van vijf verdiepingen met een grote openbare ruimte de winkels. Het atrium heeft dezelfde hoogte als de traditionele Chinese stad, terwijl de kantoortorens zich in andere sferen bevinden.

While at street level one perceives a group of buildings with different uses, the unitary use of granite in the treatment of the building gives an idea of the mass which unifies the group.

Mentre a livello della strada si può osservare un complesso con varie funzioni, l'uso del granito nella struttura dell'edificio da l'impressione di una massa che conferisce omogeneità al complesso.

Op straatniveau lijkt het een groep gebouwen voor uiteenlopende functies, maar het eenheidvormende gebruik van graniet in het gebouw geeft een idee van de totale omvang van het complex.

Above, the covered catwalk which
unites the two towers. On the right,
interior view of the shopping building
with ample public spaces and
different levels.

*In alto, la passerella coperta
che collega le due torri. A destra,
veduta dell'interno dell'edificio
commerciale con grandi spazi
pubblici e passerelle su differenti
livelli.*

Boven: overdekte doorgang die beide
torens verenigt. Rechts: blik in het
interieur van het commerciële gebouw
met veel openbare ruimte en
verschillende niveaus.

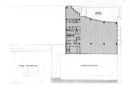

REPUBLIC NATIONAL BANK OF NEW YORK

ELI ATTIA ARCHITECTS

CLIENT / CLIENTE / OPDRACHTGEVER: EDMOND SAFRA AND REPUBLIC NATIONAL BANK OF NEW YORK.

TOTAL AREA / SUPERFICIE / TOTALE OPPERVLAKTE: 75.000 m²

FLOORS / PIANI / VERDIEPINGEN - HEIGHT / ALTEZZA / HOOGTE: 29 fl / 122 m

1984

Building projected to become the headquarters of the bank, incorporates a new building to three pre-existing buildings. Two of the previous buildings have considerable surface areas which the new diagram of the project incorporate as banking operation zones. The third, a beautiful stylish building which occupies the most significant corner of the project and which was the banks original headquarters, will become the centerpiece of the final design. The new building is the nexus linking all the others, contributing all the necessary technological infrastructures and the connections between the buildings.

Progettato per ospitare la sede centrale di questa banca, è formato da tre edifici già esistenti e da una nuova costruzione, dall'unione dei quali risulta una struttura composta: due degli edifici preesistenti, che possedevano notevoli dimensioni, sono incorporate al nuovo progetto come aree destinate ad operazioni bancarie; il terzo, un magnifico edificio ubicato nell'area più importante del progetto e che era originariamente la sede della banca, diventa l'elemento principale e più caratteristico nel nuovo. L'edificio attuale costituisce il legame d'unione di tutti gli altri, giacché apporta le infrastrutture tecnologiche necessarie ed i collegamenti tra gli edifici.

Dit gebouw werd ontworpen als nieuw hoofdkantoor van de bank. Bij de bebouwing werden drie reeds bestaande gebouwen betrokken. Twee van deze beschikken over aanzienlijke oppervlakten, die in het project zijn opgenomen als plaats voor alledaagse bankzaken. Het derde gebouw, een stijlvol en bijzonder opvallend hoekgebouw, was voorheen het hoofdkantoor van de bank en vormt in het uiteindelijke ontwerp de kern. Het nieuwe gebouw verenigt alle gebouwen en zorgt voor alle noodzakelijke technologische infrastructuren en de verbindingen tussen de gebouwen.

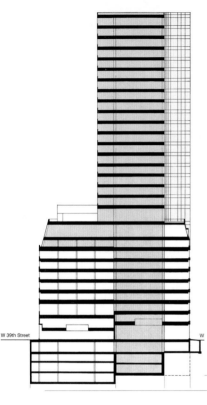

The main façade of the new tower combines bronze-toned glass, aluminum and granite, and is the formal result of the interaction of a positive faceted prism with a negative elliptical cylinder.

La facciata principale della nuova torre è di vetro con tonalità bronzo, da alluminio e da granito, ed è il risultato formale dell'interazione tra un prisma sfaccettato positivo ed un cilindro ellittico negativo.

De hoofdfaçade van de nieuwe toren is een combinatie van bronskleurig glas, aluminium en graniet. Het is het formele resultaat van de interactie tussen een geslepen prisma en een elliptische cilinder.

W 39th Street

W

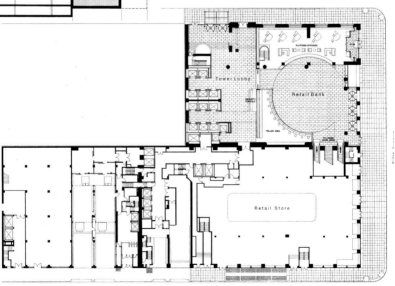

Tower Lobby

Retail Bank

Retail Store

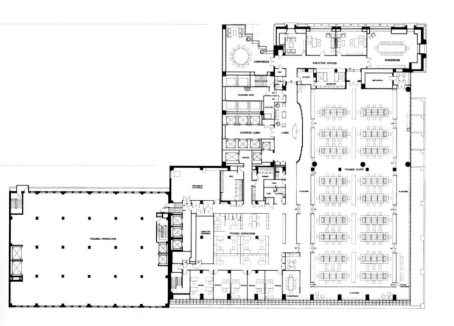

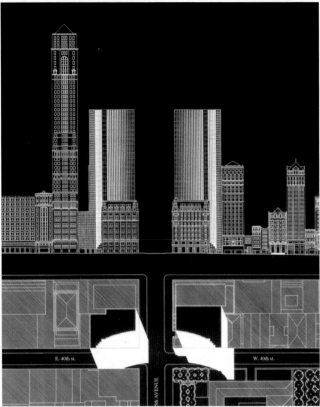

The fragmented curve embraces the representative building simply and dynamically, proposing complementary textures in shape and color.

La curva frammentata, che abbraccia l'edificio rappresentativo in un modo semplice però deciso, presenta strutture complementarie nelle forme e nei colori.

De gefragmenteerde curve va het gebouw loopt eenvoudig en dynamisch om het oude hoofdkwartier heen en biedt aanvullende texturen in vorm en kleur.

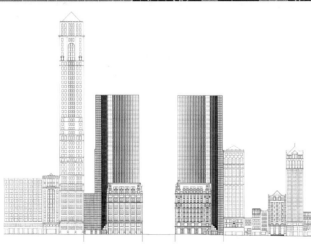

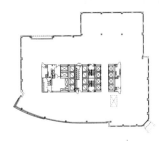

REUTERS BUILDING

FOX & FOWLE ARCHITECTS

CLIENT / CLIENTE / OPDRACHTGEVER: 3 TIMES SQUARE ASSOCIATES,LLC

2001

TOTAL AREA / SUPERFICIE / TOTALE OPPERVLAKTE: 855.000 m²

FLOORS / PIANI / VERDIEPINGEN - HEIGHT / ALTEZZA / HOOGTE: 30 fl -201 m

The new Reuters Building, also known as 3 Times Square, is situated at a strategic point, the most dynamic junction in the city, the heart of Manhattan, that of the commercial Seventh Avenue and the boisterous 42nd Street (in addition, it so happens that it is opposite a building by the same architect). At urban scale, the building is a pivot where all the energy of these two arteries converges, thus the south corner of the ground floor is cylinder-shaped. Formally, it responds to the heterogeneity of the siting, orthogonal ground plan, curved and irregular, it assembles plans and counterpoints textures, colors and languages, fighting to abandon the purity of the prism left by the Modern Movement.

Il nuovo Reuters Building, conosciuto anche come 3 Times Square, si situa in un punto strategico, nell'incrocio più dinamico della città, il cuore di Manhattan, quello della commerciale Settima Strada e la vivace 42esima Strada (oltre alla circostanza di collocarsi di fronte ad un altro edificio degli architetti). Nella scala urbana, l'edificio è un perno in cui confluisce tutta l'energia di queste due arterie, così come l'angolo sud del piano terra prende la forma di un cilindro. Formalmente risponde alla eterogeneità della collocazione, a pianta ortogonale, curva e irregolare, assemblando via via piani e contrapponendo superfici, colori e linguaggi, lottando per abbandonare la purezza del prisma che lasciò il Movimento Moderno.

Het nieuwe Reuters Building staa ook bekend als 3 Times Square e bevindt zich op een strategische loca tie aan de meest dynamische kru sing in het hart van Manhattan, tus sen de winkelstraat Seventh Avenu en de levendige 42nd Street (bover dien staat het tegenover een gebou van dezelfde architect). In stedeli, opzicht is het gebouw een ontmoe tingspunt waar alle energie uit dez hoofdaders samenkomt, hetgee wordt uitgedrukt door de cilindervor aan de zuidelijke hoek van de bega ne grond. Qua vorm weerspiegelt h, gebouw de heterogene omgeving Het orthogonale, gebogen en onre gelmatige ontwerp is uit meerde ontwerpen samengesteld en plaat texturen, kleuren en uitdrukking vormen tegenover elkaar in ee poging de zuiverheid van het pri ma van de Modern Movement va zich af te schudden.

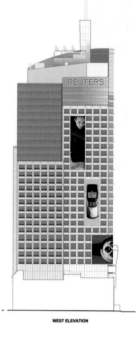

EAST ELEVATION NORTH ELEVATION WEST ELEVATION

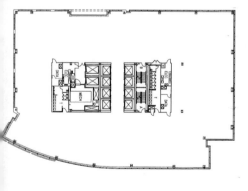

The architects confronted the unusual site of this building with the idea of designing a building that required the elegance of a 7th Avenue office block combined with the popular, commercial and theatrical charisma of New York's 42nd street.

Gli architetti affrontarono l'eccezionale collocazione di questo edificio con l'idea di disegnare una costruzione che rispondesse all'eleganza che necessita un edificio di uffici della Settima Strada con il carisma popolare, commerciale e teatrale della 42ª Strada di New York.

De bijzondere plaats van dit gebouw bood de architecten de uitdaging om een gebouw te ontwerpen met de elegantie van een kantoorgebouw aan de 7th Avenue en het populaire, commerciële en theatrale karakter van de 42nd Street.

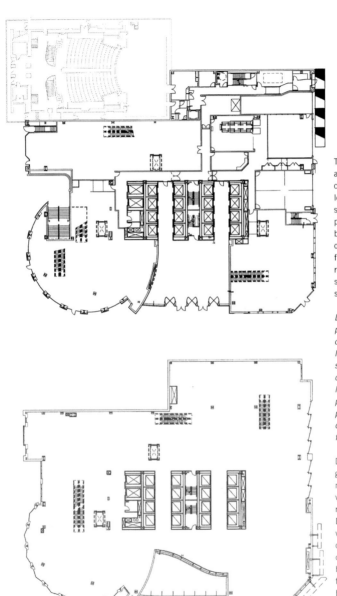

The floor plan is organised around a central communications core, leaving the rest of the space towards the perimeter of the building bare. The formal evenness of the lower, more public floors contrasts with the rest of the building, which seeks a more functional shape.

La pianta si organizza a partire da un nucleo di comunicazioni interno lasciando libero il restante spazio fino al perimetro dell'edificio. Contrasta l'eterogeneità formale dei piani inferiori, quelli più pubblici con il resto dell'edificio che cerca una forma più funzionale.

De plattegrond is georganiseerd rond een kern met centrale communicatie-voorzieningen, waarbij de rest van de ruimte vrij blijft. De heterogeniteit in vorm van de lagere, meer openbare verdiepingen contrasteert met de rest van het gebouw, waar een meer functionele vorm de boventoon voert.

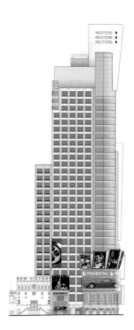

The façades of the building, Cubist in their plasticity, offer several views at each 45 degree turn. The building itself is clothed in different outfits that represent the diversity of its urban surroundings.

Le facciate dell'edificio, plasticamente cubiste, offrono diversi punti di vista che si dispiegano ad ogni giro di 45 gradi. L'edificio in se stesso si veste con differenti abiti rappresentando la diversità della sua realtà urbana circostante.

De façaden van het gebouw zijn kubistisch in hun plasticiteit en bieden bij elke draaiing van 45 graden een ander uitzicht. Het gebouw zelf is op uiteenlopende wijze 'aangekleed', een afspiegeling van de diversiteit van zijn stedelijke omgeving.

RITZ-CARLTON HOTEL

ZEIDLER GRINNELL PARTNERSHIP

CLIENT / CLIENTE / OPDRACHTGEVER: THE BOWMORE GROUP OF COMPANIES

2004

TOTAL AREA / SUPERFICIE / TOTALE OPPERVLAKTE: 79.000 m²

FLOORS / PIANI / VERDIEPINGEN - HEIGHT / ALTEZZA / HOOGTE: 65 fl / 300 m

The program of the building includes a 219 room hotel, 112 company rooms, 300 apartments – including a luxurious duplex on the deck -, gymnasium with spa on two floors, hotel reception and all kinds of habitual services, conference halls and two dancehalls. Formally, the building is a square prism which loses section as it gains height, highlighting the corner between Adelaide and Bay streets, its main focus of attention. On a stone entrance base, the building starts with an exterior structure of limestone to give way to glass and aluminum on the final floors.

Il progetto di questo edificio prevede un albergo di duecentodiciannove stanze, centododici stanze per società, trecento appartamenti –compreso un lussuoso appartamento su due piani sull'attico- una palestra con un servizio termale su due piani, la reception dell'albergo ed ogni tipo di servizi, sale riunioni e due sale da ballo. Da un punto di vista strutturale, l'edificio è un prisma quadrato che diminuisce con l'altezza, e rende l'incrocio tra le strade Adelaide e Bay il centro di attenzione. Su un basamento di pietra, dove si trova l'ingresso, si innalza la struttura esterna di pietra calcarea che mano a mano scompare lasciando posto al vetro ed all'alluminio.

Het project voor dit gebouw omvat onder andere een hotel met 219 kamers, 112 bedrijfskamers, 300 appartementen – waaronder een luxe maisonnette op de top –, een fitnessruimte met baden, op twee verdiepingen, een hotelreceptie en alle mogelijke gebruikelijke services, congreszalen en twee danszalen. De vorm van het gebouw is een vierkant prisma dat bij toenemende hoogte aan omvang afneemt en de hoek tussen de straten Adelaide en Bay tot een punt maakt waar de aandacht naartoe wordt getrokken. Op een stenen basis met de toegangshal begint de toren met een structuur van kalksteen die geleidelijk plaats maakt voor glas en aluminium op de bovenste verdiepingen.

The building, built from reinforced
concrete, has a façade covered in
limestone, glass and aluminum.

*La facciata dell'edificio, costruita in
cemento armato, è ricoperta da
pietra calcarea, da vetro e da
alluminio.*

Het bouwwerk is opgetrokken uit
gewapend beton en heeft een façade
bedekt met kalksteen, glas en
aluminium.

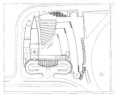

SEA HAWK
HOTEL & RESORT

CESAR PELLI & ASSOCIATES INC.

1995

CLIENT / CLIENTE / OPDRACHTGEVER: FUKOKA DAIEI REAL ESTATE INC

TOTAL AREA / SUPERFICIE / TOTALE OPPERVLAKTE: 140.000 m²

FLOORS / PIANI / VERDIEPINGEN - HEIGHT / ALTEZZA / HOOGTE: 34 fl / 143,2 m

The building is found on the bay of Hakata, an old fishing village which now forms part of the city of Fukoka. Its design responds to the place, the program and the role as a social center that hotels play in Japan. It was necessary for the property to play the role of hotel as holiday place in an urban environment. The diversity of forms that make up the parts of the building respond to a design which reinterprets traditional concepts of the imagery of holiday places offering an escape from the routine of the city.

L'edificio si trova nella baia di Hakata, un antico villaggio di pescatori che attualmente fa parte della città di Fukoka. Questo progetto risponde al luogo, al piano ed alla funzione di centro sociale che svolgono gli alberghi in Giappone. Era essenziale, per i proprietari, reinterpretare la funzione di albergo come luogo di villeggiatura nell'ambito della città. La varietà delle forme che compongono le varie parti dell'edificio presentano un design che ripropone i concetti tradizionali dell'immaginario tipico del luogo di vacanza. In questo modo, l'edificio offre una via di fuga dal tran-tran quotidiano della città.

Het gebouw bevindt zich aan de baai van Hakata, een oud vissersdorpje dat nu deel uitmaakt van de stad Fukuoka. Het ontwerp is afgestemd op de omgeving en de actuele stijl van Japanse hotels, die ook tegelijkertijd een rol spelen als sociaal centrum. De opdrachtgever achtte het van buitengewoon belang om met dit hotel de functie van een vakantiecentrum te midden van een stedelijke omgeving te scheppen. De uiteenlopende vormgeving van de delen van het gebouw zijn het resultaat van een ontwerp op basis van het traditionele concept van vakantiebestemmingen en biedt zo een ontsnapping aan de dagelijkse sleur van de stad.

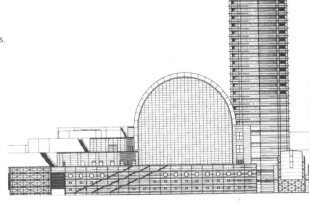

The complex has 1044 bedrooms and different leisure areas like the Atrium, the terraces and the gardens.

Il complesso è costituito da 1044 abitazioni e varie aree ricreative come l'Atrium, le terrazze ed i giardini.

Het complex is uitgerust met 1044 slaapkamers en verschillende vrijetijdsruimten, zoals het atrium, de terrassen en de tuinen.

The façades are covered with ceramics of different colors and designs. At night the building throws out reflections of warm tonalities.

Le facciate sono rivestite da ceramiche dai vari colori e forme. Di notte, l'edificio è illuminato da riflessi dalle calde tonalità.

De façaden zijn bedekt met keramiek in uiteenlopende kleuren en ontwerpen. 's Nachts reflecteert het gebouw met warm tinten.

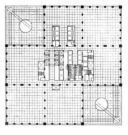

SEARS TOWER

SKIDMORE, OWING & MERRILL LLP (SOM)

CLIENT / CLIENTE / OPDRACHTGEVER: SEARS ROEBUCK & CO.

1974

TOTAL AREA / SUPERFICIE / TOTALE OPPERVLAKTE: : 410.000 m²

FLOORS / PIANI / VERDIEPINGEN - HEIGHT / ALTEZZA / HOOGTE: 110 fl - 450 m

The Sears Tower is close to the Chicago Loop and is currently the second-tallest private office building in the world. It is the property of a department store company, and contains 109 floors of offices, ground floor entrance and three basement floors which house shopping areas, cafeterias and restaurants, a gymnasium, service areas and a large loading and unloading dock for trucks. It was designed attending to the needs of the property which required the combination of ample office floors with other smaller ones to be rented out. Starting out from a ground plan type comprising a reticle of 9 squares, it arrives at different combinations of full and empty spaces which disintegrate the solid mass of the building.

La torre Sears si trova vicino al Loop di Chicago ed è attualmente il secondo edificio privato di uffici più alto del mondo. Proprietà di un'impresa di grandi magazzini, contiene 109 piani di uffici, piano terra di accesso e tre piani sotterranei che ospitano zone commerciali, caffetterie e ristoranti, una palestra, aree di servizio e una grande banchina di carico e scarico merci per camion. Si diesgnò rispondendo alle necessità della proprietà che chiedeva la combinazione di ampi piani di uffici con latri di minore grandezza da affittare. Partendo da un piano tipo composto da un reticolo di 9 quadrati si arriva a differenti combinazioni di pieni e vuoti che disintegrano la solida massa dell'edificio.

De Sears Tower staat niet ver van de Chicago Loop en is op dit ogenblik het op een na hoogste particuliere kantoorgebouw ter wereld. Het is eigendom van een warenhuisconcern en heeft 109 verdiepingen met kantoren, een toegangshal op de begane grond en drie ondergrondse verdiepingen met winkels, cafetaria's en restaurants, een fitnessruimte, servicevoorzieningen en een groot platform voor het laden en lossen van vrachtwagens. Het ontwerp van het gebouw werd afgestemd op de behoefte van de eigenaar aan een combinatie van ruime kantoorverdiepingen en kleinere verhuureenheden. Beginnend met een basisplan dat is samengesteld uit negen vierkanten kwam men tot verschillende combinaties van volle en lege ruimten die de solide massa van het gebouw kleiner doen lijken.

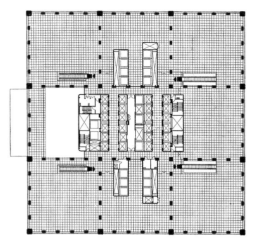

The basic floor plan is a grid of 9 blocks measuring 22 metres on each side, with pillars on the perimeter. The first 49 floors form a compact block made up of 9 squares, and from there on it is layered at intervals, removing two corner squares at every 16 and 23 storeys alternately. At the 109th floor there are only two squares

Il piano tipo sorge da un reticolo di 9 quadrati di 22,8 m. di lato, dove i pilastri sono collocati sul perimetro. primi 49 piani generano un blocco compatto formato da 9 quadrati e da qui la torre va scalando, sopprimendo due quadrati d'angolo ogni 16 e 23 alternativamente in modo che arrivino fino al 109esimo piano soltanto due quadrati.

Het basisontwerp bestaat uit een patroon van negen blokken die aan elke zijde 22,8 meter meten. De steunpijlers bevinden zich aan de rand. De eerste 49 verdiepingen vormen een compact blok van de negen vierkanten. Boven dit punt rijst de toren in fasen, waarbij afwisselend om de 16 of 23 verdiepingen twee vierkanten aan de hoek wegvallen. Op de 109e verdieping bestaat de toren uit nog maar twee vierkanten.

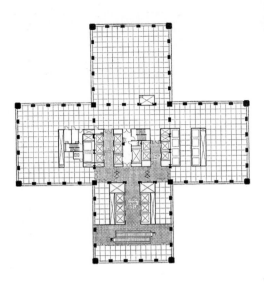

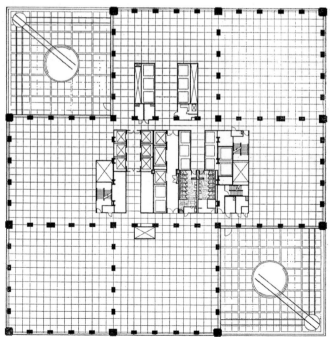

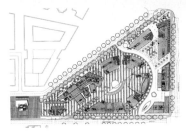

SONY CENTER - BERLIN

MURPHY / JAHN INC. ARCHITECTS

CLIENT / CLIENTE / OPDRACHTGEVER: CLIENTE: SONY

2000

TOTAL AREA / SUPERFICIE / TOTALE OPPERVLAKTE: 159.000 m²

FLOORS / PIANI / VERDIEPINGEN - HEIGHT / ALTEZZA / HOOGTE: 26 fl / 103 m

In the reconstruction of the Berlin of the 21st Century, the Sony-Center was proposed as a complex of buildings for the "new millennium". It is a cultural forum, a place for meetings and social interchanges, activity center, residential area and business center where the most advanced technology has been used in both its construction and its fitting out. It aims to be a virtual city within the city, where light (natural and artificial) is one of the essences of the design. Façades and roof work as tissues: transparent, permeable, reflective and sophisticated tissues which allow a constant succession of images, both night and day.

Durante la ricostruzione della Berlino del XXI secolo, il Sony Center venne progettato come un complesso di edifici per il "nuovo millennio". Si tratta di un foro culturale, un punto di incontro e scambi sociali, un centro di attività, una zona residenziale e centro di affari nel quale è stata impiegata la più moderna tecnologia sia nella costruzione che nelle dotazioni. Aspira ad essere una città virtuale nella città, nella quale la luce (naturale ed artificiale) è uno degli elementi essenziali del design. Le facciate ed i tetti sembrano tessuti: trasparenti, permeabili, riflettenti, raffinati, e permettono una successione sempre uguale di immagini sia di giorno che di notte.

Het Sony Center werd ontworpen als een complex van gebouwen voor het 'nieuwe millennium' in de wederopbouw van het Berlijn van de 21e eeuw. Het is een cultureel forum, een plaats voor ontmoetingen en sociale interactie, een centrum voor uiteenlopende activiteiten en er zijn woningen en een zakencentrum. De meest geavanceerde technologie is gebruikt bij de bouw en in het uiteindelijke resultaat verwerkt. Het gebouw wil een virtuele stad in de stad zijn, waarin licht (natuurlijk en kunstmatig) een van de hoofdrollen speelt. De façaden en het dak wekken de indruk van een doorzichtig, poreus, spiegelend en geraffineerd omhulsel, dat voortdurend beelden opneemt en weergeeft, zowel overdag als 's nachts.

Ground floor, ground plan and interior of the lobby of one of the four towers of offices. They are positioned at the corners of the lot, locating the medium and low buildings between them.

Pianoterra, piano-tipo e interno dell'atrio di una delle quattro torri di uffici. Sono disposte agli angoli mentre gli edifici di altezza media e bassa si trovano nel mezzo.

De begane grond, basisontwerp en het interieur van de lobby van een van de vier kantoortorens. Ze bevinden zich op de hoeken van het perceel, terwijl de middelhoge en lage gebouwen ertussen staan.

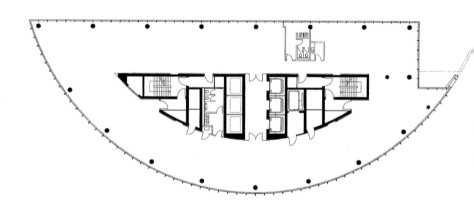

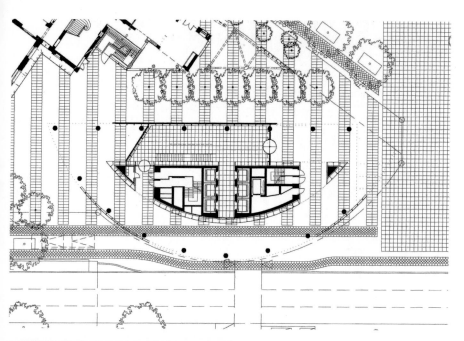

The complex consists of different buildings and various uses: homes, offices, shops, cultural activities (music, cinema, exhibitions), leisure centers and restaurants.

Il complesso riunisce edifici diversi e varie funzioni: abitazioni, uffici, negozi, attività culturali (musica cinema, esposizioni), zone ricreative e di ristorazione.

Het complex bestaat uit verschillende gebouwen met uiteenlopende functies: huizen, kantoren, winkels, culturele activiteiten (muziek, bioscoop, tentoonstellingen), vrijetijdscentra en restaurants.

Both the glass (which is the predominant material in the façades of the towers) and the steel elements (mullions) are the most advanced available technology.

Sia il vetro (che rappresenta il materiale più usato per la facciata delle torri) che gli elementi di acciaio (le colonnette), sono frutto della più moderna tecnologia.

Zowel het glas (het overheersende materiaal in de façaden van de torens) en de stalen elementen (de pijlers) maken deel uit van de meest geavanceerde technologie.

SUYOUNG BAY TOWER 88

KOHN PEDERSEN FOX ASSOCIATES PC (KPF)

CLIENT / CLIENTE / OPDRACHTGEVER: DAEWOO CORPORATION	**1988**

TOTAL AREA / SUPERFICIE / TOTALE OPPERVLAKTE: 256.000 m²

FLOORS / PIANI / VERDIEPINGEN - HEIGHT / ALTEZZA / HOOGTE: 102 fl / 462,1 m

This tower project would be located in the coastal area of Pusan. It forms part of an urban plan to transform the bay of Suyong and the Landfill area. The plan will bring about an image of modernity by converting this part of the Korean coast into tourist and leisure areas. The program is complex and varied because it includes offices, hotel, apartment hotel, shops, museum, center for contemporary art, dancehalls and a convention center. The juxtaposition of these uses in a building responds to a vertiginous and artificial form of growth which businessmen, politicians and technicians think is a symbol of the growing economic development of the Asian continent.

Il progetto di questa torre è situato lungo la zona costiera di Pusan. Fa parte di un piano regolatore il cui fine è la trasformazione della baia di Suyong e della zona di Landfill. Il progetto aspira a creare un'immagine moderna trasformando quest'area della costa coreana in una zona turistica e ricreativa. Il progetto è complesso e vario dal momento che prevede uffici, alberghi, un appartamemto hotel, negozi, un museo, un centro di arte contemporanea, sale da ballo e un centro per congressi. Il raggruppamento di tutte queste funzioni in un unico edificio è frutto della crescita vertiginosa ed artificiale che gli imprenditori, i politici ed i tecnici considerano il simbolo del crescente sviluppo economico del continente asiatico.

Dit hoogbouwproject is gecreëerd voor de kust van Pusan. Het maakt deel uit van een stedelijke planning om de baai van Suyong en het gebied Landfill opnieuw vorm te geven. Het plan zal dit deel van de Koreaanse kust veranderen in een modern toeristisch en ontspanningsgebied. Het betreft een complex bouwwerk met kantoren, een hotel, een appartementenhotel, winkels, een museum, een centrum voor hedendaagse kunst, discotheken en een congrescentrum. Het samenvoegen van deze uiteenlopende functies in één gebouw beantwoordt aan de opvatting die bij ondernemers, politici en technici leeft, dat dit symbool staat voor economische groei op het Aziatisch continent.

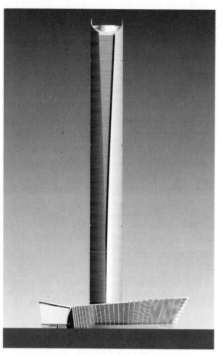

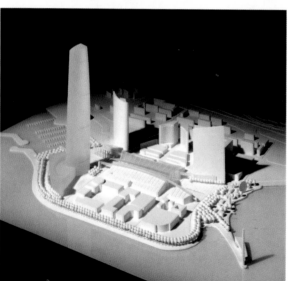

The extruding form of the tower and the curvature when reaching the ends (thus deleting two lateral façades) aim to lighten the volume of the building.

La forma della torre e la curvatura delle estremità (che eliminano in questo modo due facciate laterali) hanno la funzione di alleggerire il volume dell'edificio.

De uitgerekte vorm van de toren en de kromming aan het bovenste uiteinde (waardoor de façaden aan de zijkant wegvallen) zijn bedoeld om het volume van het gebouw lichter te maken.

In addition to the idea of lightness, the design of the tower aims to emulate the wavy lines which are produced by its reflection in the water. This is what happens with the wavy forms of the base.

Oltre all'immagine di leggerezza, la forma della torre imita le linee ondulate che si riflettono nell'acqua e difatti ottiene questo effetto nelle forme ondulate dello zoccolo.

Naast het idee van lichtheid tracht het ontwerp van de toren de golvende lijnen van het water na te bootsen. Op deze wijze is de basis golfvormig gestalte gegeven.

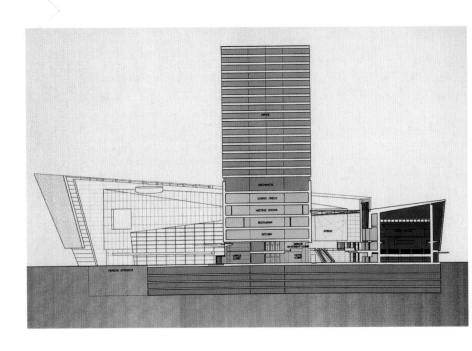

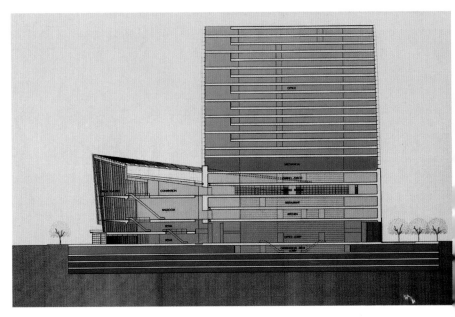

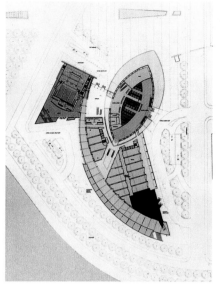

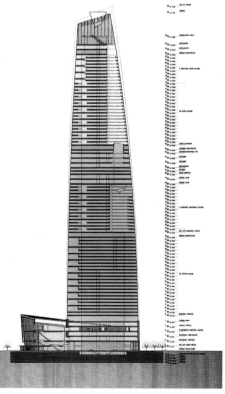

Location plans of the urban development complex of the bay. Sections of the base and the tower, on whose top floor there is a panoramic observation platform.

Piani dell'ubicazione del complesso urbanistico della baia. Sezione dello zoccolo e della torre, dove, all'ultimo piano, si trova un belvedere.

Plattegrond van de locatie van het stadscomplex in de baai. Doorsnede van de basis en de toren; op de bovenste verdieping bevindt zich een uitkijkpunt met een panoramisch uitzicht.

SWISS RE HQTRS.

FOSTER & PARTNERS

CLIENT / CLIENTE / OPDRACHTGEVER: SWISS REINSURANCE COMPANY

1997

TOTAL AREA / SUPERFICIE / TOTALE OPPERVLAKTE: 76.400 m²

FLOORS / PIANI / VERDIEPINGEN - HEIGHT / ALTEZZA / HOOGTE: 42 fl / 179,8 m

The building, which will house offices and a shopping area, will be located in a special place in the City, where the IRA demolished the Baltic Exchange. Conceptually, the project returns to the ideas of the "Climatroffice" projected together with B. Fuller in the 70s. Back then they proposed the harmonious relationship between nature and place of work. The scaly skin which protects the building settles from the façade to the roof. This membrane and the interior gardens of the building would create macroclimates which would render practically unnecessary the use of mechanical means to condition the interior temperature of the building during most of the year.

L'edificio che ospiterà uffici ed un centro commerciale, si trova in un punto particolare della City, nel luogo in cui l'IRA distrusse il Baltic Exchange. Il progetti riprende, concettualmente, l'idea del "Climatroffice" progettato con B. Fuller negli anni settanta. Proponeva, già da allora, un rapporto armonioso tra la natura ed il luogo di lavoro, difatti questo edificio possiede una pelle a squame che lo protegge, estendendosi dalla facciata fino al tetto. Questa membrana, insieme ai giardini interni dell'edificio, sarebbe in grado di creare un microclima e renderebbe praticamente superfluo l'uso di mezzi artificiali di climatizzazione interna per la maggior parte dell'anno.

In dit gebouw zullen kantoren en een winkelcentrum worden ondergebracht. Het bevindt zich op een bijzondere plaats in de stad, namelijk op de plek waar de IRA de Baltic Exchange verwoestte. Conceptueel keert het project terug naar de opvattingen van de 'Climatroffice' die in de jaren 1970 met B. Fuller werden uitgewerkt. In die tijd promootte men een harmonieuze relatie tussen de natuur en de werkplek. Het gebouw wordt van onder tot boven door 'schubben' beschermd. Dit membraan en de tuin in het interieur scheppen microklimaten, waardoor het gedurende het grootste deel van het jaar praktisch niet meer nodig is om de binnentemperatuur middels mechanische middelen te reguleren.

The shape of the tower responds to the constraints of the city, making it more slender than a rectangular building of equivalent surface area.

La forma della torre riflette la costrizione della città, giacché che è più snello di un edificio rettangolare con la stessa area.

De vorm van de toren past in de compactheid van de stad. De afgeronde conische structuur is aanzienlijk ranker dan een rechthoek gebouw met een zelfde oppervlakte.

TAICHUNG TOWER II

KOHN PEDERSEN FOX ASSOCIATES PC (KPF)

CLIENT / CLIENTE / OPDRACHTGEVER: TZUNG TANG DEVELOPMENT GROUP CO. LTD.

2000

TOTAL AREA / SUPERFICIE / TOTALE OPPERVLAKTE: 55.000 m²

FLOORS / PIANI / VERDIEPINGEN - HEIGHT / ALTEZZA / HOOGTE: 47 fl / 176 m

The design of this hotel is inspired by the symbolism of Chinese culture. The ground plan reproduces the form of a fish oriented towards the east, a figure believed to be a good omen. The levels of the tower become reduced as they rise, curving towards the inside of the glass curtain wall and giving the building great poetic simplicity. The communication and service cores are situated to the west of the ground plan, freeing the rest for views of the park and minimizing the action of the setting sun. On September 21st 1999 this building, almost finished, faultlessly overcame an earthquake of 7·3 on the Richter scale, a situation which is by no means unusual in Taiwan.

Questo albergo presenta un design ispirato all'ambiente urbanistico ed al simbolismo della cultura cinese; la base, infatti, rappresenta la figura di un pesce rivolto verso est, che è un simbolo di buon augurio. I vari piani della torre, che si riducono progressivamente quanto più si sale, si incurvano verso l'interno della parete a cortina vetrata e conferiscono a questo edificio una grande e romantica semplicità. I nuclei di passaggio e di servizio si trovano nella zona ovest, mentre il resto del piano, nel quale è ridotta al minimo l'azione del sole di ponente, gode del magnifico panorama del parco. Il 21 settembre 1999 questo edificio, che era quasi finito, superò illeso un terremoto del 7,3 gradi della scala Richter, un avvenimento affatto raro a Taiwan.

Het ontwerp van dit hotel is geïnspireerd op het symbolisme van de Chinese cultuur en heeft de vorm van een op het oosten gerichte vis. De vis staat voor een goed teken. De niveaus van de toren worden naar boven toe kleiner. De glazen façaden buigen licht naar elkaar toe en verlenen het bouwwerk een fantastische poëtische eenvoud. De communicatie- en servicevoorzieningen bevinden zich aan de westkant van het gebouw, waardoor de overige ruimte een onbelemmerd uitzicht biedt op het park en de invloed van de ondergaande zon minimaal is. Op 21 september 1999 doorstond het bijna voltooide gebouw met glans een aardbeving van 7,3 op de schaal van Richter. Aardbevingen komen op Taiwan vrij veel voor.

The tower consists of two glass-covered ground plans, slightly curved towards the sides and the summit raised on big pillars.

La torre è costituita da due superfici di vetro, poggiate su enormi pilastri e leggermente ricurve ai lati e verso la sommità.

De toren bestaat uit twee glazen façaden op hoge pijlers, die licht naar de zijkanten en de top afbuigen.

The building is calculated to
withstand earthquakes of great
intensity and last 475 years.
In 1999 it had the opportunity to
demonstrate the first point.

*L'edificio venne progettato per
sopportare terremoti di notevole
intensità e durare 475 anni. Nel
1999 ebbe l'opportunità di
dimostrare il primo punto.*

Het gebouw is erop berekend hevige
aardbevingen te kunnen doorstaan; de
levensduur is geschat op 475 jaar. In
1999 kreeg het al de gelegenheid om
het eerste punt te demonstreren.

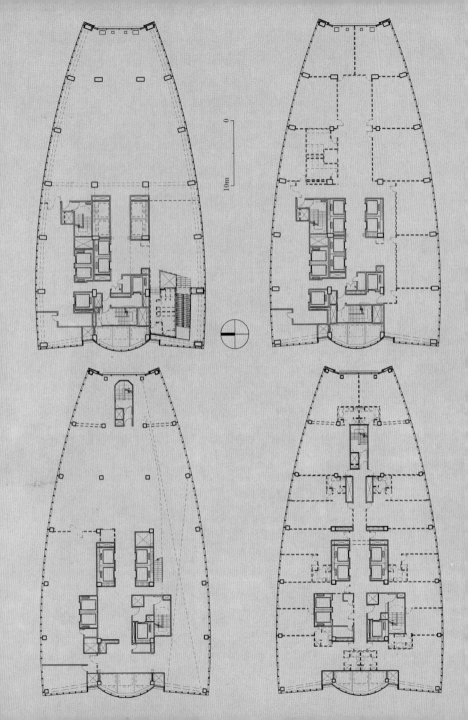

10m

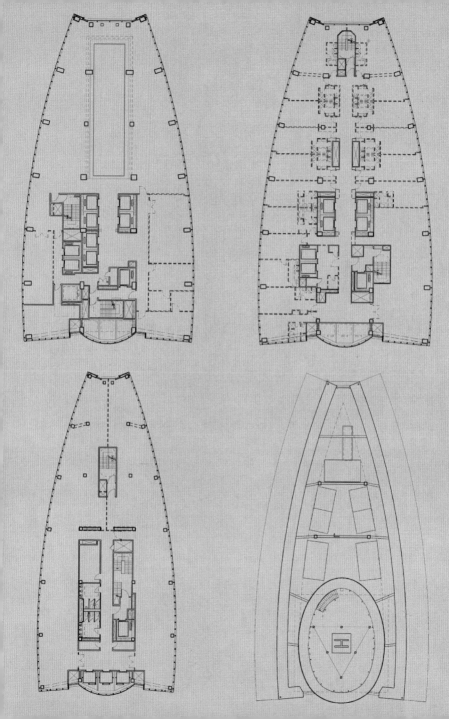

The beautiful and pure form of the building makes it recognizable from anywhere in the city, making it a landmark building.

La magnifica e semplice struttura dell'edificio lo rende riconoscibile da qualsiasi punto della città e ne fa un vero e proprio simbolo.

De prachtige en zuivere vorm van het gebouw is overal in de stad te herkennen en daardoor een oriëntatiepunt.

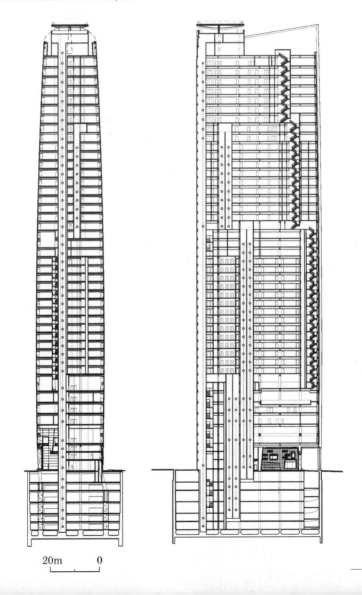

20m   0

TAIPEI FINANCIAL CENTER

C.Y. LEE & PARTNERS

CLIENT / CLIENTE / OPDRACHTGEVER: TAIPEI FINANCIAL CENTER CORPORATIC

2003

TOTAL AREA / SUPERFICIE / TOTALE OPPERVLAKTE: 350.000 m²

FLOORS / PIANI / VERDIEPINGEN - HEIGHT / ALTEZZA / HOOGTE: 101 fl / 488 m

In Taipei, the government has donated a large area where a director plan has been proposed which contains the Taipei Financial Center as a launching point. Formally, the tower places groups of eight floors on top of each other as a unit, assimilating the Chinese aesthetic with economic prosperity. Developed from the concepts of high technology and energy saving, it incorporates novel vitreous materials in the curtain walls of the façades of the tower, which confer on it transparency during the day and the appearance of a lighthouse - a new metaphor - at night.

A Taipei, il governo concesse una vasta area, per la quale venne proposto un progetto che aveva nel Taipei Financial Center il suo punto forte. Per quanto riguarda la struttura, la torre è formata da unità di gruppi di otto piani che assimilano il benessere economico all'estetica cinese. Realizzato secondo i criteri della più alta tecnologia e del risparmio di energia, presenta materiali vetrosi innovativi nelle pareti a cortina delle facciate della torre che gli conferiscono trasparenza di giorno e l'aspetto di un faro –una nuova metafora– di notte.

In Taipei heeft de regering een uitgestrekt terrein voor bebouwing ter beschikking gesteld en in het totale plan geldt het Taipei Financial Center als hoogste punt. Qua vorm is het gebouw een stapeling van groepen van 8 verdiepingen. Op deze wijze wordt de Chinese esthetica gekoppeld aan economische welvaart. Het gebouw is ontwikkeld met inachtneming van geavanceerde technologieën en besparing op energieverbruik. De glasmaterialen van de façade zorgen overdag voor transparantie en wekken 's nachts de indruk van een vuurtoren – een nieuwe metafoor.

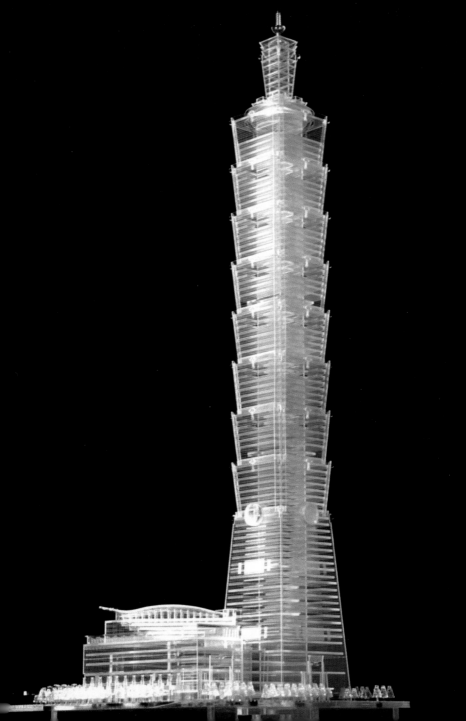

The tower will be complemented at ground level by a building which contains the most public uses; shopping center, leisure areas, conference hall, etc...

La torre, al pianterreno, è complementata da un edificio con funzioni pubbliche; un centro commerciale, zone ricreative, centri per congressi...

Aan de voet wordt de toren gecompleteerd door een gebouw met de meeste openbare functies: winkelcentrum, ontspanningsplekken, een congreszaal enzovoort.

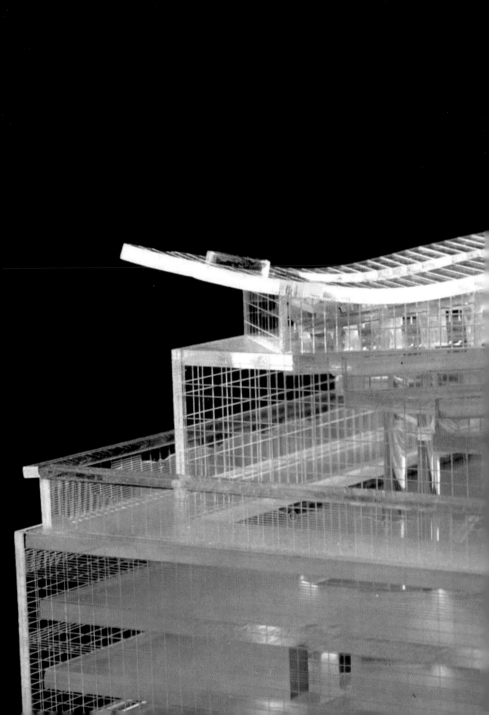

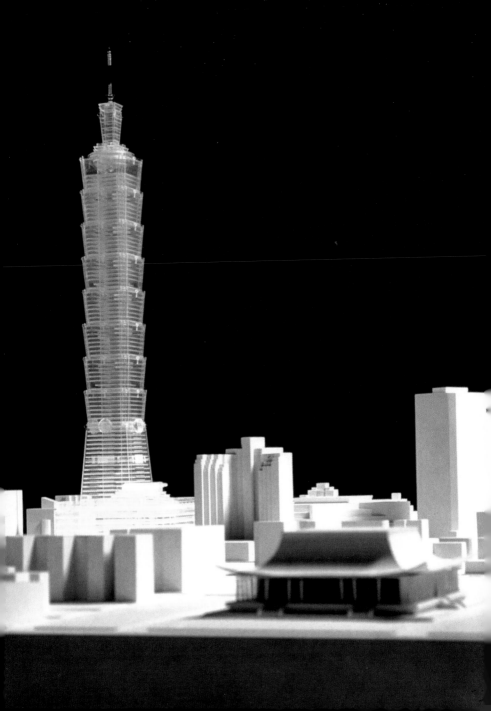

This building reproduces the constants of the firm of architects; the importance of the landmark, the formal Chinese language and being the tallest building in the world in 2003.

L'edificio riassume le costanti di questo studio architettonico: l'importanza del simbolo, l'estetica cinese e la volontà di essere l'edificio più alto del mondo nel 2003.

Het architectenconsortium heeft in dit gebouw de volgende doelstellingen willen verwezenlijken: het belang van het oriënteringspunt, een Chinese uitdrukkingsvorm en het oogmerk om het Taipei Financial Center anno 2003 het hoogste gebouw van de wereld te laten zijn.

THE CENTER

DENNIS LAU & N.G. CHUN MAN
ARCHITECTS & ENGINEERS (H.K.) LTD.

CLIENT / CLIENTE / OPDRACHTGEVER: URBAN RENEWAL
AUTHORITY AND CHEUNG KONG LTD.

1998

TOTAL AREA / SUPERFICIE / TOTALE OPPERVLAKTE: 130.000 m²

FLOORS / PIANI / VERDIEPINGEN - HEIGHT / ALTEZZA / HOOGTE: 78 fl / 346 m

This is currently the third highest building in Hong Kong. Characterized as an "intelligent building", it incorporates several service systems, including raised floors and technical paving, the first automatic gondola (hanging basket for façade maintenance) in Hong Kong and computer-controlled façade illumination. Formally, the building presents very pure volumes which accentuate their regularity with the totally glass-covered treatment of the curtain wall, with the sole exceptions of the meeting with the ground to allow access and the culmination.

Attualmente il terzo edificio più alto di Hong Kong. Classificato come "edificio intelligente", offre diversi servizi, come il suolo elevato, il pavimento tecnico, la prima "gondola" automatica di Hong Kong (una cesta sospesa che serve per la manutenzione della facciata) ed il controllo dell'illuminazione esterna eseguito da un computer. L'edificio presenta volumi estremamente semplici che accentuano la loro regolarità con la lavorazione della parete a cortina, interamente di vetro, eccezion fatta per la parte inferiore, dove si trova l'ingresso, e per il coronamento.

Dit is op het ogenblik het op twee na hoogste gebouw van Hongkong. Het wordt gekarakteriseerd als een 'intelligent gebouw', waarin verscheidene voorzieningen zijn ondergebracht, zoals verhoogde verdiepingen, Hongkongs eerste automatische installatie voor het lappen van de ramen en een computergestuurde belichting van de façade. De puristische vormgeving wordt benadrukt door het feit dat het gebouw volledig door glas is bedekt, met als enige uitzonderingen de ingang op de grond en de kroon op het dak.

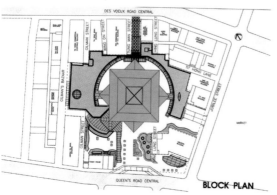

BLOCK PLAN

The form of the base of the building corresponds to two equal squares positioned at 45°, forming a star-shaped polygon.

La forma della base dell'edificio corrisponde a due quadrati uguali disposti a 45° che formano un poligono a stella.

De plattegrond van de basis van het gebouw bestaat uit twee gelijke vierkanten die in een hoek van 45 graden ten opzichte van elkaar staan, zodat een stervormige polygoon ontstaat.

In its contact with the ground, the basic prism of the building dispenses with enclosure, allowing access through the trunk of a cylinder.

Il prisma che forma l'edificio, a contatto con il terreno, prescinde del tramezzo e permette l'ingresso attraverso un tronco cilindrico.

Op de plaats waar de toren contact maakt met de grond wordt de structuur van zijn omhulling bevrijd. De toegang verloopt via een cilindervormige constructie rondom de toren.

The totally glass-covered treatment of the façade and the height of the building give it a great capacity for domination over its surroundings.

L'aspetto della facciata, interamente di vetro, e l'altezza dell'edificio producono un notevole impatto sull'ambiente.

De volledige bedekking met glas en de hoogte van het gebouw zorgen ervoor dat het gebouw in zijn omgeving domineert.

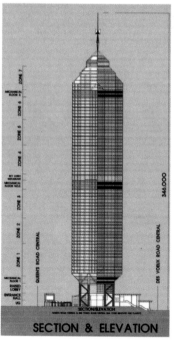

SECTION & ELEVATION

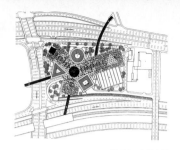

THE SHALOM CENTER

ELI ATTIA ARCHITECTS

CLIENT / CLIENTE / OPDRACHTGEVER: CITY OF TEL AVIV AND CANIT

2002

TOTAL AREA / SUPERFICIE / TOTALE OPPERVLAKTE: 255.000 m²

FLOORS / PIANI / VERDIEPINGEN: 38, 42, 46 fl
HEIGHT / ALTEZZA / HOOGTE: 153, 168, 184 m

This regionally, nationally and internationally important project develops a very wide program, shopping center, theatres and community spaces in a low Y-shaped volume which contains all the public activities (plus a garage for 3500 cars in three basement floors) and three tall towers which contain the most private activities, such as office spaces and residential areas on the top floors. This complex is situated in an important communications hub, which makes it extremely accessible at the same time as isolating it from the rest of the city.

Progetto di grande importanza a livello regionale, nazionale ed internazionale, è frutto di un vasto progetto che prevede un centro commerciale, teatri e spazi comunitari in una struttura di scarsa altezza a forma di "Y", che riunisce varie attività pubbliche, un parcheggio per 3.500 macchine su tre livelli sotterranei e tre alte torri destinate ad attività private e, agli ultimi piani, zone per uffici ed aree residenziali. Questo complesso si trovaubicato al centro di un importante nodo di comunicazioni, che lo rende estremamente accessibile e allo stesso tempo lo isola dal resto della città.

Dit project is van regionale, nationale en internationale betekenis en is zeer breed van opzet: een winkelcentrum, een theater en gemeenschappelijke ruimten op een Y-vormig terrein (waaronder een ondergrondse garage van drie verdiepingen voor 3.500 auto's). Daarnaast worden drie torens opgericht, waarin kantoren en op de bovenste verdiepingen wooneenheden zijn ondergebracht. Het complex bevindt zich aan een belangrijk verkeersknooppunt, waardoor het gemakkelijk te bereiken is maar tegelijkertijd van de rest van de stad wordt geïsoleerd.

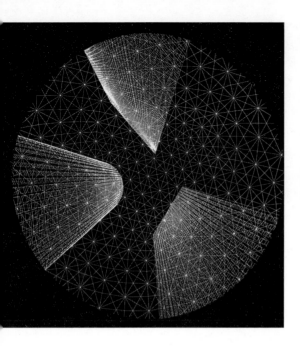

The three towers have very differentiated simple forms: square, circular, triangular; together they make up a harmonious group.

Le tre torri presentano forme semplici e molto diverse, il quadrato, il cerchio, il triangolo che, insieme, costituiscono una struttura armoniosa.

De drie torens bezitten zeer verschillende en eenvoudige vormen: vierkant, cirkel en driehoek. Tezamen resulteren ze in een harmonisch geheel.

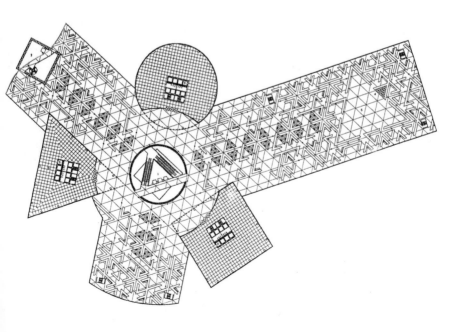

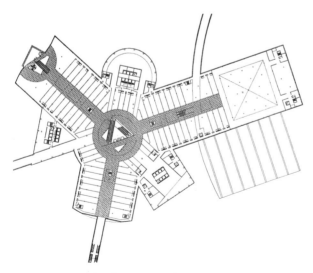

The Y-shaped base signals three directions: Jerusalem, Yaffo and the north.
It symbolizes the convergence of people united in a common objective.

La forma ad "Y" della base che indica tre direzioni –Gerusalemme, Jaffa ed il nord– simboleggia la confluenza delle genti accomunate da un unico obiettivo.

De Y-vorm van het terrein wijst in drie richtingen: Jeruzalem, Yaffo (Jaffa) en het noorden. Het symboliseert het samenkomen van mensen met een gemeenschappelijk doel.

Shalom Center - 2nd Floor Plan - Shopping Mall
Eli Attia Architects New York

The low body presents a hexagonal structure, the ideal container for diverse uses. The towers present a nuclear structure, which frees up the rest of the ground plan.

Il corpo inferiore presenta una forma esagonale, ed è un edificio adattabile a varie funzioni. Le torri, la cui struttura ècaratterizzata da un nucleo, liberano in questo modo il resto del piano.

De basis vormt een hexagonale structuur, ideaal voor het onderbrengen van diverse functies. De torens bieden een compacte structuur, die de rest van het complex bevrijdt.

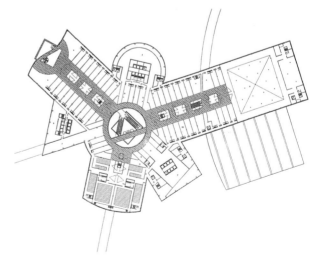

Shalom Center - 3rd Floor Plan - Shopping Mall
Eli Attia Architects New York

The blue-colored metallic curtain wall, combined with windows and skylights made of reflective blue glass, remind one of the idea of Tel Aviv as "White City".

Il muro-tenda metallico color bianco, combinato con finestre e lucernari di vetro riflettente celeste, si rifanno all'idea di Tel Aviv come "Città Bianca".

De wit metalen façade in combinatie met de vensters en blauw reflecterende glazen dakramen herinneren eraan dat Tel Aviv ook wel de 'witte stad' wordt genoemd.

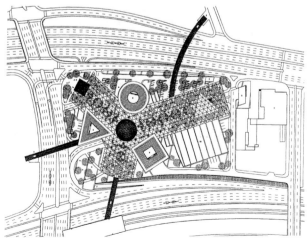

TOKYO

TOKYO-NARA TOWER

T.R. HAMZAH & YEANG SDN BHD

1994

CLIENT / CLIENTE / OPDRACHTGEVER: TRIENAL DE NARA	
TOTAL AREA / SUPERFICIE / TOTALE OPPERVLAKTE: 1.155.000 m²	
FLOORS / PIANI / VERDIEPINGEN - HEIGHT / ALTEZZA / HOOGTE: 210 fl / 800 m	

This project is an investigation of the nature and evolution of high-rise buildings. It is the result of the application of concepts such as vertical landscaping. Part of the façade becomes a hanging garden, sustained and maintained through a spiral which wraps around the building. The spiral movement of the habitable containers generates terraces, the hanging oasis and flat community gardens every few floors.
The situation of the technological infrastructure concentrated in the culmination of the building and the layout of the materials, openings and communication cores contributes to the thermic warmth of the building.

Questo progetto è il frutto delle ricerche e dello studio sulla natura e l'evoluzione degli edifici di notevole altezza; frutto dall'applicazione di concetti quali la paesaggistica verticale, parte della facciata è trasformata in un giardino pensile, sorretto e mantenuto per mezzo di una spirale che avvolge l'edificio; la collocazione a spirale delle abitazioni, che danno origine alle terrazze, le oasi pensili; i giardini comunitari situati ogni determinato numero di piani, l'ubicazione dell'infrastruttura tecnologica concentrata sulla parte superiore dell'edificio e la distribuzione dei materiali, delle aperture e dei nuclei di comunicazione il cui fine è contribuire alle condizioni ambientali dell'edificio.

Dit bouwwerk is het resultaat van natuuronderzoek en de evolutie van hoogbouw. Hier worden concepten als verticale landschappen toegepast. Een deel van de façade bestaat uit hangende tuinen, die door een spiraal rond het gebouw worden gedragen en onderhouden. De spiraalvormige indeling van de bewoonbare delen creëert een bepaald aantal verdiepingen terrassen, hangende oasen en vlakke gemeenschappelijke tuinen. De technologische infrastructuur is geconcentreerd in de top van het gebouw en de lay-out van de materialen, openingen en voorzieningskernen dragen bij aan de thermische kwaliteit van het gebouw.

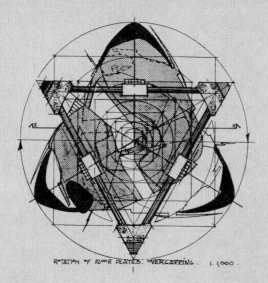

ROTATION OF FLOOR PLATES: OVERLAPPING. 1:1,000.

Landmark Tower
Yokohama (295 m)

Empire State Building
New York (381 m)

La Tour Sans Fins
Paris (419 m)

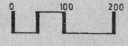

Height Comparisons

ears Tower
hicago (457 m)

Petronas Towers
Kuala Lumpur (450 m)

Millennium Tower
Japan (800 m)

Tokyo-Nara Tower
Tokyo-Nara (880 m)

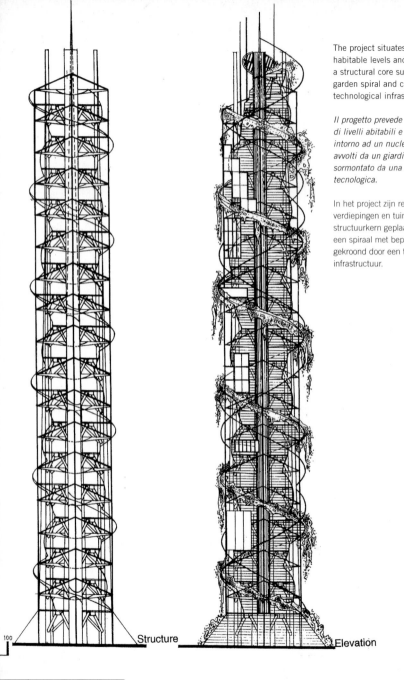

The project situates series of habitable levels and gardens around a structural core surrounded by a garden spiral and crowned with technological infrastructure.

Il progetto prevede una serie di livelli abitabili e di giardini situati intorno ad un nucleo strutturale e avvolti da un giardino a spirale sormontato da una infrastruttura tecnologica.

In het project zijn reeksen bewoonbare verdiepingen en tuinen rondom een structuurkern geplaatst, omringd door een spiraal met beplanting en gekroond door een technologische infrastructuur.

Structure

Elevation

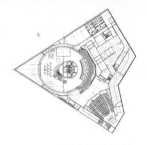

BARCELONA

TORRE AGBAR

ATELIER JEAN NOUVEL + b 720 ARQUITECTOS

CLIENT / CLIENTE / OPDRACHTGEVER: AGBAR (COMPANYIA D'AIGÜES DE BARCELONA)	**2003**
TOTAL AREA / SUPERFICIE / TOTALE OPPERVLAKTE: 47.500 m²	
FLOORS / PIANI / VERDIEPINGEN - HEIGHT / ALTEZZA / HOOGTE: 31 fl / 142 m	

This building, which forms part of the urban planning operation that the city council has promoted for the year 2004, will be the tallest skyscraper to interrupt the city's silhouette. "It is not a tower, nor a skyscraper in the American sense of the term: it is a unique emergent volume in the middle of a more or less peaceful city" J. Nouvel has written to explain the meaning of the building, which aims to accentuate the symbolic and singular character of the corporate building, emphasizing through the treatment of the building's enclosures, which cancel out the concept of roof and façade underneath a single skin.

Questo edificio, che fa parte dell'intervento urbanistico cheil Comune della città ha approvato per il 2004, sarà il grattacielo più alto nel profilo della città. "Non si tratta di una torre, né di un grattacielo nel senso americano del termine: è un volume emergente unico nel bel mezzo di una città piuttosto tranquilla" scrisse J. Nouvel per spiegare la natura di questo edificio, la cui intenzione è sottolineare il carattere simbolico e peculiare del-l'edificio corporativo, enfatizzato, inoltre, dalla lavorazione delle coperture della costruzione che annullano il concetto di tetto e di facciata sotto un'unica pelle.

Dit gebouw maakt deel uit van een stedelijke planning die het stadsbestuur heeft voorzien voor het jaar 2004. Het zal de hoogste wolkenkrabber zijn in het silhouet van de stad. 'Het is geen toren, maar ook geen wolkenkrabber in de Amerikaanse betekenis van het woord: het is een uniek element, dat in het midden van een min of meer vredige stad zal verrijzen,' schreef J. Nouvel om de betekenis van het gebouw te verklaren. Het streven is om het symbolische en bijzondere karakter van een zakengebouw te benadrukken. Het concept van dak en façade wordt vervangen door de uitzonderlijke vorm met een enkelvoudige omhulling.

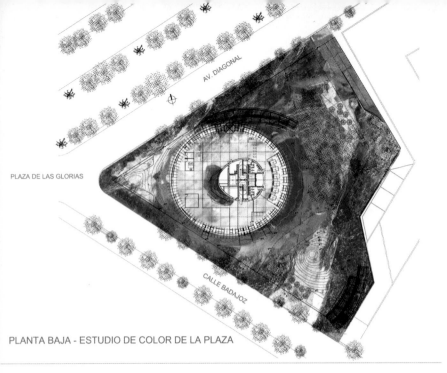

PLAZA DE LAS GLORIAS

AV. DIAGONAL

CALLE BADAJOZ

PLANTA BAJA - ESTUDIO DE COLOR DE LA PLAZA

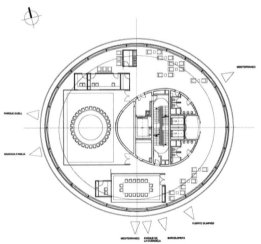

PLANTA 26 - PLANTA DE ALTA DIRECCION

Above, siting of the tower whose base is surrounded by a very special green area, with ponds, waterfalls and a mineral area which functions as a moat which separates the building from the road.

In alto, ubicazione della torre la cui base è circondata da un'area verde particolare, con stagni, cascate ed una zona minerale che funge da fossato e separa l'edificio dalla strada.

Boven: de locatie van de toren. De basis wordt omringd door een bijzondere groenvoorziening met vijvers, watervallen en rotspartijen, die het gebouw van de straat scheidt.

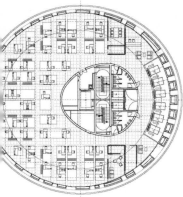

NTA TIPO DE OFICINAS - DISTRIBUCION LIBRE

The building can be divided into two
stretches, a concrete shaft in the
first 25 office type floors and a glass
dome in the top 6 floors for top
management which crown the
building.

*L'edificio può essere diviso in due
parti, un fusto di cemento ospita i
primi venticinque piani-tipo di uffici,
e una cupola di vetro gli ultimi sei
piani dell'alta.*

Het gebouw is op te splitsen in twee
delen: een betonnen schacht voor de
eerste 25 verdiepingen met kantoren
en een glazen koepel op de laatste 6
verdiepingen als kroon op het gebouw,
waarin de directie van het bedrijf
wordt ondergebracht.

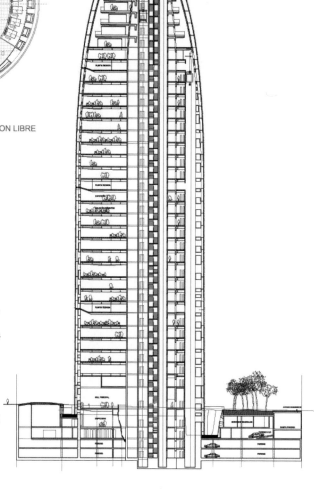

SECCION OESTE - ESTE

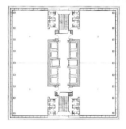

TORRE MAPFRE

ORTIZ LEON ARQUITECTOS

CLIENT / CLIENTE / OPDRACHTGEVER: MAPFRE

1992

TOTAL AREA / SUPERFICIE / TOTALE OPPERVLAKTE: 70.000 m²

FLOORS / PIANI / VERDIEPINGEN - HEIGHT / ALTEZZA / HOOGTE: 43 fl / 153,5 m

The holding of the Olympic Games in Barcelona 1992 meant a series of urban planning interventions which substantially changed the city's image. One of the most representative architectural elements of that transformation are the "Mapfre" and "Hotel de les Arts" towers in the Olympic Village, a newly created residential neighborhood where the athletes were housed during the games. The Mapfre Tower is not only a business center, its surface area is laid out in two low building used for shopping and offices. This tower is characterized by the square ground plan and the uniform treatment by means of horizontal bands on the façades.

La celebrazione dei Giochi Olimpici di Barcellona nel '92 comportarono una serie di interventi urbanistici che trasformarono sostanzialmente il volto della città. Uno degli elementi architettonici più caratteristici di questa trasformazione sono le torri Mapfre e l'Hotel de les Arts della Villa Olimpica, un quartiere residenziale di nuova creazione dove si alloggiavano gli atleti dei giochi. Le Torri Mapfre non sono solo un centro d'affari, la loro area si estende su due edifici bassi di uso commerciale ed uffici oltre alla torre. Questa è caratterizzata dalla base quadrata e dalla lavorazione omogenea con le fasce orizzontali dellefacciate.

De organisatie van de Olympische Zomerspelen in Barcelona in 1992 betekende een aantal ingrepen in de stadsplanning, die het stadsbeeld aanzienlijk hebben veranderd. Een van de architectonische veranderingen zijn de torens 'Mapfre' en 'Hotel de les Arts' in het olympische dorp, een nieuwbouwwijk waarin de atleten tijdens de Spelen werden ondergebracht. De Mapfre-toren is niet alleen een zakencentrum, maar herbergt in de beide lage gebouwen winkels en kantoren. Deze toren kenmerkt zich door zijn vierkante opzet en gelijkmatige horizontale banden op de façaden.

The problems of image, exposure to the sun, energetic transmission, comfort, maintenance and cleaning have been basic conditioners in the design of the façade.

I problemi di immagine, soleggiamento, trasmissione di energia, comfort, manutenzione e pulizia sono stati criteri essenziali nella progettazione della facciata.

Bepalend voor het ontwerp van de façaden waren met name de vraagstukken van beeldvorming, blootstelling aan zonlicht, energieoverdracht, comfort, onderhoud en reiniging.

The structure is mixed, with a concrete core and highly resistant metallic perimeter pillars separated from the rigid core.

La struttura, mista, è composta da un nucleo di cemento e piloni metallici perimetrali, estremamente resistenti,separati dal nucleo duro.

De gemengde structuur bestaat uit een kern van beton en zeer resistente stalen dragers aan de randen die van deze kern zijn gescheiden.

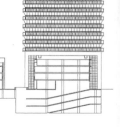

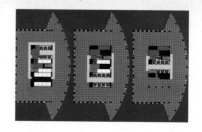

TORRE MAYOR

ZEIDLER GRINNELL PARTNERSHIP

2002

CLIENT / CLIENTE / OPDRACHTGEVER: ICA REICHMANN TORRE MAYOR

TOTAL AREA / SUPERFICIE / TOTALE OPPERVLAKTE: 140.000 m²

FLOORS / PIANI / VERDIEPINGEN - HEIGHT / ALTEZZA / HOOGTE: 57 fl / 225 m

This building, which will dominate the Chapultepec Park, has been designed to stand out in the skyline of the city as one of the tallest buildings. The play between the rectangular stone volumetry of the façade with its curved curtain wall will be visible and changing as one moves along the Paseo de la Reforma. The main façade breeches the curtain wall in the floors closest to the ground, creating an impressive entrance through the square. The podium, designed as two lion's claws which embrace and open the square towards the Paseo de la Reforma, was designed to give life to the entrance space, with shops and restaurants.

Questo edificio dominerà il Parque de Chapultepec. Venne ideato con l'intenzione di farne una delle torri più alte nel panorama urbanistico di città. Il gioco tra il volume rettangolare di pietra e la superficie del muro curvo di vetro sarà visibile e mutevole mano a mano che avanziamo lungo il Paseo de la Reforma. La facciata principale ritrae il muro-cortina all'altezza dei pianipiù vicini al suolo, creando così un magnifico ingresso sulla piazza. Il basamento, progettato a forma di artigli di leone che abbracciano ed aprono la piazza verso il Paseo de la Reforma, è stato ideato con il fine di apportarevitalità alla zona dell'ingresso, con negozi e ristoranti.

Dit gebouw zal in het Chapultepec Park komen te staan en een van de hoogste gebouwen in de skyline van de stad zijn. Het samenspel tussen het rechthoekige stenen deel en de gebogen façade blijkt steeds duidelijker als men het gebouw over de Paseo de la Reforma nadert. De façade wijkt op de laagste verdiepingen terug en zorgt zo voor een indrukwekkende ingang die over een plein wordt bereikt. De verhoging is ontworpen als twee leeuwenklauwen die het plein in de richting van de Paseo de la Reforma openen. Er worden winkels en restaurants in ondergebracht om de toegangsruimte tot het gebouw te verlevendigen.

The project concentrates the greater part of its efforts in approximating the scale of the building to the user by means of its entrance.

Il progetto concentra tutti gli sforzi nel tentativo di avvicinare la scala dell'edificio al cittadino per mezzo dell'entrata.

Het project concentreert zich met name op de ingang en tracht daarmee het gebouw van een dergelijke omvang dichter bij de gebruiker te brengen.

The curtain wall withdraws, leaving the structure of the façade exposed, the square and the shopping center bring the building closer to the Paseo de la Reforma.

Il muro-cortina si ritrae, lasciando la struttura della facciata isolata, la piazza ed il centro commerciale avvicinano l'edificio al paseo de la Reforma.

De façade blijft open en laat de structuur zien. Het plein en het winkelcentrum brengen het gebouw dichter bij de Paseo de la Reforma.

The main façade repeats on the deck the breeching of the entrance, generating a skylight under which the floors are staggered.

La facciata principale ripete sul tetto la rientranza dell'entrata, creando così un lucernario al di sotto del quale si dispongono a gruppi i piani.

Aan de bovenkant van de hoofdfaçade herhaalt zich de open structuur, waardoor een dakraam ontstaat waaronder de verdiepingen zichtbaar zijn.

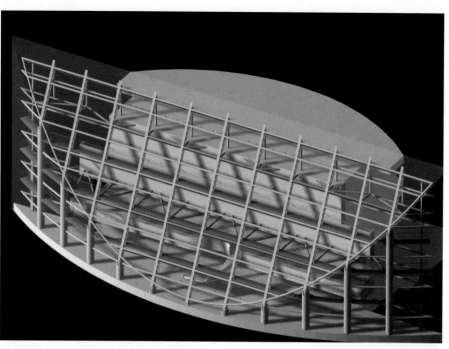

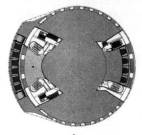

TOUR SANS FINS

ARQUITECTURES JEAN NOUVEL

CLIENT / CLIENTE / OPDRACHTGEVER: SCI TOUR SANS FIN	**1989**
TOTAL AREA / SUPERFICIE / TOTALE OPPERVLAKTE: 91.000 m²	
FLOORS / PIANI / VERDIEPINGEN - HEIGHT / ALTEZZA / HOOGTE: 92 fl / 460,60 m	

This is the winning project of a competition which proposed the construction of a building in a lot next to the Grand Arch, in La Défense, the district where the high-rise buildings of Paris are concentrated. This singular tower, which aspires to be the slenderest in the world when it is built, has been conceived from the idea of ascension and fainting. From the choice of materials for the façade (granite, stone and glass make up a gradation) to the relation width/height with which it has been designed, the idea of the project is materialized. The building responds both to the concept (Tour sans fins) and the urban context, working as a ball and socket joint which articulates the complex presided over by the Grand Arch.

Questo è il progetto vincitore di un concorso che proponeva la costruzione di un edificio in un'area edificabile vicina al Grand Arch, a La Défense, il distretto dove si concentrano gli edifici più elevati de Parigi. Qiesta torre singolare, che aspira ad essere la più snella del mondo quando sia costruita, è stata concepita sull'idea dell'ascensione e dello svanimento. Dalla scelta dei materiali della facciata (granito, pietra e vetro compongono una digradazione) alla relazione ampiezza/altezza con cui è stata disegnata, materializzano l'idea del progetto. L'edificio risponde tanto al concetto (Tour sans fins) quanto al contesto urbano; funziona come una rotula attraverso cui si articola il complesso che presiede il Gran Arch.

Dit is het winnende project in een competitie voor de oprichting van een bouwwerk op een perceel naast de Grand Arch in La Défense, de wijk waarin de hoge gebouwen in Parijs zijn geconcentreerd. De bijzondere toren zal bij voltooiing de meest ranke ter wereld zijn. Het ontwerp is gecreëerd vanuit het idee van opstijgen en vervagen. Het project wordt verwezenlijkt in de keuze van de materialen voor de façade (graniet, steen en glas zorgen voor de gradaties) en de relatie breedte/hoogte. Het gebouw beantwoordt aan zowel het concept (Tour sans fins) als de stedelijke context en functioneert als een scharnier die het gehele complex benadrukt, met in het centrum de Grand Arch.

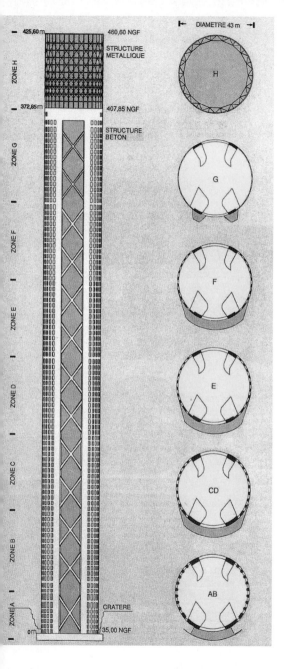

DIAMETRE 43 m

425,60 m   460,60 NGF

ZONE H

STRUCTURE
METALLIQUE

H

372,85 m   407,85 NGF

STRUCTURE
BETON

ZONE G

G

ZONE F

F

ZONE E

E

ZONE D

CD

ZONE C

ZONE B

AB

ZONE A

CRATERE

0 m   35,00 NGF

The peripheral, mixed structure frees the entire interior constructed surface area without conditioning the interior distribution. Made of perforated reinforced concrete at its base, the structure becomes lighter as it rises in height through the use of crossbeams, ending with a lightweight metallic structure at the top floors.

La struttura periferica e mista consente di liberare tutta la superficie costruita interna senza condizionare la distribuzione interiore. Dal cemento armato perforato alla sua base si alleggerisce progressivamente nella misura in cui si eleva attraverso tiranti trasversali, terminando come struttura metallica leggera negli ultimi piani.

De gemengde randstructuur bevrijdt de gehele oppervlakte van het interieur zonder daarbij de distributie in het interieur te bepalen. De toren bestaat uit geperforeerd gewapend beton en de structuur wordt naar boven toe geleidelijk aan lichter door middel van dwarsbalken, om te eindigen met een lichte stalen structuur op de bovenste verdiepingen.

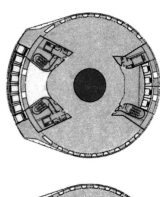

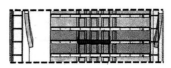

Niveau avec patio central

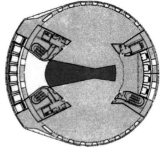

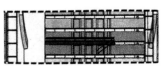

Niveau avec rue centrale

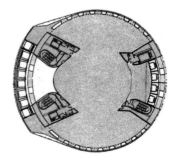

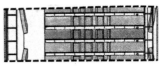

Niveau courant

Plan/coupe

Plateau
Noyaux
Patio central
Rue centrale
Vide sur fenêtres urbaines

LES NIVEAUX SUPERIEURS

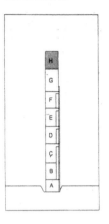

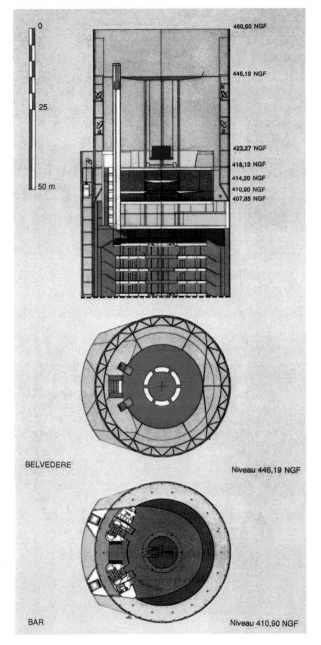

0

25

50 m

460,60 NGF

446,19 NGF

423,27 NGF
418,13 NGF
414,20 NGF
410,90 NGF
407,85 NGF

BELVEDERE

Niveau 446,19 NGF

BAR

Niveau 410,90 NGF

COUPE / PLANS

- Belvédère
- Bar
- Panoramique
- Terrasse
- TMD
- Poste de sécurité avancé
- Locaux techniques
- Bureaux
- Ascenseurs publics
- Ascenseurs belvédère

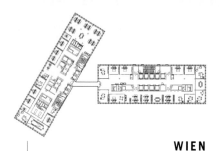

TWIN TOWER

MAXIMILIANO FUKSAS ARCHITETTO

2001

CLIENT / CLIENTE / OPDRACHTGEVER: IMMOFIANZ IMMOBILIEN ANLAGEN AG
WIENERGERGER BAUSTOFFINDUSTRIE AG

TOTAL AREA / SUPERFICIE / TOTALE OPPERVLAKTE: 139.500 m²

FLOORS / PIANI / VERDIEPINGEN - HEIGHT / ALTEZZA / HOOGTE: 34 fl / 127 m

These glass towers united by means of a base contain offices and leisure areas. The architect's initial research was based on specifiying a solution which would enrich the skyline of the city and help to grant Wienerberg (a newly created area) a mechanism for its own identification. Articulated in a street which evokes the sinuous lines of the road ("landscaped street"), the project works from two architectural typologies (the tower and the base as two juxtaposed buildings) eluding the monotony of the complex and at the same time allowing the user a functional recognition of the whole (offices and leisure areas) in the distribution by independent elements.

Queste torri di cristallo unite mediante una base a mo' di zoccolo, contengono uffici e zone destinate all'ozio. La ricerca iniziale dell'architetto si basò nell'individuare una soluzione che arricchisse lo skyline della città e contribuisse a dotare il Wienerberg (un'area di nuova creazione) di un meccanismo di identificazione proprio. Articolato in una via che evoca il sinuoso tracciato del cammino ("landscaped street"), il progetto lavora a partire da due tipologie architettoniche (la torre e lo zoccolo come due edifici giustapposti) eludendo la monotonia del complesso e, allo stesso tempo, permettendo all'utente un riconoscimento funzionale dell'insieme (uffici e zona di ozio) nella distribuzione per elementi indipendenti.

Deze glazen torens zijn verenigd door een basis en herbergen kantoren en vrijetijdsruimten. Het onderzoek van de architect was in eerste instantie gericht op het vinden van een oplossing die de skyline van de stad zou verrijken en de Wienerberg (een nieuwbouwwijk) een eigen identiteit zou geven. Het bouwproject ligt aan een straat die is aangelegd als een slingerende landweg en bestaat uit twee architectonische typologieën (de toren en de basis als twee naast elkaar geplaatste gebouwen) waarmee de monotonie van het complex wordt doorbroken en de gebruiker tegelijkertijd in staat wordt gesteld om de functionaliteit van de afzonderlijke elementen te herkennen (kantoren en vrijetijdsruimten).

Located in a transition area between the density of the city and a greenbelt, the towers possess and praise the theme contained in the early sketches, the development of the urban landscape.

Situate in un'area di passaggio tra la densità della città e le zone verdi, le torri riassumono ed esaltano allo stesso tempo la tematica presente nelle prime bozze e lo sviluppo urbanisitco del paesaggio urbano.

De torens staan in een overgangsgebied tussen de compacte stad en een groene gordel en vormen een verwezenlijking van het thema in de vroege schetsen voor het ontwerp, dat betrekking had op de ontwikkeling van het stedelijke landschap.

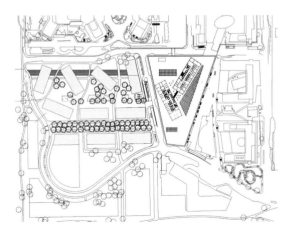

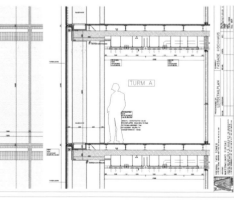

TURM A

The architect researched the converging paths of art and architecture. We can see contributions of Land Art in the square set out as a "landscaped street", evoking winding country roads in the midst of vegetation.

L'architetto ricerca le vie d'incontro tra arte e architettura. Troviamo interventi di Land Art nella piazza articolata come una "landscaped street" che evoca cammini rurali dai percorsi sinuosi immersi nella vegetazione.

De architect zocht het raakvlak tussen kunst en architectuur. De zogenaamde 'Land Art' is toegepast op het plein, dat als een 'landscaped street' beelden oproept van slingerende landweggetjes omzoomd door dichte vegetatie.

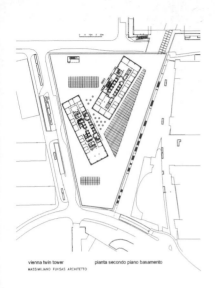

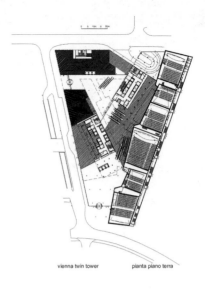

vienna twin tower   pianta secondo piano basamento
MASSIMILIANO FUKSAS ARCHITETTO

vienna twin tower   pianta piano terra

The project for the building was conventional – an office block and a shopping centre. The proposal satisfies the need with differentiating elements, the tower and the base as two juxtaposed buildings, avoiding the conventional layout. At the same time it provides a clear, functional recognition of the base and the tower.

Il programma dell'edificio era convenzionale, torre di uffici e centro commerciale. La proposta risponde con differenti tipologie, la torre lo zoccolo come due edifici giustapposti, eludendo il complesso convenzionale. Allo stesso tempo consente un un chiaro riconoscimento funzionale tra la base e la torre.

Het ontwerp voor het gebouw was conventioneel – een kantoortoren en een winkelcentrum. De toren en de basis zijn als twee afzonderlijke elementen naast elkaar geplaatst en wijken op deze wijze af van de gebruikelijke opbouw. Tegelijkertijd biedt het ontwerp een duidelijke functieherkenning van de basis en de toren.

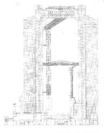

UMEDA SKY BUILDING

HIROSHI HARA ATELIER

1993

CLIENT / CLIENTE / OPDRACHTGEVER: JOHN HANCOCK MUTUAL LIFE INSURANCE CO.	
TOTAL AREA / SUPERFICIE / TOTALE OPPERVLAKTE: 260.000 m²	
FLOORS / PIANI / VERDIEPINGEN - HEIGHT / ALTEZZA / HOOGTE: 100 fl - 128 m	

A skyscraper is a building which has symbolic meaning from both the economic and urban planning points of view. The promoters of this building wanted it to be an icon of Omeda City, an area in the industrial belt of Osaka. At the same time, the architects proposed it as a prototype of a building typology where the building generates a new form of urban development. This will be the city of the future where buildings like this are raised, tall towers connected by means of their upper floors via a horizontal platform.

Il grattacielo è un edificio che si impone come un simbolo sia dal punto di vista economico che urbanistico. I promotori di questo edificio volevano creare il simbolo di Omeda City, città alla periferia di Osaka. Inoltre, gli architetti ne fecero il modello di una nuova tipologia architettonica. L'edificio, inoltre, da origine ad un nuovo tipo di sviluppo urbano. Si tratta della città del futuro, dove verranno costruiti altri edifici simili, slanciate torri collegate a livello dei piani alti mediante una piattaforma orizzontale.

Een wolkenkrabber is een gebouw dat zowel in economisch als planologisch opzicht een symbolische betekenis heeft. De promotors van dit gebouw wilden een icoon oprichten van Omeda City, een wijk aan de rand van Osaka. Tegelijkertijd presenteren de architecten het bouwwerk als een prototype van moderne stedelijke bebouwing. In de stad van de toekomst zullen dit soort gebouwen – hoge torens, die op de bovenste verdiepingen door een horizontaal platform verbonden zijn – verrijzen.

Siting plan of the building.
It spreads vertically, generating wide
green spaces. The glass façade
reflects everything which surrounds
it, from the sky to the ground.

*Planimetria dell'edificio che,
elevandosi verticalmente, lascia
ampie zone verdi. La facciata di
vetro riflette tutto ciò che lo
circonda, sia il cielo che la terra.*

Plattegrond van de locatie van het
gebouw. Het verheft zich loodrecht en
biedt rijkelijk plaats voor groene
ruimten. De glazen façade
weerspiegelt al het omringende, van
de hemel tot de aarde.

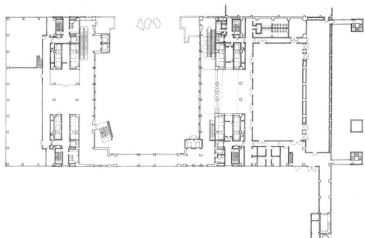

The observation platform which unites the two towers is perforated by a circle from which escalators descend down the empty central space.

La piattaforma-belvedere che unisce le due torri è attraversata da una circolo all'interno del quale le scale mobili scendono verso la zona centrale vuota.

Het uitkijkplatform dat beide torens verenigt, bevat in het midden een enorme cirkelvormige opening waar roltrappen doorheen lopen.

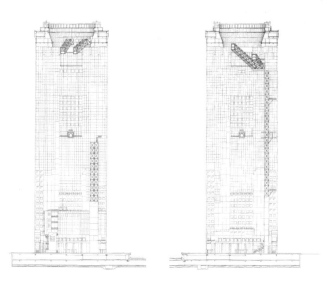

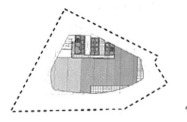
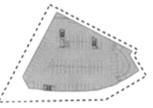

WATERFRONT HOUSE

T.R. HAMZAH & YEAN SDN BHD

CLIENT / CLIENTE / OPDRACHTGEVER: WATERFRONT HOUSE SDN BHD	**2000**
TOTAL AREA / SUPERFICIE / TOTALE OPPERVLAKTE: 41.000 m²	
FLOORS / PIANI / VERDIEPINGEN - HEIGHT / ALTEZZA / HOOGTE: 26 fl -130 m	

This tower, an office building of high standing which had to take maximum advantage of the possible constructed volume, was thought up by the client and the architect as an object which had to present a sustainable alternative model for the growth of the neighborhood (marked by the Petronas towers) in the heart of a city where the greatest building growth of the Asian continent of the last few years has taken place. Apart from being the company's headquarters, it is a meeting place for the clients, presenting a fresh and innovative corporate image. Apart from being a formidable contemporary object, its bioclimatic design is based on minimizing as much as possible the use of heating and air conditioning, promoting an urban culture which is sensitive to energy saving.

Questa torre, un edificio di uffici di alto standing che doveva approfittare al massimo il volume costruito, fu pensata dal cliente e dall'architetto come un oggetto che doveva presentare un modello sostenibile alternativo per lo sviluppo del quartiere (contraddistinto dalle torri Petronas) nel cuore di una città dove si è portata a termine la maggior crescita costruttrice del continente asiatico degli ultimi tempi. Oltre ad essere la sede della compagnia, è un luogo di incontro peri clienti che presenta un'immagine corporativa fresca e innovatrice. Oltre al fatto di essere un oggetto formalmente contemporaneo, il suo disegno bioclimatico si basa sulla massima riduzione dell'uso del riscaldamento e dell'aria condizionata, fomentando una cultura urbana sensibile al risparmio energetico.

Dit is een kantoortoren van hoog niveau die optimaal moest profiteren van het beschikbare volume. Het gebouw werd door de opdrachtgever en de architect uitgedacht als een goed alternatief model voor de groei van het stadscentrum (die wordt gedomineerd door de Petronas Towers), want in de afgelopen jaren wordt in Kuala Lumpur meer gebouwd dan waar ook op het Aziatische continent. Het gebouw vormt het hoofdkantoor van het bedrijf, maar geeft de bezoeker tevens de indruk van een moderne innovatieve ontmoetingsplaats. Het is een fantastisch hedendaags object met een bioklimatologisch ontwerp, gebaseerd op een zo groot mogelijke reductie van het gebruik van verwarming en airconditioning. Op deze wijze wordt een energiebesparende stadscultuur gepromoot.

The tower is located in the heart of the city next to the Petronas Towers, in an area of recent urban development. Ground floor of the building and main entrance that leads to the foyer that distributes users and the public.

La torre si trova nel cuore della città insieme alle torri Petronas, una zona di recente sviluppo urbanisitico. Piano terra dell'edificio e accesso principale che porta al vestibolo a partire dal quale si distribuiscono gli utenti e il pubblico.

De toren staat in het hart van de stad naast de Petronas Towers, in een gebied met recentelijk veel stedelijke ontwikkeling. De begane grond van het gebouw en de hoofdingang die naar de foyer leidt worden gebruikt door zowel het werkend personeel als bezoekers.

Conceptually, the building is divided in three different sections. The four-storey base houses comercial space, restaurants and bars. The displaced pillars from the perimeter of the façade result in open floors destined to office space.

Concettualmente l'edificio parte da tre sezioni differenti. La base di quattro piani di altezza dove ci sono spazi commerciali e di ristorazione (bar, ristoranti). I pilastri dislocati sul perimetro della facciata che offrono piani liberi per uffici.

Het gebouw is conceptueel opgesplitst in drie delen. In de basis van vier verdiepingen zijn winkels, restaurants en bars ondergebracht. De pijlers aan de rand van de façade zorgen voor open verdiepingen die als kantoorruimte zullen worden gebruikt.

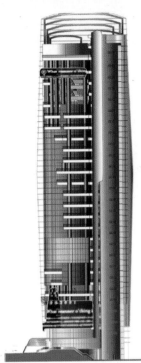

The last four floors house the company's headquarters and include a roof garden. Vegetation is a constant element throughout the entire building; it is a part of the climate control system and is psychologically a beneficial factor among the building's users.

E gli ultimi quattro piani dove si trovano gli uffici centrali della compagnia che includono un giardino sul tetto. La vegetazione è una costante in tutto l'edificio che forma parte del sistema del controllo climatico e, a sua volta, comporta psicologicamente un fattore positivo per gli utenti.

De bovenste vier verdiepingen vormen het hoofdkantoor van de onderneming en bevatten een daktuin. In het hele gebouw vormt beplanting een constant element, want ze maakt deel uit van het klimaatbeheersingssysteem en heeft een positief psychologisch effect op de gebruikers van het gebouw.

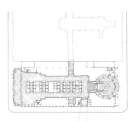

WELLS FARGO CENTER

CESAR PELLI & ASSOCIATES INC.

CLIENT / CLIENTE / OPDRACHTGEVER: HINES INTERESTS LTD PARTNERSHIP & NORWEST BANK	**1989**

TOTAL AREA / SUPERFICIE / TOTALE OPPERVLAKTE: 188.000 m²

FLOORS / PIANI / VERDIEPINGEN - HEIGHT / ALTEZZA / HOOGTE: 57 fl / 235,6 m

In 1982, a fire destroyed the 16-floor headquarters of the Northwestern National Bank. The new building, the Norwest Center (currently Wells Fargo), is the prototype of American skyscrapers designed to capture in their architecture the soul of the city. Its imposing presence is marked by the dominant vertical rhythm of the facade, where the Minnesota stone predominates over the glass. Starting out from a rectangular base of granite, the building ascends in a slender way by means of a light lateral breeching, thus characterizing its silhouette which is topped with a light crown of glass and marble.

Nel 1982 un incendio distrusse l'edificio di sedici piani del Northwestern National Bank. Il nuovo edificio, il Norwest Center (attualmente Wells Fargo) è il prototipo del grattacielo americano progettato per catturare nella sua architettura l'anima della cittá. Il suo aspetto imponente è caratterizzato dal ritmo dominante della facciata, nella quale la pietra del Minnesota predomina sul vetro. L'edificio, costruito su una base rettangolare di granito, si stringe, mano a mano che si innalza, grazie ad una lieve rientranza laterale, che gli conferisce così la sua forma caratteristica. L'edificio culmina con una leggera corona di marmo e vetro.

In 1982 verwoestte een brand het zestien verdiepingen grote hoofdkantoor van de Northwestern National Bank. Het nieuwe gebouw, de Norwest Center (momenteel Wells Fargo) is het prototype van Amerikaanse wolkenkrabbers die ontworpen zijn om de ziel van de stad in architectuur te vangen. De dominante aanwezigheid wordt uitgedrukt door de loodrecht verrijzende façade uit Minnesota-steen en in mindere mate glas. De rechthoekige basis is van graniet. De toren verheft zich rank doordat zijgedeelten licht terugwijken. De lichte kroon bestaat uit glas en marmer.

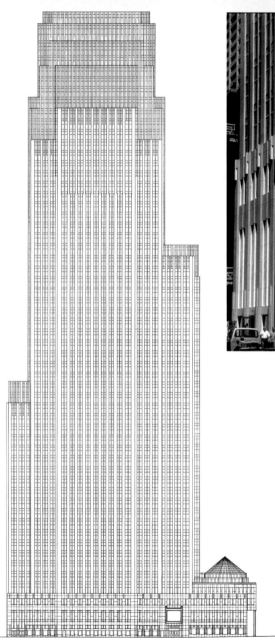

Front elevation of the building.
Despite the rectangular shape of the
lot, the vision of the building varies
according to the point of view of the
observer.

*Prospetto frontale dell'edificio. Dal
momento che la forma della base
è rettangolare, l'immagine
dall'esterno è diversa a seconda del
punto di osservazione.*

Voorgevel van het gebouw. Ondanks
de rechthoekige vorm van het perceel
varieert het uitzicht op het gebouw
met het gezichtspunt van de kijker.

The base of the tower, which occupies more than half a block, is connected by means of a bridge to a public space designed together with the sculptor Siah Armajani.

La base della torre, che occupa più di mezzo isolato, è collegata grazie ad un ponte facente parte di uno spazio pubblico progettato in collaborazione con lo scultore Siah Armajani

De basis van de toren beslaat meer dan een half huizenblok en is door middel van een brug met een openbare ruimte verbonden, welke in samenwerking met de beeldhouwer Siah Armajani werd ontworpen.

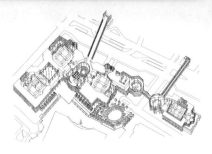

WORLD FINANCIAL CENTER

CESAR PELLI & ASSOCIATES INC

1985

CLIENT / CLIENTE / OPDRACHTGEVER: OLYMPIA & YORK	
TOTAL AREA / SUPERFICIE / TOTALE OPPERVLAKTE: 790.000 m²	
FLOORS / PIANI / VERDIEPINGEN - HEIGHT / ALTEZZA / HOOGTE: 34, 51 fl / 225,3 m	

This complex was built on land reclaimed from the sea, forming part of the World Trade Center of Manhattan, between the Hudson River and the West Side freeway.

On the other side, the Twin Towers contrast with the reflective façades and copper decks of the W.F.C. The two complexes form one of the most recognizable silhouettes of the city. The four office towers are connected by means of the lower floors, giving rise to a very large site with very varied uses, such as a winter garden, shopping spaces, stage and a bridge which links it with the Twin Towers.

Questo complesso, costruito su terreni sottratti al mare, fa parte del World Trade Center di Manhattan, tra il fiume Hudson e l'autostradadella West Side. Sull'altrasponda, le Twin Towers con le facciate a specchio ed i tetti di rame del WFC. I due complessi costituisconouna delle sagome più caratteristiche della città. Le quattro torri di uffici sono collegate a livello dei piani inferiori,che formano un recinto notevolmente esteso destinato a vari usi, vi si trovaun giardino d'inverno e spazi commerciali, inoltre fa da scenario e collegamentoalle Twin Towers.

Dit complex is gebouwd op land dat op de zee werd veroverd en maakt onderdeel uit van het World Trade Center van Manhattan, tussen de Hudson River en de West Side-autosnelweg. De façaden van de gebouwen spiegelen en de daken zijn belegd met koper. Eens vormde dit complex samen met de Twin Towers een van de meest herkenbare silhouetten van de stad. De vier kantoortorens zijn verbonden door middel van de lagere verdiepingen, waardoor een zeer groot geheel ontstaat dat voor allerlei doeleinden wordt gebruikt, zoals een wintertuin, winkelruimten en voorheen een brug die het complex met de Twin Towers verbond.

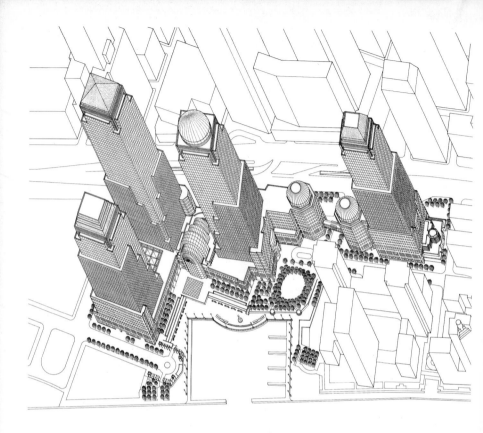

On the right, view of the great glass vault which covers the Winter Garden. On the left, boats at the Hudson River dock.

A destra, veduta della grande volta di vetro che ricopre il Giardino d'Inverno. A sinistra, imbarcazioni sul molo del fiume Hudson.

Rechts: uitzicht op de magnifieke glazen boog die de wintertuin bedekt. Links: boten aan de kade van de Hudson River.

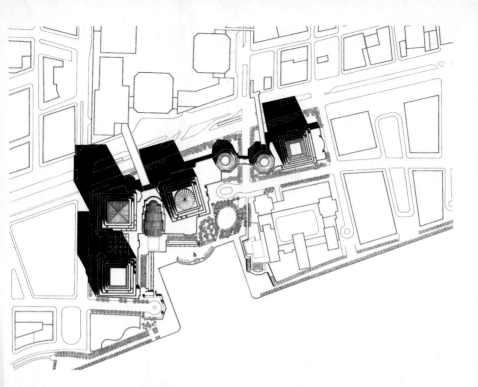

On the left, inside the Winter Garden. Above, axonometric projection of the group with the study of the shadows thrown by the buildings.

A sinistra, interno del Giardino d'Inverno. In alto, assonometria dell'insieme con lo studio delle ombre proiettate dagli edifici.

Links: in de wintertuin. Boven: axonometrische projectie van het complex met een studie van de schaduwval van de gebouwen.

IN MEMORIAM

This mythical image of Manhattan has been drastically altered since the attacks of September 11th 2001, when two airplanes crashed into the two towers, causing their subsequent collapse.

Il leggendario panorama di Manhattan è cambiato completamente dopo l'attentato dell'11 settembre 2001, quando due aerei si scagliarono contro le torri gemelle provocandone il crollo.

Dit mythische beeld van Manhattan is drastisch gewijzigd door de aanvallen op 11 september 2001, toen twee vliegtuigen zich in de beide torens boorden, waardoor ze instortten.

PHOTOGRAPHIC CREDITS / *REFERENZE FOTOGRAFICHE* / FOTOVERANTWOORDING

©Richard Payne FAIA (53 Rd at Third) ©Eli Attia, ©Judith Turner (101 ParkAv, Republic National Bank, Shalom Center) ©James Yochum, ©Jon Miller/Hedrich-Blessing (181 West Madison) - ©G.Murphy, ©G.Lambros (311 S.Wacker Drive) ©Peter Sutherland, ©Mark Lohrman, ©Timothy Hursley (777Tower) ©Daria Scagliola/stijn Brakkee, ©Luc Boegly/Archipress ©PCF&P (ABN-Amro) ©T.R.Hamzah & yeang sdn.Bhd (Al Asima shopping Center) ©Joe Poon (Al Faisliah Complex) ©Lend lease/Martin Van Der Wal, ©RPBW/Jad Sylvester, ©RPBW/John Gollings (Aurora Place) ©Timothy Hursley (Bank of America) © Cervera & Pioz WPA (Bionic Tower) ©Zeidner Grinnell Partnership (BNI City) ©Jeff Goldberg/Esto Photographics (Carnegie Hall) ©Ian Lambot, ©Martin Charles (Century Tower) © Roco Design Limited (Citibank Plaza) ©Ian Lambot, ©Nigel Young, ©Richard Davies (Commerzbank) ©Holger Knauf, ©Steinakmpa-Ballog, ©Murphy/Jahn (Deutsche Post) ©Andrew Gordon (Condé Nast) © Murphy / Jahn (Deutsche Post) ©Dennis Gilbert (DG Bank) ©Christian Korab/Balthazar Korab Ltd, ©PCF&P, ©Philip Prowse (First Bank Place) ©Aker/Zvonkovic Photography, ©Jane Lidz, ©Nick Merrick/Hedrich-Blessing, ©PCF&P, ©Waren Aerial/PCF&P (First Interstate World Center) ©Architecturalphotography.com, ©David Williams, ©PCF&P, ©Thorney Lieberman (Four Seasons Hotel) ©Lourdes Jansana (Gas Natural) © Hedrich-Blessing, ©Bruce Stewart (Gas Company Tower) ©Murphy/Jahn (General Bank) © Ian Lambot (Hong Kong & Shanghai Bank) © Anna Puyuelo, © James H.Morris (Hotel Arts) © Marc Mascort i Boix, ©Càtedra Gaudí (Hotel Attraction) ©Cuxart (Hotel Diagonal 1) ©Eamonn O'Mahony, ©Richard Rogers Partnership (Hotel Hesperia) ©Chris J.Roberts, ©James Carpenter Ass, ©Zimmer Gunsul Frasca (IDX) © Lu Yun Studio (I & C Bank of China) © Hedrich-Blessing (Jin Mao) © Kerun Ip (Jiushi Corp.) ©Timothy Hursley/Esto Photographics, ©Timothy Hursley, Ezra Stoller©Esto Photographics, ©Hedrich-Blessing (John Hancock) – ©Tamotsu Kurumada (JR Central) ©Richard Payne FAIA (Key Tower) ©Lawrence S.Williams Photography, ©Matt Wargo Photography (Liberty Place) ©Nicolas Borel (LVMH tower) © Murphy / Jahn (Max Building) © T.R.Hamzah & yeang sdn.Bhd (Menara Umno) ©Facade Gartner, ©Roland Halbe, ©Tod Swieachowski (Messeturm) -©Richard Davies (Millennium) ©Wolfang Hoyt/Esto Photographics, ©SOM (National Commercial Bank, Jeddah) ©Cesar Pelli, ©Kaneaki Monma, ©Mitsuo Matsuoka (NTT) Ezra Stoller©Esto Photographics, ©Brian Nolan/Esto Photographics, ©Wolfgang Hoyt/Esto Photographics, ©Alexander Georges, ©Chase Manhattan Archives (One Chase Manhattan Plaza) ©Bo Parker/Esto Photographics, Ezra Stoller©Esto Photographics (One Liberty Plaza) ©Kouji Okamoto (Osaka WTC) ©Osamu Murai (Oub Center) © J.Apicella/CP&A, ©P.Follett/CP&A (Petronas Towers) ©Jock Pottle (Plaza 66/Nanjing Xi Lu) © Andrew Gordon(Reuters) ©Cesar Pelli, ©Osamu Murai, ©Taizo Furukawa, ©Yukio Yoshimura (Sea Hawk Hotel) ©Timothy Hursley/Esto Photographics, ©Timothy Hursley, Ezra Stoller©Esto Photographics (Sears) ©Engelhardt/Sellin-Aschau i.CH., ©H.G.Esch (Sony Center) ©Jock Pottle(Suyoung Bay Tower 88) ©Foster & Partners (Swiss Re) © T.R.Hamzah & yeang sdn.Bhd (Tokyo Nara) ©Artefactory (Torre Agbar) © Georges Fessy(Tour Sans Fins) © T.R.Hamzah & yeang sdn.Bhd (Waterfront House) ©Balthazar & Christian Korab, ©George Heinrich, ©Steven Bergerson (Wells Fargo) ©Jeff Perkell, ©Olympia & York, ©Peter Aaron/Esto Photographics, ©Timothy Hursley (World Financial Center)

ANCHOR BOOKS

ANCHOR BOOKS - UK INSPIRATIONS 1999

Edited by

Kelly Deacon

FOREWORD

Anchor Books is a small press, established in 1992, with the aim of promoting readable poetry to as wide an audience as possible.

We hope to establish an outlet for writers of poetry who may have struggled to see their work in print.

The poems presented here have been selected from many entries. Editing proved to be a difficult task and as the Editor, the final selection was mine.

Anchor Books - UK Inspirations 1999 is a compilation of poetry which has been assembled using the work of poets who reside in the United Kingdom. The poems vary in style and content, ranging from what they like about their town or city to pleasant memories in life and the joys of the world today. Each poem is a unique inspiration reflecting on the true emotions from each poetic heart.

A delightful collection for one and all to read time and time again.

Kelly Deacon
Editor

CONTENTS

MAN OVERBOARD

She said goodbye.
She didn't use the word itself;
A thousand whispered observations
Dripped for years
Upon the fabric
Of his soul
And seeped at last
Through a pinprick hole

He made a pilgrimage
To shrines deep in the shattered heart
And held discussions with his fallen gods
Which fell apart.

That night it rained across the stars
And poured in torrents through
A hole in space
The photos of his life swirled all
About him
Debating the cause of situations
Arguing with eloquence against the motion
Which was carried all the same.

And by degrees he drifted out to sea.
They searched all night but he was never found.
His soul, once seeing that it could be free,
Waved fondly and stood smiling as he drowned.

Michael J Browne, Bedfordshire

THE SUB CONTRACTOR

The sweat that oozes from my brow,
in rivulets, soon freely flow,
on scaffolds dusty, where I bow,
      in toil.
That lesser men, will never stay,
make quick their words, to get away,
ne'er last the pace, for just a day,
      but go.
But we stay, just bite the lip,
when hourly labours ease the grip,
as foreman's tongue, the pharaoh's whip
      us lash.
The subby stands, amid the din,
a sneering crew, lick after him,
his power warm, so wears a grin,
      and watches.
The men he watches, he seems to flay,
as bricks for him, they rush to lay,
make profits roll, make rich the day,
      for him.
Oh demons come, grab his lapel,
drag him squealing, straight off to hell,
make ranks of rogues, one more to swell,
      with him.

Ian Maclaren, Bedfordshire

GRIEF

I look at beauty, but see not beauty there,
Birds have no song,
The summer trees are bare,
Flowers have no perfume,
Grass is no longer green,
I look at beauty but beauty is unseen.

Night lifts her veil, the moon is on the wane,
Stars close their eyes, they cannot see my pain.
The world is dark, for me there is no dawn,
My love is gone and I am left to mourn.

Muriel Johnson, Devon

FANCY THAT

The air was foul with hazy smoke
And voices harshly roared,
From giant men who filled the bar and common curses spoke.

They stood thick-set against the bar where 'whisky' was the call,
And they were tough and drank it neat
As fast as it was served it seemed, with hardly pause at all.

No woman ventured in that bar unless on business bent,
Those men were rough and had a way
Of taking what they wished - though all their cash was spent.

The locals stayed away from there, though battle had been done.
When first the riggers came to town
They fought with fist and boot and knife but found they had to run.

That night the bar door opened and entered in two men
Who dwarfed those present by their size,
Which made them huge indeed for many there stood six foot ten.

They forced their way through to the bar, those present seemed to sense
That here were men to hold their own
Against all odds in harshest strife, if given slight offence.

Up to the bar they broadly stood, the barman did attend,
As one spoke up in dulcet tones, and many heard him say-
'A glass of dry white wine for me and lime juice for my friend.'

S R Ramsden, Bedfordshire

WINTER WINDS

In the grip of winter's blast
Shrieking seabirds bouncing on bitter biting winds
A passing ship with twinkling lights
Pitching, tossing in the night
Raging seas of freezing foam
Lashing the pier on rusting stilts
Barren slopes above the shore
And coastal roads deserted

In the grip of winter's blast
Empty parks, street lamps shine bright
Shedding light on windswept pavements
The silent stare of a lonely tramp
Idle newspapers float in heaven's way
Wafting sounds of a distant hooter
In the cold night air and everywhere is deserted

Raymond J Hobbs, Berkshire

THINK BEFORE YOU JUMP

Abandon ship, it's going down they shout.
It's running out of oil, the engine will stop.
The shouting goes on, then panic sets in.
They all jump overboard, but alas it's far too soon.
You see this little ship stays floating till the new moon.
Then a big wave a big as you've seen,
takes our little ship past those who abandon him.
Our little ship sails on happily to bigger seas.
And those who abandon our little ship,
are now stranded in puddles and weeds.

Alan Brunwin, Surrey

DECEPTION

A sudden tear escapes, unchecked
from a mournful pair
of ice blue eyes
to betray the veneer
of polished sheen.
A gloved hand flicks by
to wipe it unseen
from beholder's gaze
as she stands, serene.
The moment has passed.
The mask returned
yet the feelings beneath
still turn and churn
her composure to jelly
while a statue of stone
is portrayed to the world
so all we can see
is a dignified widow
alone now - and *free!*

Kate Smith, Buckinghamshire

THE LAST WHALE

Being the last of your kind
You might as well be blind
Are you to be held by the ocean
Just to be cut open
Are you to beach
For something just out of reach
And will the world marvel at your isolation
Always somewhere to go but no destination

P Lowe, Lincolnshire

PEACE

She lives here,
peace,
in the whisper of the summer flowers
she is the humming of the bees.
Her breath of serenity
filters through the trees,
she is the rustle on the autumn leaves.

She is the frost
the glorious morning dew,
her hands of sunlight
reaching for skies blue.
Her kiss is the silence
before the chorus of the dawn,
as sweetly as the birds sing
she is the new day that is born.

She is the restfulness
in all that sleeps,
cradled in her arms
gently, she rocks me to peace.

C Leith, Buckinghamshire

HEAVENLY EYES

You stole my heart,
with just one glance.
You touched my soul,
didn't stand a chance.

You fill my mind,
I want you too much.
You're not mine to hold,
not mine to touch.

You're in my dreams,
I long for your kiss.
My desire is a sin,
I shouldn't feel like this.

I pray for my soul.
I look to the skies.
But all I see,
are your heavenly eyes.

Deanna Lorraine Dixon, Lincolnshire

ONCE UPON A TIME

Once there were fields, where now the houses stand,
Stretching for endless miles across the land,
Spring-dressed with daisies. Slowly moving herds
Chewed ceaselessly, whilst like a shining lake
The bluebells swayed b'neath trees whose leaves would make
A curtain for the newly nesting birds.

In dried-out ditches, halfway up the slope,
Purple and white, violets spread a cope
Fit for a king, or God. Their gentle heads
Demurely bowed, as if in constant prayer.
From the wire fence, the birds would glean the hair
Left by the horse, to line their infants' beds.

Where are you now, resourceful little birds,
And where the horse, and silky dairy herds?
Bulldozers tore the royal violet cloak
To shreds. Only the daisy, desolate,
Refuses to accept the common fate
Of nature's beauty, faced with modern folk.

D Davis-Sellick, Dorset

JUST A DOG

A labrador from Upper New York State
Looks at me with trust and love.
I respond, the same,
We do not query this rapport
Which somehow came
When I was there.
Though I'm a man
And she is just a dog.

She knows my car
As tense behind the window waits
Then scurries to the door
Where their stored greetings overflow
With yelps of joy.
I then acquire a shadow
Warm fresh from her rug
And shaped just as a Yankee dawg.

When we have used this day
Of precious finite time, together,
Between her basket and my bed
I join my hands
And thank my God
For true and constant friends.
Among the best of these, of course,
Is Emily - who's just a dog.

KAK, Cambridgeshire

AUSTRALIA

Australia is the place to be
Beautiful, warm and so heavenly
A wonderful feeling of being free
A land as far as the eye can see
The sky above so very blue
With little white clouds floating through
Around the treetops and flying high
Multitudes of birds fill the sky
Their pretty colours oh so bright
Chirping away from morn till night
Around the homesteads are grown
Colourful flowers of every tone
Roses and shrubs, fruit trees galore
Clothed by the sun for evermore
Many fields of golden wheat
Gleaming in the midday heat
Miles and miles of beautiful land
With livestock grazing all around
The eerie sounds of the crickets at night
Are gone by the early morning light
My family have lived here for many years
Three generations have grown up here
They came to seek a better life
In this far-off land of sunshine and myth
I'm really enjoying these wonderful days
Learning about Australia and its different ways

Maggie Coleby, Cambridgeshire

DRUIDS' HARBOUR

Oh yes! I knew the Druids' Harbour,
Often walked the rocky shore.
Watched the tide rush round the headland.
Felt the chill wind from the moor.

Oh yes! I knew the Druids' Harbour,
From the point they set the sail.
Goods and dreams for distant dwellings,
Searching for their Holy Grail.

Oh yes! I knew the Druids' Harbour,
The rituals in that sacred wood.
There the novices learnt the mysteries.
And against the Roman phalanx stood.

And folks met at the Druids' Harbour.
Of what wonders would you hear?
Learn of wizard, dragon and saga,
The legend of Arthur and Guinevere.

I often dream of Druids' Harbour,
Lanterns bobbing in sea's darkest night.
A small boat breaking on the horizon,
Under the winter sun's pale light.

A caravan park now scars Druids' Harbour.
Burgers, chips and amenity blocks.
Plastic things for a plastic people,
On the holy ground of Druids' docks.

So come with me to Druids' Harbour,
Journey back through all the years.
A life more meaningful and romantic.
Our golden past, have no fears.

B L Haswell, Cambridgeshire

REVENGE

I'll be here till I'm 96
They were all informed one day
I'll wear my hair down to my waist
And tie it up with string.

My dress will be below my calves
Dirty, ripped and rotten.
Below that I'll wear big black boots
All down at heel and muddy.

I will also have a bicycle
Rusty, red and shabby, with a bell!
And I will shout 'Ger out the way
I'm coming through you beggars.'

I'll go and visit my big sons
When they have friends for tea.
And plonk myself beside them all
Ignoring gasps of horror.

I'll then ask 'What's for tea?'
And when I'm told, I'll holler
'What, that again? I don't like that
Can't *you* eat that tomorrow?' And mutter

About their friends who should be home
It's time to make their supper.
Then take my leave without a word
To son and friends alike.

I'll go home riding on my bike
And ring my bell with glee
Revenge is sweet! My dear ones
But you can't shout at me.

J Wills, Cumbria

WEEKEND DAD

At ten o'clock on a Saturday morn
He calls to his kids with a beep on his horn
They have been waiting like little lost sheep
Their mother, still upset, is having a weep
His access was granted, he chose the weekends
He looks like he's happy but he really pretends
His new lady friend waits down the street
A safe distance he's chosen so the pair never meet
For the next two days they're his to command
At first it was great now he understands
That the workload involved is one constant drain
And behind every small pleasure there're oceans of pain
As their marriage broke down they all lost their smiles
Now their lives lie all shattered on solicitors' files
A few burgers and fries and trips to the zoo
Won't replace quality times of which there are so few
But if we so-called adults continue playing this game
We'll wreck their young lives and us they should blame
Because believe me it's true there's nothing so sad
As the beep on the horn from the weekend dad.

Michael Bellerby, Cleveland

HEARTBROKEN - A PERSONAL EXPERIENCE

Someone you love is always special,
So special, they're hard to describe,
They mean more to you than anyone else,
Without them, life wouldn't be life.

But when that person knows you feel for them,
Hard situations can occur,
You love that person with all your heart,
However, for you they may not care.

Harder it is when the person you love,
Shows affection back in your way,
And then you can't believe it when that same person,
Decides those feelings aren't to stay.

You live in pain,
Fearing love won't come again,
Crying in the rain,
Your heart, broken and stained.

Hajar Javaheri, Cambridgeshire

WOLF

The wolf is a majestic creature
his eyes, windows of amber
displaying a beautiful soul
his face conveys power and beauty
a sleek coat and alert pointed ears
silhouetted by moonlight, a shadow amongst the trees
powerful paws and fine sharp teeth
he is gentle, yet forthright
his ways are those of the wild,
wilderness, the essence of the Earth
his talents are swiftness, cleverness and cunning
yet amongst his fellows, there exists
a perfectly ordered society
the society of wolves, where pack mates
model themselves on balance and perspective
the wolf pack which hunts together.

Who is the wolf that does not belong?
He is a loner, wild and free
he seeks the wilderness,
known only to the free.

Brenda Straw, Derbyshire

LOVE AND LIFE

It is said '*Love* makes the world go round,'
      That is very true.
Life also makes the world go round,
      Feeling bright or blue.

There is so much *Love* in little things,
      Which meet us on the way.
Life's worries can also come along,
      To sadden many a day.

There is *Love* in the morning,
      And in the noonday too,
Life shares it from dusk till dawning,
      They go along together, that's true.

There is *Life* in the trees
      In the grass that grows,
And in every living thing,
      Love is also behind it all.

The birds on the wing,
      The flowers in the garden,
Along with animal friends
      Bring *Love* and *Life* to all generations.

Love and *Life* go hand in hand together,
      As we journey day by day,
But there comes a time when a *Life* passes on,
      And *Love* carries on in her own sweet way.

Gwen Banbury, Cheshire

CORNISH SUMMER

Golden sands reaching out
towards the sea.
Crystal pools glinting
in the sunlight.

Jagged rocks stark against
the bright blue sky.
Towering cliffs rise
in granite splendour.

Seashells and pebbles
of iridescent hues.
Washed by the sparkling waters
of the stream.

Rippling and gurgling
on its way to the sea.
Past the rocks and pools
to mingle with the waves.

Sand dunes as far
as the eye can see.
Mauve heather covered,
a haze of muted colour.

Seagulls, yellow beaks
and pure white plumage.
Soaring against the clear blue
summer skies.

Lydia E Stanton, Cornwall

DEPEND UPON SHE
(for Sheri)

You who lie crippled, helpless, sightless, speechless there
Nursed by a carer full of heart
Depend upon she who lifts and cleans with care.

You can only lie and grunt with sightless stare
You were made this way from your very start
You who lie crippled, helpless, sightless, speechless there.

Born into a world far from fair
You lie upon a special wheeled cart
Depend upon she who lifts and cleans with care.

Many there are who talk over your wheeled chair
And speak about a priceless work of art
You who lie crippled, helpless, sightless, speechless there.

For you it's hard to even breathe the air
And for every entry on your daily chart
Depend upon she who lifts and cleans with care.

You need a constant flow of drugs to keep you from despair
To keep you from that last depart
You who lie crippled, helpless, sightless, speechless there
Depend upon she who lifts and cleans with care.

John Aldred, Cheshire

MUM (1998)

A Mum is the greatest gift the dear Lord gave to you
She cheers you up when you're sad and blue
She stands by your side when you have done wrong
She has been there for you since the day you were born
You owe her your life so be there for her
Give her your love and your tender care.

As when the time comes to say your goodbyes
You won't feel the guilt when you have tears in your eyes
As after she has gone you will break your heart
But her spirit lives on even though you are apart
But you never forget things that Mum did for you
As the memory remains of a Mum good and true.

Frances Llewellyn, Grampian

A WARNING

Imperceptibly at first the thought processes accelerate
Then faster and faster the spinning skater of the mind draws in her arms
Adrenaline pig swills around the arteries
Praying hands shake like a mantis in search of lunch
The mind's protective filters fall away
All the senses clamour for attention like kids in a sweet shop
John's new heaven is revealed in the full glory of the universe
Celestial colours clash like Titans
Talismanic details are examined on a bus ticket
Hearing becomes as acute as an owl's
Faster, ever faster screams the high command intoxicated by its
                                                own power
The football of reality drifts away down the river of delusion
A new reality is constructed from half-forgotten myths
A false framework into which facts are straight-jacketed
Numerology counts out the tardy minutes
The Bible delays the devil's advance
Flashes of paranoia illuminate its letters
Fearfully-fingered crosses are made on windows and doors
Too loquacious to listen, good advice goes unheeded
Too busy to eat, weight falls away like autumn leaves
Too excited to rest, a day lasts half a week
Too far from reality to return, the mind's maze unravels
Prepare yourself then - for the end of your world is nigh

James E Cragg, Lancashire

PERFECTION

(For Anne and Jen with love)

Wouldn't life be perfect
If we could hold it in our hand
If we could shape and mould it
Like a castle in the sand

Wouldn't life be perfect
If we could write the script
To turn the page with confidence
Wouldn't that be a gift

Wouldn't life be perfect
If we could weave the way
Take each step by our own design
So we always have a say

But life just isn't perfect
It's often harsh and cruel
Just as we gain momentum
We run right out of fuel

Yet though life's often hurtful
I'm better of than a few
Because my life's a little richer
Since I found a friend in you.

D Finkel, County Durham

NORTHLANDS

In the distance fat sheep grazing,
further south are cattle lazing.
Touring traffic to-ing, fro-ing
past the busy farmer sowing
seeds to feed his needs.

Grassy hillsides stretch away,
age-old dry dykes line the way.
Here and there an ancient stone
against the blue sky stands alone,
where wandering weaves of weeds have grown
- proud proof of days gone by.

Endless clear skies meet the sea,
blue and grey and white and free.
Gentle waves roll in to shore,
tossing stones and bringing more
seashells to speck the sands.

With peace and quiet all around
such calm, contentment can be found.
As sunset spreads a crimson ray
to end another carefree day,
the city life seems far away
from Scotland's old Northlands.

Iris Anne Perrin, Highlands

SUMMER'S DAY AT PORTH JOKE BAY, CORNWALL

Old weathered bench, deep etched by seasons swiftly passing
In turn caressed by summer sun, then lashed by wintry rain
No tumbling seas this tranquil day, cliffs lapped by gentle surf
So rest awhile, and in reflective mood, gaze on this rich domain

Distant figures wend their way up clifftop paths so steep
Then downhill stride, more easy now, the children gaily run
Along the edge of sandy coves, gouged deep from granite rocks
Such treasured days of childhood joy, a time for carefree fun

A gentle breeze, a gossamer touch, soft stirs tall grassy stems
And deep 'midst purple tamarisk fronds, the summer bees make play
Their gentle hum soft mingling with the cries of distant lambs
Grazing on the grassy slopes across the narrow bay

Gentle slopes climb upwards to time-weathered ridges bare,
To Kelsey's Heights, where ancient eyes looked on this very scene
Will future eyes, in fleeting time, like us with pleasure gaze
Where ocean wide meets rugged cliffs, and fields of emerald green?

Brightly coloured windbreaks nestle close 'neath lofty cliffs
Like Bedouin encampments on Saharan shifting sands
Excited children's cries echo shrilly through the air
As on the sands their frisbees fly, evading outstretched hands

From cloudless skies the sun smiles down on sands and opal seas
Round shell-clad rocks the children play in pools of clearest jade
The busy world is strangely stilled, and seems to hold its breath
So rest awhile in this fair place, let care and tumult fade.

Francis Sawyer, Cornwall

MILLENNIUM - YEAR TWO THOUSAND

M any years have passed us by
I n great expectation we can give
L ife has so many forms we can but try
L earn to share, love and live.
E ngaged in hope of things to come.
N ot prepared for sudden change,
N or despair if leaving home.
I n maturity of time there is a range
U nexpected honours to proclaim
M illennium rise to fame.

Y ears of planning from day to day.
E nrich the life of all who care,
A nd produce the joys to share.
R emember the memories of years gone by.

T ake note of changes all around.
W ork in faith one can but try,
O nce again temptations will abound.

T his is the time to prove yet again
H ow family life is so secure
O ne can rely on help to sustain
U nder pressure, yet very sure.
S o be prepared in thought and deed
A lways learn from those who lead
N ot doubt and cause affray
D o something great to help each day.

A Joan Hambling, Devon

WINTER FUN TIME

Winds and weather blend together,
Like blossom upon a tree.
Winter snowballs shall be seen in the Wild West.
If you watch you will see,
A little robin sitting on a tree.
When the blossom starts to fall,
Then you know that winter is just round the corner.
The waves crash upon the rocks,
And it makes the train tracks all slippery,
And the storms are the best part for me.
The warm fires in the houses,
And people eating chicken curry,
Round the lovely warm fire.
The winter loves to be here,
Shall I tell you why?
Because it loves the cuddly warm feet of the children.
Thank you God for making winter,
Every day you are with us in winter.

Katie Hocking (12), Cornwall

NUCLEAR COLOURS

Rats by the million, cockroaches too,
why's the sky orange? It used to be blue.
Why is my body all purple and red?
Why are the bodies all tortured or dead?

It just couldn't happen, this nuclear war.
'We're safe with these weapons,' the leaders all swore.
Those still living wished they were dead,
with nothing to live for, a place of plain dread.

The rich had their shelters, they were alright,
the simple had nothing save only for flight,
but the poor did better if only they knew,
the rich just died slower midst buckets of spew.

What of the unborn awaiting their fate?
Warn the mutations what future awaits,
no one to aid them, no one to save
their misery stretching from cradle to grave.

R F Walker, Norfolk

THOUGHTS ON A RAINY DAY

Raindrops running down a window pane,
God's tears for you and me,
And for all of struggling humanity.
He set the universe in motion,
Like crossing some uncharted ocean.

What does it mean for you and me?
Why are we here?
He is out there, alone, unseen,
He does not intervene!

There is no dimension,
It is beyond our comprehension;
So we go on, into the future,
With hope and fear, but with love from Him above.

Towards our destiny,
Into eternity.

Stanley Crook, Lancashire

WHERE GOES THE TIME?

Where goes the time?
Where goes the blossom of spring?
Where goes the song I sing?
Where goes time?

Where goes the time?
Where goes the sparkle of eyes?
Where goes joyful surprise?
Where goes time?

Where goes the time?
Where goes the flowing river?
Where goes the arrow's quiver?
Where goes time?

Where goes the time?
Where goes the swallow's flight?
Where goes the starlit night?
Where goes time?

Where goes the time?
Where go the summer days?
Where go the summer rays?
Where goes time?

Where goes the time?
Where goes money?
Where goes honey?
Where goes time?

Where goes the time?
Where goes love?
Where goes the dove?
Where goes time?

Where goes time . . . ?
Gone!

A B Mossta, Cumbria

SEE ME AS I AM

Do not look at the colour of my face
Look at the smile on my lips
The friendliness in my eyes
Because my hand offered in friendship
Is the same as anyone's

Do not laugh at the way I speak
Listen to what I say
Is not what I say just as important
As what anyone else has to say

Do not laugh at what I wear
I am clothed and warm and clean
If everybody dressed the same
The world would have no colour

So be my friend
Because one day you may need me
When someone doesn't like you
For who you are
Then you will need my smile
And my hand in friendship.

Ann Norris, Suffolk

SEASONS

January brings the snow,
It also brings the rain,
We know that spring is on its way,
And we shall see the sun once again.

The children love to see the snow,
Falling gently from the sky,
They clap their hands and jump with joy,
As they go skipping by.

They've built a snowman and he stands,
As proud as he can be,
They borrowed one of Dad's pipes,
And a scarf that belongs to me.

We know that spring is on its way,
We've seen a lark or two,
And the bulbs are bursting through the ground.
The birds are beginning to sing too.

The snowdrops and the daffodils,
Spring flowers will all be in bloom,
The crocuses with their purple heads,
The white and yellow ones too.

The buds on the rose trees are bursting out,
To remind us that June is near,
Then every rose on every bush,
Will suddenly appear.

Their perfume is so very grand,
Each one is special too.
And if I would have a special rose,
I'd send one to all of you.

So spring will pass and summer too,
Then autumn will appear,
The leaves will fall from off the trees,
Now we know that winter is near.

Norah Stevenson, Cumbria

THE BARN OWL

There's a farmer's cottage across the way
With a little green gate and a window bay.
There at the end of a muddy track,
An old barn stands with broken thatch.
The barn inside is very quiet,
Only darkness reigns, there is no light,
Way up through broken wooden beams,
A shaft of sunlight can be seen.
For there upon a rafter high,
A barn owl sits with watchful eye.
He sleeps until the daylight fades,
And sunlight takes to evening shade.
But as the daylight fades away,
Moonbeams shed their silver rays.
Through open window makes his flight
Into the shadows of the night.
With outstretched wings he glides away
Without a sound to seek his prey.
His screech is loud and often heard,
He is a wise old clever bird.
Although he is a bird of prey,
As a farmer's friend in the barn he will stay.

E Parker, Essex

LOST YOUTH

Oh where did my youth go?
I look in the mirror and see
The reflection of a stranger looking back at me,
Who is this person with an old and wrinkled face
The wispy hair and glasses look strangely out of place
Then something stirs inside me
And vaguely in my brain
Is a picture of someone I once knew,
A pretty girl again,
A small but shapely figure
With eyes the shade of blue
The fair hair long and wavy
And a zest for living too.
What happened to this lady?
The answer will enthral,
She's living here inside me
She hasn't changed at all.

Anna Wilson Moore, Derbyshire

SPRING IN ENGLAND

I want to shout it out clearly
For this land we love dearly
What a picture is now to behold.
The new shoots on the bush
With tree greens all so lush
A variety of colour untold.
The painter's palette can't gather
Enough room to manoeuvre
God's colours so brilliant and wide.
Yet content we must be
To enjoy spring as we see, and
Taking all in with our stride.

J Ward, Lancashire

ME

I look in the mirror
And, what do I see?
That funny old creature
Cannot be me;
All wrinkled and worn
And off-white with age
I just look like
A very old sage! But,
What lies beneath
Is much more alive -
There's a mind that's
Racing, with thoughts
That fly,
Hither and thither
Right up to the sky.

Shirley B Allan, Somerset

WHAT AWAITS ME?

As I sit in my room and ponder
What awaits me in the world out yonder?
While I am shopping and people pass by
Will they be happy or want to cry?
I know myself I have good days and bad
Some days when I feel cheerful some when I'm sad,
Most of the time I'm healthy and fit
Other days I feel like crying because of the pain in it,
But whatever the feeling of that day
I know our Lord Jesus is with me all the way,
He lifts me up when I'm feeling down
Laughs with me when I'm happy or playing the clown,
Even now while I am writing these words
Jesus is watching over me making sure they are preserved.

George Reed, Derbyshire

The Big 'C'

Sitting alone in the waiting room
Waiting to hear my results,
I felt my heart beating
When the consultant entered the room,
Then he spoke the dreaded word
'It's *cancer* I'm afraid,'
Will I die like my husband did?
But there are no guarantees.
'Why me,' I thought, 'it isn't fair,'
And my tears started to fall.
The anger swelled inside of me,
'But I will fight it tooth and nail.'

I had the radiotherapy,
And hoped it would go away
But then I was caught unaware
As it appeared there once again,
My hopes were dashed
But I must fight on,
No matter what they say.

As the shock subsides
With my breast removed
I feel I may have won,
I may be disfigured,

'But I am alive!'

And I think what a small price to pay.
But if it returns I'll fight it again,
I will fight it all the way.

S Raven, Devon

SNOW

Flake
By flake
It silently falls
On fields and walls,
On temples, palaces and towers
In blanketing, smothering, ghostly showers.
Life holds its breath -
Afraid of death,
Flake by
Flake.

Drift
Upon drift
On mountain sides
It whirls and glides,
It heaps, rolls and rumbles,
Then glissades slides and tumbles.
There's nowhere to go
To escape snow,
Drift upon
Drift.

Slowly
But slowly
The glistening flakes
Become amorphous, melting shapes,
Then the smothering blanket breaks
And dormant life unfurls, awake.
Its fears now go
With melting snow,
But slowly,
slowly.

Joan Boulton, Devon

NATURE WITH ITS BEAUTY

Looking out across the bay, the sea mist gently rolling ashore
Bringing a feeling of tranquillity, a message to adore.
The tide gradually brings in flotsam, seaweed and driftwood
Beaten and weathered by the elements, conditions they've withstood.
Footprints are left on virgin sand by gulls and varied seabird,
The sound of water singing joyfully - listen - it can be heard.
The rivers inland again mirror the striated sky - dawn soon,
Then as evening draws nigh, a cloud drifts across the moon.
Breathtaking - this scene - no words have truly described,
But in one's heart, one's mind, it's there - nature has inscribed.
Voices, laughter, can be heard - carried on the evening breeze,
The air so still, scented from fragrant blossom on the trees.
Onshore a church spire silhouetted against the evening sky
Of grey, blue and pink - such colours and a beauty to defy.
When night arrives, again the world becomes a different land,
All around becomes so silent - listen, for silence it does command.
A single image suddenly in the moonlight, appears to become two
As the peace of night awakes - and reflections come into view.
Lights twinkle and shine, becoming brighter and draw the eye,
Moonbeams filter through trees onto the water - from the sky.
Foxes bark, rodents scamper, owls hoot, they are nocturnal - unseen,
Take time to enjoy nature's beauty, absorb all around and dream.
Day or night, evening or dawn - be aware of all that here is given,
Then where'er you are, its imprint to forget, will not be forgiven.

Irene J Mooney, Devon

REFLECTION

Is there a man who can be said,
Could others guide - the righteous tread,
But he himself was easily led,
And often strayed.
Here linger at this resting place,
Wherein he's laid.

The wretched dweller here below,
With dextrous mind was wise to know,
And sharply felt the welcome glow,
And cushioned flame,
But grave misdeeds, with crushing blow,
Did bring him shame.

So read the lettered stone with care,
And let thyself - thyself beware!
The lesson heed, that's here portrayed -
And give it voice,
For circumspection here abounds,
As wisdom's choice.

Padraig, Ayrshire

THE WATERFALL

Down down down and down
The water hits the lower ground
And slaps the rocks with slapping sounds
Then swirls round stones and mossy mounds
Until silently and mysteriously nature puts on her brake
And the water lies still in the slate-covered lake.

Pauline Scragg, Liverpool

THE OTHER SIDE OF NOWHERE

I'm lost on the other
Side of nowhere
A place where I hide
When I hurt deep inside

I came here to mend
A heart that is broken
There's only me here
And no word is spoken

There is no one to share
My grief and my sorrow
No yesterday today or
Even tomorrow

I dream my dreams
All day to pass the time away
Just stare at the sky
And try not to cry

I try to forget when I am a sleeper
But the wound in my heart
Only seems to get deeper

If I don't come to terms
With the cause of my pain
It could cause me trouble
Again and again

No friends are allowed
And two is a crowd

No doctor it seems
Can cure what I've got
That's why I'm here
I haven't forgot

So until I find my way
I guess it's here I stay
Lost on the other
Side of nowhere.

James Valentine Sullivan, Norfolk

WHAT'S THE POINT?

Mankind struggles against inevitability of demise,
We are destined to destruction,
Sure as the leaf that departs a tree will one day strike ground,
Mother Earth will reclaim that which we stole.

Why are innocents punished?
And guilty get away?
Right or wrong is a function of timing and money.

Born,
Die,
Life is just something to spread the words,
A measure of time.

We bomb,
We kill,
We allow atrocity,
Apathy is the name for our ignorance,
Apathy is the name of our enemy,
Apathy is the cause of our pain.

We are alone,
We are to blame,
We can make no difference,
The Earth will rise again,
Without the destruction of us.

Paul M Howlett, Devon

MAY

Emerging from dank winter, like a daughter from the womb,
This lovely May cries 'promise', softly hung with sweet perfume.
A bride dressed for her wedding, wearing all her finery,
A tantalising vision in her chaste virginity.

Dew-fresh is her complexion, with an aura calm and still,
Unsullied by dark storm clouds, and unravaged by the chill.
Shy flowers, unblemished gemstones, nestle deep in downy hair,
Caressed with gentle fingers by the breezes blowing there.

She treads a springy carpet, shower-washed and raindrop clean,
While overhead sweet music drifts from canopies of green.
Gay posies vie for colour; dancing petals cloud the aisle,
Reflecting warmth and sunshine from the rosebud of her smile.

Her touch is light and fleeting, like a butterfly-wing kiss,
As fragile as a rainbow and elusive as a wish.

The freshness of her beauty takes the wondering breath away,
Leaving memories, to be cherished, of a perfect bridal day.

Rosemary A Shaw, Dorset

6TH SEPTEMBER 1997

quick father, quick father! come father! see!
poison imps pilot petrol push bikes
as our princess is buried on the bbc
camera guns shoot daily price hikes

many black borders birth moneyed authors
big issue, big tissue, big papered lie
stranger friends blush to testify
multi-paged specials piling high

practised mirror tears outrun young years
pushing protocol swelling an aisle
lorded gents 'n' ladies calm populous fears
haunt the bereaved . . . hey did he smile?

tills jingle spangled for a harried flash
hurling dead gardens at a slowing hearse
stick on supermarket cd grief, for cash
good for charity, of course.

John Fairley, Grampian

ONLY CHILD

Deep as green forests the rooms of her growing,
the walls castle ramparts
of swallows and brown paper leaves.
In plaster and cracked alabaster the map of Infinity.
She shares the dark stairwell
with banshees and murderers and thieves.

All day through the keyhole dustmotes come visiting,
carrying portmanteaux
and rucksacks too small for the eye.
Her children and forebears
stretch forwards and back in brass doorknobs,
her ancestors sombre, her children all smiling and shy.

She envies their stillness, their certitude,
their yellow dominions.
She studies the map by the hour.
Supposes the sunbeams stream in through the cracks to anoint her
and dreams every night that she'll wake
to a stairwell in flower.

Shirley McDermott, Shropshire

DEAD MEAT

His hands lay still across his chest
Lying motionless with no thoughts or feelings
As if time had stood still in an eternal peace
This dead body that lies before me
Is no longer the friend that I once knew
But a cold piece of meat that has been put on
Display like a showroom dummy
These people that surround me weeping into their
Hands with the mourning that they feel
Feeding on their own self-pity
To the delight of the chosen few
They that congregate inside these walls of worship
Standing as an icon to the thousands that flock
In the belief that they believe
As they lower the coffin into the ground
The maggots gather waiting for the
Feast that beholds them
Dead meat in a box
Like the takeaway consumed each Friday night
With bones discarded before we choke
Dead meat is all we are
Rotting flesh that lies interred

Graham Hagger, London

KOSOVO

Beware, the Alliance is coming
The world police are out
To the sound of a soldier drumming
Limy beside the Kraut.

There are Yanks in mighty fine warplanes
Hollywood film next year
We will watch the killing and crying
Then down to the pub for a beer.

It is all an armchair war theatre
The countries do change sides
In a world of television pictures
Where can refugees hide?

The drone of a warplane flying near
Bombs dropped away from below
To the sounds of cold screaming anger
Bury your dead . . . Kosovo.

Peter Mitchell, Sussex

FAMILY LIFE

From when we're born to the time we marry
No one knows what burdens we'll carry
Teething, crawling, learning to talk
Tumbles we have when learning to walk
School days spent with friend or foe
Nobody knowing how far we'll go

Teenage years, when we start to mature
Learning all about love and allure
Meeting and marrying our partner for life
Bearing children, overcoming strife
Working hard for children and spouse
Seeking promotion, buying a house

When retirement comes around
Peace and tranquility can be found
Put your feet up, that's the best
Leave the rushing to the rest.
Grandchildren come, bringing joy
Be it girl or robust boy
Enjoy it all from start to finish
Before your energy does diminish

Marion Pollitt, Lancashire

SENTENCE REPEALED

Winter returned at April's noon-day
And covered the sun with clouds of grey.
The fresh, green landscape of hope and cheer
Was shrouded with a mantle drear,
Just as my heart was cloaked with fear.

Daffodils and crocus ceased to glow;
Their heads were buried 'neath the snow.
New buds were smitten by the frost,
Just as all hope in me was lost:
It seemed too late to count the cost.

A dreadful chill struck through the air
With icy fingers of despair.
Depression deepened, despondency grew,
All dreams of future summers flew:
The years before had been too few.

But new-dawning sun caused clouds to flee,
Its warmth embraced and set me free
From restraining doubts and suppressing woes.
The tide of joy and thankfulness flows,
My faith's renewed, my spirit glows.

Once more the flowers raise their heads,
The gloom of winter is finally shed.
The bird's song gaily heralds the morn
Of new hope, new life. My flesh that was torn
Is healed as new. Spring is reborn.

Jean M Warren, East Sussex

LITTLE JACK

I'm all alone and I'm only five
I wish I had a family like my friend Clive,
A mummy to cuddle me on her knee
A daddy who'd take me walks by the sea,
A sister to read me stories at night
And a big brother so we could fight.

We could all go on outings
Or play games in the park
Watch bonfires and fireworks in the dark,
Play cowboys and Indians, then make a den
Or walk with my puppy, he's called Ben.

There's a swing in my garden and a tent on the grass
My pocket's full of marbles all coloured glass,
I've an Action Man soldier and a football outside
Guess what for my birthday - a new bike to ride!
Clive and me try to climb trees
We get lots of scratches and quite dirty knees
We collect big spiders and things from the streams
When I show aunty she runs off and screams!
I'm good at gambols and can stand on my head
But sometimes I'm naughty and sent up to bed.

I'd love a daddy who would teach me to swim
A mummy who'd be there to tuck me in
A sister and brother so we could share
My very own family to love me and care.

Lilian France, Leicestershire

DESPAIR!

Black clouds hover in an ever darkening sky,
Menacing, doom-filled, angry and wild,
As they gather slowly, drifting by
Catching the very essence of my own rancorous
     Dark thoughts, which threaten to wreck the
     Peace of my inner soul,
Tearing at my heart strings,
In one abusive mad moment,
Ending my goal . . .
Everything for which I have strived, and
Fought for in a bitter battle of love and hate!
Is this, then, the end of my dream?
'Is it now too late?' to myself, I scream,
To recapture the feelings which once we shared!
My heart tells me that your love has indeed flown,
Leaving me now so sad and alone . . .

Freda Ringrose, Lincolnshire

THE CLOCK

My life begun and the clock struck 1.
Then I grew and the clock struck 2.
I was young and free then the clock struck 3.
Got a key for my door and the clock struck 4.
I was still alive when the clock struck 5.
Walking with sticks when the clock struck 6.
Died and went to heaven then the clock struck 7.
Standing by a Pearly Gate when the clock struck 8.
I thought heaven was fine when the clock struck 9.
Born again and then the clock struck 10.
Grew up in Devon and the clock struck 11.
Then the clock stopped at 11.56,
So I smashed it into tiny bits.

Jason Foulkes, East Sussex

WATCHING, WAITING

Flight of fancy spread your wings like eagles flying high,
Strong intrepid visions, seeing tiny things move nearby.
Watching, waiting patiently for a visitor to pay a call,
Swooping silently in the night, take care you do not fall.
Counting every second, hearing every little sound.
floating on the warm winds night-time brings around.
Movement, very graceful, like the ballet of Swan Lake,
Closes in now on her prey, some chance she has to take.
She cleans her meal most carefully and enjoys her fill,
Then returns to dark night air and flies on until,
It's nearly dawn and time for home, it's also time to rest.
Owl looks around and says to herself 'My home is the best.'
She takes a last look before she sleeps all through a beautiful day,
This becoming creature looks so grand, as in her tree she'll stay.
Small creatures can roam around freely as owl falls asleep,
But when she's awake they must take care as on the ground they creep.
Rest beautiful bird, save energy while you can.
While you sleep keep one eye open though, for that dreaded man.

Denise Threlfall, Lancashire

SOUTHERN CASTLES

Herstmonceux Castle in the early morning light
Stands proudly magnificent and a wonderful sight.
Golden hued battlements dappled with snow,
A drawbridge creaking and ready to go.
Turrets gleaming in the mid-winter air
Creating an aura of long ago.
The moat frozen over gives the illusion of glass
But with the return of the sun the deception
Will pass.

Melissa Farnham, East Sussex

RAIN

The drumming on the window
Wields its soporific beat
On the old man in the rocker
Beside the glowing fire of peat.
The gently drooping eyelids
Hide his thoughts of wet days past
When he ran precipitando
Over saturated grass.
These limbs that once were agile,
Now permanently bent,
Won't bound through sodden meadow
Where his boyhood days were spent.
For now when heavens open
And the elements conspire
To make little boys don wellies,
Longevity seeks the fire.

Helen Logie, Orkney

TWILIGHT'S A'COMING

Oh faithful stars I see before me
I feel your presence even when
I am blind to your beauty

Oh trusted moon I view
Your power turns the tides
As your fullness possesses minds

And as day sees rejuvenation
Night falls to requiem
Welcome daybreak welcome
But be assured
Twilight's a'coming.

D Tomlinson, Essex

A LEAVE-TAKING

Calm waters cool and wide
below the mountain's eagle side
whisper soft enticingly

      Here you may abide.

Clouds in the high blue
beyond the touch of seabirds' wings
trace their echoless journey through
the voids of air.

      Must you follow over the hill?
      Peace is not there.

Beside these waters I would stay
but into the morning leads my road
half a thousand miles away.

      Come back - come back -
      one day.

David Poole, Essex

SEASIDE COTTAGES

Chocolate-box cottages, clustered round a creek.
Is it here we'll find the joy that most of us still seek?
Cries of the seagulls, crashing of the waves,
Water rushing in and out of all those little caves.
Colour-washed walls of pink and green and blue,
Sparkling bright windows where the sun shines through.
We imagine peace behind these walls, beneath a crown of thatch,
But do we think that dreams and life can ever really match?
It's all ideal in so many different ways,
Still, maybe we should keep the dream just for holidays.

Anne Haines, Herefordshire

CHILDHOOD MEMORIES

As I watch a plane travelling across the summer sky
Leaving two white lines in the blue
I'm reminded of my childhood
And the happy time I knew

The days were always sunny or it always seemed that way
Playing in the garden, my mother never far away
Paddling in the paddling pool, swinging on my swing
Although now I can't remember the words I used to sing

A feeling of contentment
No worries to cloud my day
With my dolls and other toys
All day long I'd play

The dog would sit and watch me
And sometimes she'd join in too
Especially if there was food about
Biscuits, sweets - she liked a few

My brother would make up water games
A fountain he'd make with the hose
Although how he thought it all up
Heaven only knows

And then as evening would draw near
Dad would suddenly appear
Home from work the grass he'd mow
My family all here - security I'd know

It's sad that nothing stays the same
But now I watch my children play their own games
And I try my best to make their time
As happy a childhood as mine.

Corrinne Calvert, Essex

EASY TARGET

They opened the door
And out she walked
The press took some pictures
And then they talked.

As she walked towards
Her car
The bomb squad watched
From afar.

She turned and stopped
As if something was wrong
She turned back to her car
Her life was gone.

The bomb exploded
In her face
All that remained
Was the lawyer's briefcase.

Panic arose
The place went mad
The char broiled body
Looked dead and sad.

The police arrived
In squads of three
But they were too late
There was nothing to see.

The woman was dead
But no one would forget
How Rosemary Nelson
Was an easy target.

C Julians (12), Essex

MY LOVE IS ALWAYS TRUE

Girl,
Don't despair.
I want to show you I care.
I Want to give you my love.

Girl,
Please don't cry.
Just wipe the tears from your eyes.
I've got to give you my love.

I want to say a prayer for you.
You know my love is always true.

Girl,
Come with me.
Let's take a chance and be free.
Like birds let's both fly away.

Girl,
Can't you see?
Let our romance truly be.
The love we have will not stray.

I want to say a prayer for you.
You know my love is always true.

Peter Steele, Gloucestershire

FOR WHAT TIME'S LEFT

My aching heart thumps inside my weary breast
My tongue lolls out, rasping breaths I take
Where can I hide? I long for rest
Under hedges, in ditches, the barns, the lake
I've tried them all, for pity's sake
Why pick me out? What did I do?
I only kill to eat - to live, like you.

The hunt is on, the dogs draw near
The river's too far but where else to go?
I cannot think, that they will tear
Me limb from limb, my blood shall flow
Down through the meadows, oh! no - please no.
Instead - I'll bend my ears and drag my tail, bereft
Through the long grass, for what time's left.

Doreen Brooks, Fife

LITTLE THINGS

We are but a drop in the ocean of life,
That is all we can ever be.
But millions of drops all together,
will form a mighty sea.

We are but a grain of sand,
That is all we can ever be,
But millions of grains on a sandy beach,
Make a wonderful place to be.

We are as one small shining star,
Up there in the galaxy.
But millions of stars shining together,
Are a wonderful sight to see.

Just one poor lonely soldier
Stands gazing across the sea
But if he has an army behind him
Then they can march to victory

Just one small piece in the puzzle of life,
That is all we will ever be.
But if one small piece is missing,
Completed that puzzle can never be.

Iris E Covell, Lincolnshire

LUKE

(A dedication to someone I love)

I want him back, the lad I had
Happy, young and free,
And the years we spent together in perfect harmony.
Innocent and trusting, enthusiastic too,
Listening to what I had to say
Compromising, accepting and agreeing things
     should be done in such a way
So as we could live together, knowing we could get along.
But years pass, the lad became someone I do not know,
A scruffy, grumpy kid
Argumentative, unruly, unresponsive to everything I said.
Noisy, loud, abusive, a know-it-all too,
Where, oh where did I go wrong, and now what do I do?
'Talk it through, it'll pass,' I'm told, but when all's said and done,
After all, how are they to know it's like talking to a brick wall -
Besides, he's not *their* son!
Well I've waited and I'm waiting but there doesn't seem to be
An end in sight, or, we're over the hill - at least not yet for me.
So I shall suffer on again, suffocating all my fears
And hope that we come through unscathed his *awful* teenage years.

Beverley Griffin, Gloucestershire

BLUEBELL TIME

They always grew here when I was a girl.
Dainty, yet splendid, in a blue coloured swirl.
Where have they gone? I cannot find one.
They loved the shady woods, away from the sun.

Walking onward beside the small stream,
memories rekindle as if in a dream.
I can picture us all laughing, running, playing.
Paddling, fishing in the stream, jam jars swaying.

Smiling and thoughtful, I wander on,
yet thoughts of bluebells almost gone
until, with delight, just ahead in the dell,
I see banks and banks of lovely bluebell.

Seated among them on a fallen tree,
my youth I recalled, I felt young and free.
I gathered some bluebells just for the memory,
my heart full of joy, as I dreamed of yesterday.

Valerie Ansell, Suffolk

THE SOLDIER AND HIS SWEETHEART

Crooked and bent over, walking with a stick
he doesn't get around a lot, he can't walk very quick
arthritic fingers, bent and twisted round, walking with his
sweetheart, that long ago he found
handlebar moustache, he kept from long ago, for a smart young
soldier once was he, everyone used to know
he fought for his country, and left his sweetheart behind
but in those days it was the thing to do, no one seemed to mind
but on returning home again, many tears were often shed
until the very happy day, the sweetheart and soldier wed
fifty years have passed now, and marching through the street
all ex-soldiers and comrades unsteady on their feet
coats hung full of medals all shined the night before
but the soldier and his sweetheart can't march with them no more
because time is a great healer, that's what we often find
but for this poor young soldier, the war has made him blind
but in his heart he is happy, because all that he can see
is the way he left his sweetheart in 1943.

Margie Hill, East Yorkshire

MARK

The pain goes so deep,
All I can do is weep.
No peace to be found,
My head spinning around.
No food can I eat,
I just want to retreat.
I took all the blame,
No one else came.
Deserted by all,
I feel I could fall.
Made to lie,
I too want to die.
The love I have lost,
At such a cost.
I love you, you know,
Come back and make my life glow.
I love you, you know,
Did you really have to go?

Jackie Turner, Gloucestershire

DECEIT

You will feel me
Soft in my rage.
Lonely without you
But lonelier with you.
Gnawing on the inside of my emotion.
A fetish of exasperation.
Time does not heal
But kills the patience.
Love is a loss taken daily
To be renamed a different person
To a familiar face.

Louise O'Keeffe, Kent

CALL GIRLS

Of the maidens who call around yearly,
They're consistent, that's all I can say.
But June is too bold, April blows hot and cold,
And one can never be certain of May.

I see more of Eve who comes daily,
A persistent, reliable madam;
For Eve never misses, with those succulent kisses,
I can see how that girl tempted Adam.

She may arrive late in the summer,
But in winter it's mid-afternoon.
Only briefly she lingers and with cold, icy fingers,
She lowers the heat in my room.

She makes the sky blush with her beauty;
With her smile she can calm all my fears;
But, try as I may, I can't get her to stay,
And she leaves before black night appears.

When she's gone, all those ghosts and hobgoblins,
With nightmares on black wings are borne,
And deep darkness doubles my fears and my troubles,
And I long for the first glimpse of morn.

For my favourite, Dawn, calls each morning,
To melt all the troubles and gloom;
Rosy-cheeked and beguiling, she appears ever smiling,
And crashes right into my room.

Some call her a brash, brazen hussy,
Who robs many a man of his rest,
But of ladies that call, though I treasure them all,
Sweet Dawn is the one I love best!

Norman Ford, Gloucestershire

STILL LOVE

Still Love,
That has to be the cruellest kind.
Still Love,
That makes some streets so lonely.
Still Love,
An incurable epidemic.
Still Love, Still Born.

There's still love in these eyes,
There's still love in these hands,
Still love, still love in these lips,
Still love, still love in this heart.

Do you denounce that such ever
Existed in this world for you?
Do you doubt there ever
Being another soul for you?

Lay down your burden,
Stretch out your hands,
To receive the love of another,
That has been close all the while,
All the time of your sadness,
A cure was only a kiss away.

Look into my eyes,
Do mine show the same as yours?
I can't make any apology,
For all that has flowed and flown
for us, in our lives to date.
All I ask is why wait, why wait,
While there is still love.

Richard Gould, Hampshire

FOR GINNY - THE COMFORT OF NIGHT'S SHADE

Somewhere a saxophone moans its sadness
Into the deep blue of night's sharp air.
But beauty still destroys her,
No protection there -
The angelic softness of her skin,
The soft and sexual symmetry of her curves
The lustre of her eyes
Or the wonder of her deliciously scented flesh -
No matter what the hour of day,
Her beauty still destroys her.

In that evening tide
Washed in like a sea of emotional fear
This low and lusted after Venus tries to hide:
Blistered by the distant sax's sobs
In a dark untidy room
She crouches in a corner,
Her perfection compromised
By self-loathing and shame -
Flagellation of the soul
For all those covetous glances,
Those burning looks fairly frothing with desire,
Those groping hands
Birthed by contact of passing passion's fire.

All for what?
She'd never sought this devotion and desertion:
Merely born to this shape and form
She now despised,
Cowering in a corner of night's shade -
And still,
Her beauty destroys her.

Paul B Whittaker, Lancashire

ENTRY AND EXIT

To enter, then to leave life's stage,
An ephemeral span to play,
What limits set the memories
To curb a remembered page.
Snapshots that time will ever yield,
Forgotten in a strange and twisted way.

Who counts the seconds yet to come,
With the ticking of life's clock,
In rhythm with the beating heart,
Happiness and love for some,
Yet muted, slowed, the ticks,
As the reaper gathers his flock.

Whilst I have lived, loved, and been,
Is both a vision set,
Of memory and oblivion,
The unseen and the seen;
Easy perchance to remember,
Yet far simpler to forget.

Can the mind forever sever,
Happiness, love, so fleetingly, passed,
As a twinkling of starlight,
Gone in a flash for ever,
Though memory retains, retrieves,
To make a passing moment last.

As remorselessly through life we move,
Through the lows and then the highs,
Passing shadows come and go,
Hopes, ambitions to dash or prove,
Yet life and love, we finally see,
Are quick helloes, and long goodbyes.

Iolo Lewis, Hertfordshire

ALL IN DUE SEASON

All the seasons in their turn
Bring their special charm,
Snowdrops, roses, ripening fruit,
Harvests from the farm

The warmth of sun to burst each bud
First heralded the spring,
Then summer brought the lovely flowers
To brighten everything

Then autumn comes, and in its way
It gives us shades of gold,
The corn, now gathered from the field
Is stored safe from the cold

Soon winter comes, and colder days,
Sleet, snow and frost abound,
The leaves which once adorned the trees
Now lie deep on the ground

The sun, once high in bright blue skies
Now lies low in the sky,
The hours of daylight now are few
As weeks go slowly by

Although all nature seems at rest
Till winter brings its storms,
Beneath the rock hard earth there stirs
New life in bulbs and corns

Yet, in due time the winter's grip
Will ease, and then the sun
Will bring us springtime round again
A new year has begun

Horace Hartley, Kent

SWEET MOTHER OF MINE

Sweet Mother of mine I thank you for that gift of life
and for wanting me in your life

Thank you for understanding me
when I was wrong
and for taking care of me
when I needed someone

Thank you for helping me in my life
and for every tear that I have cried

Thank you for all your love
now I shall give you all mine

Thank you for being
that sweet mother of mine

Rachel Wake, Hertfordshire

DREAM ON

In your dreams you are wrapped in satin veils
As you float on petals in summer streams
You board your ship with its golden sails
And a loved one's touch lasts forever it seems.
In your song is a note that the bluebird hears
And is carried to the isle where the onyx grows
In a distant sky an azure light does shine
And your heart is in tune with angelic throes
With the light of the moon the diapason rings
And as it fills the air it caresses your soul
Through the mist of earth's eternal springs
Time stands still, as never before, your fullness whole
A tranquility that glides in like a fawn
Love rests with you and you sail upon.

G Hodson, Lancashire

DECOMPOSE

Will you hang
little caged man?
Neck and rope
in close proximity.
Hope you choke.

Are you scared?
Death is here,
enter hell unprepared.
See you later
little caged man.

See you never.
You are rotting,
you are burning.
What of justice?
You've escaped it.

All you have
discovered by vandals
while you decompose.
Flesh weeping, peeling
your bones revealing.

You're not forgotten -
it's not forgotten,
a horrible memory.
You are released,
you've been uncaged.

A dead man -
but you're free.

K Reid, Grampian

TIME BUS - FUNERAL

Two old ladies in their best,
Both so subdued, demurely dressed.
They take their places on the bus
And both are making quite a fuss.
One dabs her hanky at her eyes
The other says through mournful sighs,
'Now don't cry dearie, it was grand,
Although I should have liked a band -
The flowers, dear, were luverly,
I hope they'll do as well for me.
The sermon, it was simply great
It worked me into such a state.'
The other nudged her - 'Hurry dear,
I think we've got to change just here
And Time Bus drivers just won't wait,
For Temporal Transport's never late.'
She said, 'Your funeral was divine -
We'll meet next week and go to mine.'

Clifford Pyves, Kent

MOONRISE

The evening shadows congregate
And exaggerate their moods
Before settling down suspiciously for a brief nocturnal reign
The exhausted sun manipulates its weak and ailing rays
Supplying expected beauty till the fleeing light does wane

The darkness creeps mercilessly
Smothering the maternal fire
And night shall finally confiscate the spirit of the sun
And from the perennial silence the seeds of mythology shine
The arriving stars announce themselves to the eyes of everyone

Into this rural atmosphere
Does rise a possessive heart
Inviting eager constellations in her company for a while
The moon navigates her favours with a regal loyalty
Providing a friendly guardian for the lonely lost exile

Her presence liberates romance
And burns a spiritual flame
Having nightly coronations till the final prayer is nigh
As a proud celestial ornament born into slavery
The priestess of eternal night does cultivate the sky

David Bridgewater, Merseyside

SUNRISE

Waves come rolling in
Crashing on the beach,
White crest splaying
As they meet.
Cry of gulls in the wind
Over the dark, living sea.
Spreading far away
Into the distance,
Meeting with the sky.
A sky full of promise,
Shades of pink and orange,
Turning crimson, bleeding.
Blending into cotton swirled clouds,
Tinted with sun's blood.
Amid are dots of blue and white
Thus begins a brand new day,
Complete with radiant dawn.

Zoë Fail, Kent

THERE WAS A KING

There was a King in the land of Nod
Who said 'I don't believe in God'
Taken aback his people cried
Where will you go to when you die?
The King said 'I won't die I'm sure
I know of every single cure
for aches and pains and runny noses
My life will be a bed of roses
I'll drink and bauch 'til the old cock crows
May even punch the devil's nose!'
So he went on throughout his life
Carousing there with many a wife
A King he was with never a care
Until he trip-toed down the royal stair
With his legs in the air his head quite bent
The devil crept in with no argument.

Patricia Battell, Kent

PILGRIM'S REGRESS

'Hello,' said the pilgrim to those who could not hear
But the tremble in his voice, gave away his fear
He pushed through the door and on down the hall
Blissful, unaware, riding for a fall
For the house was built across a well
Which ferried souls between Heaven and Hell
And far away in the celestial dark
God and the Devil watched him as a spark
God shrugged, on sunbeams he was up to speed
But a spirit like that, the Devil had a need
So Satan smiled at the pilgrim's frown
He touched his soul and he took him down.

Douglas Lawrie, Glasgow

REFLECTIONS

When village schoolboys once demanded
'Which lass dost thou like best?'
To fairest Meg I raised my standard,
and named from all the rest.
I had never felt so bold,
but she was not impressed.
Her faded schoolday photograph
for me still smiles the best.

The smell of new-mown hay relayed
a passing youthful zest
for Joan, a lately bosomed maid,
sloe-eyed, and black hair tressed:
And even now do I recall
with backward glance suppressed,
One sun-bright day, long far away;
The yearning in my breast.

Now in grimy town residing
young Lucy was my joy,
until dismissingly confiding
she found another boy.
To me she told of love grown cold,
and thought it for the best
that we should ever say goodbye
ere love was put to test.

O! of those distant years behind
when time, slow taking wing
our growing, youthful ways defined
with languid hours beguiling;
my thoughts awaken, to collect
lost memories flooding in,
of long past days that did enthral,
and each new day was spring.

J Maurice Wilson, Lancashire

WHITSTABLE BEACH

(A response to Matthew Arnold's Dover Beach)

The sea is calm tonight,
The tide is full, the moon lies fair
Upon the estuary, as far away
The lights of Sheppey shine
In testament to man's conquest of the Night.

The Night that holds no fears, confusion or bewilderment
No phantasms, ghosts nor terrors.
No nightmares
And no dreams.

Our dark imagining is spent; we have our light, our certitude within,
Our confidence of control, of measured time.

And now the lights across the waves
Begin to twinkle and blink out.
Soon all will be still
And black.
The sun has set, its golden path to Heaven in its setting blaze upon
                                                    the waters
Is gone.
The world is dark
And empty.

Alone, standing alone amid the night
Gazing out into infinity
Where dark meets dark at the horizon.
There is certitude - all must end
In nothing.

And yet
Alone upon the naked shingle of the world,
Walking out into the darkest deeps
Of sea and sky:
Is it Nothing,
Or Eternity?

Helen Marsh Jeffries, Kent

TEST TRANSMISSION

Scintillating sunlight
on tides, gulls' wings,
on sea-rinsed sands of
bronzed estuaries.
Mutely the helicopter's
all-seeing eye
scans golden land
possessively.
Cruising seawards,
it oversees a clutch
of seagulls white,
its carefree progeny,
while mesmerically
synthesized song
weaves its tranquil spell.
This godlike eye
scans hills, fields,
beaches, wind farms,
the tanned interior
of a quiet church,
and humbly leaves
as the lemon sun
dies mightily
beneath the splintered clouds.

Wes Ashwell, London

Resolution

Ring out the old
Ring in the new
So many things I have to do
This is the year
That I will swim
This is the year
My diet begins
No more chocs in front of the telly
No more cakes inside my belly
Fruits and salads
Are the key
To a healthier slimmer me
For the first week
Things went fine
Until I turned
My thoughts to wine
I would sip whenever able
Drink my mates
Under the table
Now I laugh a frolic
A slim but perfect alcoholic

Elizabeth Thorpe, Manchester

The Fight

My head is spinning, I'm going mad,
My insides are crying, I feel so sad,
I've made the break now I must carry the cross,
I must grieve alone for it is my loss.

The days are hard, the nights are long,
I feel I've done right but something's wrong,
The laughter, the cheering it still goes on,
I must be alone, I must be at one.

I can feel it now trickling down my throat,
Pure, smooth and silky, is it my antidote,
But alas it can never be,
like a ship out of water it must be dry like me.

They say god is the healer of them all,
I've been picked up please don't let me fall,
For in the distance I can see a light,
Give me the strength to win this fight.

G Gormley, Surrey

THE WILLOW

Along the River Ely
There's a great big willow tree
Branches just touching the water
As if it had eyes to see
Look at the graceful way it bends
You can hide beneath its boughs
With a picnic and a good book
You can while away the hours
A romantic tree is the willow
You just have to shut your eyes
To imagine boats and punting
'Neath golden summer skies
Or maybe even music
Or cricket on the green
While the river laps about you
And the birds sing all unseen
Yes, a romantic tree is the willow
With a magic of its own
A place so green and secret
When I want to be alone.

June Davies, South Glamorgan

HOME SWEET HOME

Home sweet home
a dear little nest,
Warm and comfy to give pleasure and rest,
a place for love, content and happiness,
Welcome to visitors who pop in for tea,
or wine and dine as the case may be

Flowers and plants to soften a room,
rugs and cushions to be given a groom,
books and pictures to give much pleasure,
delicate china and things to treasure,
family photos, old and new
perhaps if you like them - a pet or two!

A pretty garden, through the window to see,
soft green lawns and a shady tree
Springtime blossom a sheer delight,
quite suddenly, everything is so bright,
beautiful flowers of every hue
sparkle with diamonds from the morning dew

Autumn comes, mellowed with golden days,
the trees magnificent in their shaded ways
Lovely carpets of yellow, gold and brown
as their shedded leaves come falling down

The snow is here with dazzling light
making etchings, black and white,
Sparkling frost h as touched all things
A little robin hops along - then suddenly takes wings

Now it is cold, with cosy fires burning bright,
another year has passed, it is Christmas night!
A new year begins
with a promise of many things!

Edna Parrington, Lancashire

THE LAST DAY OF MAY

Sweet May, once more your course is run,
Again with glory you filled the earth,
Bestowing on us your abundance of beauty,
You month of loveliness and mirth,
With sweetly scented blossoms cascading
And lovesick songbirds serenading.

The hedgerows you dressed in bridal whiteness,
And the woodlands with bluebell carpets laid,
Perfumed purple sprays of lilac,
And cherry trees with blossom arrayed;
You hung laburnums with tassels of gold
And the blackbird's song your praise extolled.

You painted the fields with buttercup yellow,
The daisies spread like summer snow,
While golden kingcups in water meadows
Swayed to the streamlet's gurgling flow;
From the spinney trees the cuckoo called,
And I stood there, bewitched, enthralled.

By the wayside you wove the keckflower lace,
Red clover and cowslips you brought into bloom,
Lit candles on the horse chestnut trees
And revealed the glory of gorse and broom;
You made the swallows wheel and dive
As though ecstatic to be alive.

But now your reign is nearly done
And I with sweet nostalgia must wait
Another year, till you return again
In all your glory, your beauty inviolate;
Farewell, lovely May, while still in splendour clad,
You must depart, and I am sad!

Bernard Laughton, Leicestershire

UNTITLED

Were you there, the time we sailed across a strip
that lead directly above the stars
and into an abyss of planetary bliss?
We flew above technology and below sanity
bordering on an impossible place
where love was love,
place was place,
time was time
and darkness was light.
We rolled in fields of scented blackness
and choked on the dust of life's motorbike.
We danced on the ocean
and loved on a star.
Then to take off again back to life,
back to time, back to place.

D T Morgan, Surrey

SONG OF THE SEA

The waves move over the silver sand
A gentle swish, a murmur slow
They sigh, they glide and then are gone
The tide will come and go.

The waves crash over the cragged rocks
They thunder, roar and are never still
Like a lion they creep up on their prey
All ready to pounce for the kill.

Whether calm or rough, the seas move on
The breeze can be gentle or a hurricane blow
Twice a day they will always be there
For the tides will come and go.

Patricia Jones, Lancashire

TODAY, BEYOND YESTERDAY

Today I closed a door and left behind,
The ghosts of the past that were unkind,
The fear of stepping beyond that door,
Chilled me through to the very core.

The spirits reached out and grasped my mind,
I hesitated, then left behind,
The spectres of a night in hell,
Which turned me into an empty shell.

A whole person can now begin to grow,
Kindled with friendships that add a glow,
To the new life that started that day,
I closed a door and walked away.

Elena Kingsley, Lancashire

A BOX WITH A PHONE

A box with a phone or a phone with a box
Who are you calling all on your own
Will it take very long
Who can tell what is going on.

A box with a phone or a phone with a box
Who too who is having a moan
Or who too who is asking who out
Just one more thing to phone up about.

A box with a phone or a phone with a box
Are you asking quite a lot
While not sure just what you have got
When you put down the telephone oh yes
When you put down the telephone.

Keith L Powell, Lincolnshire

WALSINGHAM

A place of wonder,
A place of peace,
A place of pilgrimage,
A place wherein lies God's Grace.

It never fails anyone
This special place of 'hearts-ease',
Strengthening the soul on each visit
Shedding its burdens like left luggage.

This shrine to Our Lady
Works its miracles quietly.
Known to a chosen few
And never forgotten by them.

Gabrielle Hopkins, Lincolnshire

POLICE MESSAGE

Baby in a telephone booth.
Only the sun kept him alive.
Male named Joe, pink cheeks soft and smooth.
Newborn, four hours? Or was it five?

His mother please to come forward.
Address unknown, description - none.
Rumoured last seen in West Norwood?
Too far off from her little son.

The police looked at that sweet smile,
Said - chance of finding her is slim.
He will be safe with us meanwhile.
We're sure she will want to keep him.

Peggy Trott, London

MILLENNIUM

The clocks all strike,
A cheer is raised,
The celebration starts.

The dark night sky
Lights up with sparks,
Disclosing the earth below.

Once covered in blackness,
Now unmasked,
On view for all to see.

Time to look back,
Share the past,
Predict the new.

Recall all the memories,
The pain and the joy
That made tears drip like rain.

Some too scared to remember,
Just lock themselves away.
Unlike the earth, they are masked.

As the world keeps turning round,
The years keep ticking over
The past will never be forgotten.

Not everything that starts
With 'Once upon a time'
Ends with 'Happy ever after'.

Antonia Spurry, Nottinghamshire

HOME TRUTHS

Striving for individuality, identity and fame
Each generation is the same.
In my day it was 'the thing' to go to a college of art
'Love peace, not war' and follow the heart.
A new era was born to the Mersey beat
And grew up with Van Morrison, acid, but not meat!
A harmless lot, or so we thought.
We broke up the family with the pill, if not babies to abort.
The stakes are much higher now, would you believe?
And technology can't control the pollution it conceives,
So grow up quickly youths of today
And accept the home truths, I here say,
Or there will be no world for your children.
Brush personal experimentation aside.
And open your eyes wide, wide!
Grasp the magnificence of creation
In all its glory, in every nation.
Look at the symmetry in a simple flower,
Wonders of the universe in dynamic power.
Be humble, with animals, make friends.
Reverse the trends!
I, who once said 'knowledge is not valid without experience'
Now say to youths of today,
Listen to your elders and don't waste time
The world is disappearing like a carcass in quick lime
Accept these home truths I plead
And don't give way to the pandemic Greed.

Adrienne Van Den Tooren, Lincolnshire

FACE IN THE SKY

Out of the night came beauty
    such beauty I had never seen,
Developing into euphoria
    made me forget the sadness that had been.

I can remember every detail
    each word each kiss each touch,
Now felt in every magic moment
    that I miss so very much.

So sad to watch love walk away
    when that love is forever in our heart,
Now is it pride or just stupidity
    that is keeping us apart?

Are the dreams a mirage of reality
    happening here and in another place?
For as I look up to the sky
    everywhere I see her face.

She turned as she walked away
    through the smile I saw the tear,
That waterfall started with that first tear
    the love seen in those tears is so clear.

So be happy be lucky be yourself
    for Clair you left me a legacy of love,
And when all the tears are counted
    they will match the stars up above.

J W Anderton, Wirral

BLUE

Immortalised in melody
     A stunning rhapsody to blue
The blue of the sea
     The blue of the sky
The blue of your eyes
     A constant surprise
God gave us this colour
     In all its fine shades
From morn's misty azure
     To midnight's parades
With stars peeping through
     A blackness of blue
Deepest blue magical
     Mystical beautiful blue
No wonder we call
     A trusted friend
        True blue

Bryn Bartlett, London

REBIRTH

Chanticleer punctuates the break of day,
Ebony fades to pearly-grey,
A bird-song crescendo embraces the air,
Wood-pigeon coos while leaping brown hare
Lopes lazily, idly, silently then
Wily Reynard slinks back to his den.
A pink stain caresses the coiffured hill
With all the beauty of an artist's skill.
A crimson flush gathers in the east
As flaming orb's sweet slumbers cease,
Then golden globe bursts forth with light
As day usurps the nigrous night.

A Richard, Grampian

THE KID

'I've lost my mummy'
He loudly declared,
While one finger explored up his nose.
Having gained the attention
Of all who stood there,
He went shy and then studied his toes.

He sucked on his thumb
And then whimpered in fear
As he thought of his mummy alone.
Without him to guide her
And show her the way,
He feared she would never get home.

His heart filled with fear,
But he tried not to cry
As he searched,
And he searched all around.
He used his coat sleeve to wipe at a tear,
He'd be brave till his mummy was found.

Did cities have tigers?
Were lions let loose?
And were monsters out roaming the streets?
He thought of his sword
And toy pistol at home.
Perhaps mummy could bribe them with sweets.

Then suddenly arms lifted him high.
He was caught in a loving embrace.
He was greatly relieved
As he offered his sleeve
To wipe tears
From his dear mummy's face.

Lynne Marie White, Manchester

WATCHING US, WATCHING HER
(For Cardiff, Group 73, Lourdes '99)

Passing through the wrought-iron gates, passing the pilgrims,
Dodging nations of faith.

The mass were heading to Mass,
To listen attentively to the multi-lingual readings,
That every now and again were in our native tongue.

So we stood amongst the groups,
Set apart from the rest, differently dressed,
And we waited. Mute.

For no words could articulate the mood,
No movement would warrant a response.
We were in a meditative state,
For which everyone would care,
                    Prayer.
                    To be in.

She stood there, *watching us, watching her.*
Adorned in blue. Flower in foot.
                    Pensive. Listening.
And amongst hundreds of people's staggered breathing,
I've never felt such a calm.

At night when the crowds had left her gaze,
She waited patiently with the few remaining.
Set back, protected in rock, that anywhere else would be cold.
But the 'grotto' was alive, breathing ancient apparitions,
Still drunk on the spring that feeds the vines,
Allowing life to thrive, allowing decoration to hang about her home.

As the spring spoke and the candles breathed,
The peace was intrusive, provoking thought.
People cried. Hugging the rock, the body of 'Our Lady'
Wet from a thousand tears.

On leaving I turned to thank her,
For all the times she had listened,
                              consoled.
Asking nothing of me.
Still sombre she stood there . . .
                    watching me, watching her.

M R Harper, South Wales

HE WILL NOT BLOOM AGAIN

Autumn's last days, the falling leaves
The dying flowers, the red red rose;
All are rotting now on nature's compost heap,
And time is standing still.
Nothing moves, all in nature is suspended
Animation, except man, that forever mobile
Being moves through nature uncorrupted,
Corrupting.

Burning the leaves; the dying flowers,
The red red rose, (polluting the air),
The beauties of May, the riches of
June, turned to grey ash.
Leaving nature bare, exposing its soul. Seemingly
Rootless but with roots stretching into the earth,
They will bring again the leaves, the flowers,
The red red rose, certain of a new spring.

Man, uncorrupted, corrupting, uncertain of his spring,
Will wither and die, be laid in the earth,
A stone to mark the spot with his name and
a piece of verse, flowers plucked and strewn
over his grave.
But he will not bloom again.

G Kenny, Dublin

TARDEBIGGE VILLAGE

In Tardebigge Village where I was born,
The church looks down from the hill
On the cut, which flows through the countryside
Where people can wander at will.

It showers a blessing on the New Wharf
Where the narrow boats moor, calm and still;
Its slender spire rises high to the sky
From the beautiful church on the hill.

The people canalling call in at the Wharf
For a meal and a chat about boats,
Where long years ago the donkeys were fed
With fresh water and bags of fine oats.

But those days have gone and the engines have come,
With power and lights through the tunnel
Which ends at Old Wharf, way under the Shaws,
No need now to foot over gunwhale.

The donkeys are gone and no longer we see
Them padding their way to and fro,
With no need for a guide, or a stick for their backs,
They always knew just where to go.

Away from the towpath and up the main road,
Turn left at the Grange's main gates,
Then up Hewell Lane till the first right turn
And down Old Wharf Lane to their mates.

If only the world was as peaceful and calm
As the waters where narrow boats go,
Where the trees give their shade over flower-studded banks
While the water voles dart to and fro.

These joys of the countryside enter one's soul
Bringing peace to the troubled mind.
The leisurely progress, so tranquil the pace,
Leaves the world and its worries behind.

I Broomfield, Worcestershire

DHAVLOS DREAMING

Legend tells us here the mythological beauty,
The gold-crowned Aphrodite, rose from the waves
And the clear, cool waters of her 'Fontana Amoroza'
Still tempts mere mortals in search of perfect love.
Richard the Lionheart pledged everlasting fidelity
To sweet Berengaria within the walls of Lemesos,
The Crusaders made Cyprus their resting place
And Makarios returned for eternal slumber.
Last night in dreams, I followed the pilgrim trail
On the often trod path of heartbroken refugees,
From Dherynia, where I lay in restless sleep,
And on in an endless search for elusive Dhavlos.
Through the maze of blockaded Nicosia streets
And onward, I warily tiptoed into no-man's land,
Drifting over the Pentadakfylos Mountains
To glimpse Morphou Bay through dawn mist.
Varosha's phantom sirens lure the weary traveller
To rest aching bones on her deserted shores,
And even the elusive prize of ancient Salamis
Seemed almost within my ephemeral grasp.
Within Kyrenia's historic harbour walls,
The resplendent galleon of my soul in full sail
And Commandaria still sweet against my lips,
I prepared to embrace Dhavlos once more.

Caren Christophorou, Manchester

NEWCASTLE, COUNTY DOWN, REVISITED

I am standing today at the foot of the Mournes
As the waves break on the shore:
But the sound of the sea has a sad refrain
For you loved this place, and oh! the pain
That you will come back no more!

The soft shades of evening are gathering now
O'er the little seaside town
And the west wind whispers a plaintive sigh
As its warm breath carries the seabirds' cry
And the setting sun goes down.

I walk by the side of the darkening sea
Making footprints in the sand
And I hear your voice from another shore
Where death and parting are no more
And you wait to clasp my hand.

Pearl Reynolds, County Antrim

SAVE OUR SOULS

The swirl of the sea and the foamy brine,
The underwater squid as it plays for time,
The Basking Shark as it swims offshore,
With bated breath and a good deal more,
The cod, the dab and the mighty bass,
That pray the fisherman will soon bypass,
These colourful fish in our deep blue ocean,
That swim around in splenderous motion,
The birds of prey that survive by diving,
And the fish that escape are glad of surviving,
Then maybe some day we will learn of their plight,
And fish carefully and only - when the time is right!

William D Watt, Ayrshire

UNWANTED GUEST

Toothpaste on the mirror,
Towels on the floor,
Tide marks in the bathroom sink,
Fingerprints on the door.
I'm tripping over clothing,
And toys upon the stairs,
Nothings ever put away,
There are wrappers everywhere.
No one ever owns up,
To these deeds and more,
I'll expose the guilty party,
My plan will work I'm sure.
I'll hide behind the curtain,
I'll crouch behind the door,
Camcorder at the ready,
When Nobody comes to call.

Helusia Shire, Somerset

BLESSINGS

We all should stop and think, where would we be
If there were no blessings for us to see?
A shaft of sunlight, the smell of a rose,
The beauty of a flower as it blossoms and grows.
The snow in winter, the miracle of spring,
The sights and sounds of each lovely thing.
The cry of a baby who's just been born,
The splendour of sunset, the freshness of dawn.
The happiness of children as they play,
Songs of birds as they welcome each new day.
So who are we to grumble and bemoan our lot?
When we think of our blessings and all that we've got!

Christine M Wilkinson, Tyne and Wear

BON VOYAGE

Stephen my son is in Aussie land,
Last I heard he was on the beach on the hot sand.
He's gone travelling around for about a year,
I do miss him because he was always here.

Trouble is there's been no mess to clear up,
Because he was always a messy pup.
Bless him I wouldn't be without him though,
Because his love and kindness he'd always show.

Once a week we try to keep in touch,
As his brother David and I miss him so much.
I'm glad he decided to see other places,
And of course he'll meet loads of new faces.

People out there are so friendly, they always greet you with a smile,
Even if you've only been there a short while.
I know there might be some snags along the way,
But be strong and keep going come what may.

All you young people enjoy yourselves while you can,
On the way you might even get a suntan.
Just make the best of your life and what you've got,
Life is for being happy and enjoying it, is it not?

Kathy Buckley, Norfolk

INFANTRYMAN

Eyes open; staring, fixed on the horizon,
Where lapwings wings lap furrowed soil.
Overhead smoke clouds blood red sunset.

Mouth open; drawing in the atmosphere.
Khaki chaos and uniform confusion,
The stench of fear here entrenched.

Shirt open; exposing body to sun's dying rays.
Razor wire reflections and gunmetal glints
Pierce dreams amidst agonised screams.

Chest open; ribs flower in crimson bloom,
Convulsed last exhalation, a groan.
Disorganised organs, died, unknown.

Andy Nicholls, Staffordshire

A SOLDIER

There is an old rugged wall where the flowers grow
A soldier lies there, who he is I do not know
He wears a beret, his face is black
Carries a rifle on his back
Mates of his not far away
Will they live to tell the tale another day
Their home for now a khaki tent
Nothing permanent, only lent
Clothes camouflaged green
So amongst the trees they won't be seen
Gunfire, bombs and snipers all around
Soldiers, they have gone to ground
Writing letters to sweethearts, wives, mum and dad
Telling them not to worry, it's not too bad
Amongst the mud and silent tears,
One wonders about their hopes and fears
How much longer is it likely to go on
Missing someone's husband, brother or son
When the fighting and troubles have ended
The wounded have been attended
Home at last with loved ones near
Thank goodness they sounded the last all clear

B W Jones, Northamptonshire

THE STANHOPE BUILDING

(Bridge Street Methodist Church, Mansfield)

A light in the window
An open door - No
Not ready. Not ready
For the homeless poor.
A building tall and erect,
But boarded up.
Not complete. The door is shut.
'Not safe' the council said.
Not fit to lay one's head.
So what do we do to open the door,
To give shelter and comfort to those
On the floor?
Work hard with God until the day arrives
When all are welcomed to the light inside.

Jennifer Barrow, Nottinghamshire

THE SUN

So special is the sun.
It brings such warmth to everyone.
It shines and makes things grow.
The sun has such a magic glow.

Even in the night when all is dark,
We can still see its fiery spark
Reflected in our sunlit moon,
To remind us, sunshine will be back soon.

And with dawn returns the sun,
Bringing light to everyone.
It shines and lets us know,
It's back again, the world's aglow.

Jackie Culley, Northamptonshire

MY LOVE, MY ALL, MY EVERYTHING
(For Debbie)

There, before me, she stands,
beaming in the warm yellow light,
she challenges the stars in beauty,
as they glisten in the night.

I watch and stare in awe,
as her seductive brown eyes follow me,
she flashes a beautiful smile,
a smile only I can see.

She touches me, softly, deeply,
I shiver, as if I'm cold,
she lightly scratches my body,
until she takes a hold.

Her arms hold me in love,
like a baby in distress,
She makes me feel relaxed and safe,
her love, never in excess.

Now, her body is in control,
she moves silently, silent as snow,
her sensual lips move towards me,
her eyes and body glow.

She sings as beautiful as the birds,
If she could fly, she'd be a dove,
she spreads peace and happiness around me,
and to her, I pledge my never-ending love.

She, is the most important thing in my life,
to my heart, joy and love she doth bring,
I devote my life, and this poem to her,
my love, my all, my everything.

R L Peters, Clwyd

DISC JOCKEY

(Dedicated to my nephew Ian)

I would love to be a radio DJ
I know I would be fine in fact OK
Listening to my favourite records
Each and every minute of the day
Being first to hear the latest hits
The good the bad the funny bits
Place them on the turntable watching them being played
And at the end of every week gladly being paid

Listen to that beat
Isn't it so sweet
Now my feet are really tappin'
Very soon I will be rappin'

In-between playing the discs
I can have my tea and biscs
And I always have to remember to say
'To all of you out there - have a lovely day'
I wish I was a DJ
On the airwaves every day
Listening to my favourite songs
Play and play and play.

Graham Macnab, Stirling

DEATH

He did not knock, this stranger tall
This stranger dressed in grey.
He did not speak a word at all
But came and took my love away.

Was he more handsome then than I
Or was her love so weak.
For she went away and gave no cry
Nor opened her mouth one word to speak.

Who was this stranger tall and dark
Who came at still of night
So silently no dogs did bark
Or birds took wing in fright.

I hate this stranger dark and tall
Woe to the day he ever came.
And yet, I think he'll visit all
Death was the cruel strangers name.

G F Thomas, Powys

WHY ME?

Is it the colour of my hair or perhaps my skin,
That's why you won't let me join in.

Maybe it's my weight,
That you just can't take.

You laugh yet I cry,
Many a tear has left my eye.

Perhaps you don't know or even care,
That's why you rip the clothes I wear.

No one knows except you and me,
The reasons why I'm late for tea.

Some days I'm in real pain,
And I really think that I'm going insane.

Is it the colour of my hair or perhaps my skin,
That's why you won't let me join in.

Sara Childs (16), Nottinghamshire

A POLO - THE MIRACLE CURE

If you had a headache at my school,
You were given a Polo,
That was the rule.
If you felt ill and you wanted to go,
You couldn't do that,
Oh no.
Give her a Polo,
That was the name of the game,
These snivelling kids,
They're all the same.
If your tummy hurt,
Or you had a toothache,
It was a Polo that you had to take.
A Polo was the miracle cure,
Trouble was when you'd had one,
You wanted some more.

Sally Hunter, Nottinghamshire

REFLECTIONS

Dark clouds gathering
Feeling of deep despair
Sun shines upon the path
Leading we know not where.

Christ's eyes upon me
Searching out my soul
You who cannot rest awhile
And wander from the fold.

How can you show example
To those upon the way
If you will not rest awhile
But dash from day to day.

Nancy Farr, Cardiff

MY LIFE

I wonder if I have any idea of who I really am
What's my purpose, hopes, dreams, where do I fit in God's plan
I have memories of a lonely childhood
And great fears as my youth came along
Then I met a man and I married, he looked so handsome and strong
I remember my vows at the altar, I promised to love and obey
But as his eyes grew cold I was frightened, what had I done that day
I waited and watched for approval, I did everything that I could
I remembered what my mother had told me, and did all the things I
should

I thought at last I'm special, important and loved at last
But, although I didn't realise then, this was just a repeat of the past
I'm almost into my fifties, and find myself living alone
My wardrobe is in two cases, and my home is not my own
It wasn't me he cared for, it was never me from the start
But I didn't know how could I, all I knew was the pain in my heart
I know that love is special, and there's no room in my heart for doubt
But whenever I show love to someone, why is it they always shout
This doesn't happen with animals, or flowers, birds and trees
They return my love in a whisper, that's as gentle as a breeze
What makes people so different, is it because they've a soul of their
own

Are they so afraid of unity, do they like to be alone
I know I'm an individual, but I'm also a part of it all
Why do some individuals, make love out to be so small
My life is at a cross-roads, God knows what my future will be
But I pray from my heart, that just one soul,
Would be willing to share life with me.

F Wright, Mid Glamorgan

GOODBYE

The tears are gently rolling,
Slowly down my cheek,
Dad doesn't know why I'm crying,
You've only been gone a week.
He doesn't seem to understand,
Now you're moving on.
Once you've settled in your flat,
You'll very soon be gone.

You know I'll always love you,
But you're not here, it's a shame.
When I'm making breakfast,
I won't call out your name.
When I'm making dinner,
Watching the clock for your train,
You won't be coming off it.
Life will never be the same.

You'll come and see us sometimes,
And you'll regularly call.
But your clothes will always be somewhere else,
Like the posters on your wall.
You're all grown up my daughter,
Now I need to let you fly,
But forgive me if occasionally,
I feel the need to cry.

P A Kelly, Ayrshire

Highland Games

Young chiels dressed in kilt and vest
Put their strength up to the test
Against one another,

To me it is a sight to savour
As they try to toss yon muckle caber
Tae twal o'clock,

And toss the weight up ower the bar
Or tak part in Tug o' War
Just tae see fa's strongest,

Then some o' them the hammer throw
Roon the heid an' let er go
Tae see fa throws the furthest,

Now they run around the track
With their numbers on their back
Just tae see fa's fastest,

Also on the boards children prance
As they demonstrate a highland dance
Before the judges,

This is a time for clans to meet
And for the fittest to compete
But me! I'll just hae a seat
Then sit an' watch.

D Parley, Grampian

ADVICE TO A JILTED FINALIST

Proud achievement lies abandoned in the dirt,
Sadness is the order of the day;
Faith and love were disabused by hurt,
The stable pillars of our life were clay.
With wish for reconciliation gone,
Decision known and temper resolute,
Distraction is the rightful option;
Abandon thought - and party absolute!
Then, when summer's madness has had its fling,
And urgent escapist lust has faded,
Reflect and give philosophy a swing -
Destiny will plot your path unaided.
Though fear and doubt return in elemental force,
The strength and love of friends will guide your course.

Dominic Coburn, Buckinghamshire

A NEW DAY

When sunshine falls upon a new day
Who knows what it'll bring, come what may

Another page of our life unfolds anew
With it new friends, new beginnings too

Just start the day as it comes to you
Go about your job and things to do

Give a smile to one, wave to another
Hug your sister and love your brother

And as the day ends and night-time falls
To morrow a new start, a new beginning for all.

Josephine Anne Dunworth

SOULMATES

People can love or be in love, and feel so strange.
But it takes a certain type of person who can touch
your soul and lift it up so high that the next breath
you take hurts with pleasure.

I don't need to be with you to know what you're thinking,
to feel what you're feeling.
We could be millions of miles apart but I know our souls
are somewhere in the middle enjoying
all the pleasures our outer shells could never dream of.

When I dream I dream of you,
whether it be day or whether it be night.
But our dreams are not true dreams, they are reality
but which no mortal can touch.
We live in it and it lives in us,
as you live in me and I in you.

Maria Conte, Surrey

A SONG IN MY GARDEN

A blackbird is here in the garden once more,
He is perched above in the old may tree,
I listen and thrill to his latest encore,
Sing on sweet bird for whatever may be.
Whistling, trilling as day follows day,
Calling, waiting and hoping that She
Of the soft brown breast will answer and stay
To cherish a brood in his favourite tree.

Alone in my garden performing each task
The future is somewhere I cannot foresee,
And then as I listen my heart dares to ask
Songbird Oh! Songbird sing also for me.

Marguerite Eyres, Sussex

HIGHLAND TAM

O Highland Tam's a mighty cow!
With horns so far out from his brow;
At twenty miles or more, a guess,
His roar is heard in Inverness.

The mountains shake when he goes by,
They see the look in that blood-red eye.
He's from the Highlands, don't you know,
The land of storm and flood and snow;

Where beasts are big and tough and wild,
And woe betide those meek and mild;
But Tam's the biggest of them all,
Can brush aside a six foot wall.

They've said before his time will come,
But when it does, there'll be a son;
Tam'll live on! He'll never die!
He'll watch that wee lad from the sky.

And when he grows up big and strong,
And in Tam's eyes can do no wrong,
You'll hear a mighty roar of joy,
Big Tam is saying - 'That's my wee boy!'

Alistair McLean, Perthshire

THE OLD SHEPHERD

He sits alone on a grassy knoll,
Grey-muzzled collie by his side,
Deep-etched lines embellish his brow,
His sadness hard to hide,
Retirement did not come easy,
To a man so used to active life,
And a yearning for his precious flock
Cuts through him like a knife,
To feel the thrill of a misty morn,
As he climbed the heathered hill,
Where rocky crags the ground has torn,
And the air is pure and still,

Rounding up his straggled flock,
With the aid of his old faithful dog,
To take them to the lower ground
To survive the dreary winter slog,
Working day and night at lambing time,
Tending to birth with loving care,
Ever heedless of the frosty rime,
That lays the countryside bare,

But now an old man's dreams come to an end
And drift away like frothy foam,
As with heavy heart he turns the bend,
To stroll back to his cottage home.

Francis O'Neill, Wigtownshire

EARLY TRAIN

Up they creep to platforms long,
Where others stand or walk around.
Near gleaming rails of metal strong
Which span a river underground.

Like a ghost a train just glides
From behind a wall of mist,
Along curved tracks for it to ride,
Brakes are on, and made to hiss.

Doors are banged and bolted fast,
Pale faces look, both young and old,
In frozen coaches made to last,
Behind a panting monster, put on hold.

In the dark a signal stares
With eyes of red and vacant look,
Some men just stand with little care
For those in lines, they need to book.

With a clank the signal's arm
Nods to the driver and points away.
A sudden cry strikes the calm,
No longer need the phantom stay.

Unleashed on green, off it goes
To clatter over turnouts made,
And rock as a boat, both to and fro
On shimmering paths, now all displayed.

Roderick Scorgie, Shropshire

BURNHAM'S LOST RAILWAY

The late lamented S & D.
Once ran to Burnham, by the sea
Where plans to make a thriving port
Through tidal problems came to naught.

The 'pier', a slipway merely now,
Was planned to show its passengers how
Easy crossing to Wales would be
By linking the south to the Bristol sea.

Marine Drive now covers the track
Where trains once travelled there and back;
A grassy bank beside the road
Marks where excursion people strode.

The sidings and the engine shed
Were where cars are now parked instead
And not a single sight remains
To show where Burnham had its trains.

But 'S & D' lives just the same;
A High Street pub proclaims its name
And on the seafront promenade
A land-train's trying very hard.

So, Somerset and Dorset lives
And pleasure to the grockles gives;
But nothing can be quite the same
As the railway that once bore that name.

Geoff Tullett, Somerset

AGE CONCERN

Old people, wrinkled faces, snow white hair
Shapeless bodies, bent, or carried in a chair
I know the day must come when I am old,
But dread the time when life is running cold,

How awful to rely on others' aid.
Not to run or climb, and to be made
To join with other old folk in a hall,
Or even worse, not to go out at all.

How awful, when you look upon your face
To see the lines that you cannot erase.
To find your body won't obey your will
And know that youth is gone, for good or ill.

I do not want to sit around all day
Looked after by the young, but in the way
So little time to come, the past long gone
And only memories of my own home.

So while I can, I'll keep a youthful heart.
Do what I may, so I won't fall apart
And I'll enjoy what life is yet to come
I will not let age win. My mind stays young.

Enid Broe, South Gloucestershire

IN SWEETEST MEMORY

(Dedicated to my nephew, Charles: 19.12.65 - 6.4.67)

Christmas was only a few days away -
How truly auspicious the world seemed that day;
A new baby brother, a cherished new son,
Robustly he cried and his life had begun;
Like gold was his hair and his eyes a bright blue,
Enchantingly mischievous all his life through -
So brief was the life that he knew.

The questions are unanswerable - of course we can't know why
A child who showed such promise should be destined just to die;
Though three whole decades have now passed since that most
                                        awful day
The memory's still vivid and it doesn't go away;
He's still thought of with wistfulness and undiminished love
And hopes that he has flourished in an after-life above.

You haven't been forgotten, Charles - your siblings know of you
And I've borne you four cousins who have heard about you too;
I hope there is a heaven (and I think there is, somehow)
You always had a cherub's face - are you an angel now?
Your life was passed in innocence - of sin you were still free;
My sweet ethereal godchild, may I hope you'll pray for me?

Rosemary Yvonne Vandeldt, Yorkshire

A DYING SHAME

Slowly my eyes open, see daylight.
Sun is rising, displacing night.
Another long night enduring pain,
Wishing my life could be lived again.
They were happy years when I was young,
Life wasn't ending but just begun.
I was healthy, strong, beyond a care,
Now I'm infirm, gasping for air.
Lying in bed day after day,
While my body withers and lungs decay.
Weight loss is drastic, I'm skin and bones,
These last few months I've lost six stones.
I'm thankful for life but I've one regret,
Inhaling smoke from that first cigarette.
I'm feeling weak, pain's getting worse,
The pain, the pain, the pain I curse.
Oh Lord I pray, Good Lord please answer,
Take my life or rid this cancer.

Ivor John Williams

THE BAG LADY

Who is this little person that wanders through the town?
She never seems to worry and never has a frown
She carries all her clothing in various kinds of ways
Just walking all round town, that's how she spends her days.

And are there any people who wonder where she is?
Do they ever worry or even care a fig?
Who is there to turn to if she should need some help?
Or is she just another one who has to help herself?

Where did she come from? Whatever did she do?
Could this ever happen to either me or you?
Whatever are the reasons that make her live this way
To travel our streets lonely, for ever and a day?

Could it be she's running from something she can't face?
Or is it that she's had enough of our weird human race?
Whatever are the reasons, it is still plain to see
That there are people like her, who need just to be free.

Fran Martin, Sussex

AT EVENTIDE

Firelight flickered in the darkened room,
Shadows danced on the walls around,
As in some tribal, primeval rite,
And, in the glow of eventide,
The questing soul, in pilgrimage, sought
An era long since laid to dust,
An age of ancient days from whose hosts
There rose up one who stood apart
Above all others, and drifting thoughts
Drew together, as focused rays,
Clothing the figure with golden light
Until, it seemed, he breathed again.
Within the room the shadows gathered
And flowed into a shape, a form,
Beside the chair, mortal to the eyes
Yet immortal, called from afar,
From Sacred Isles, by a yearning heart,
And two minds touched ere he returned,
But the joy and peace he brought lingered
Like blossom's scent on summer air.

Ralph Smith, Yorkshire

WHY CAN'T THE WORLD SLOW DOWN?

Why can't the world slow down?
People hurrying, scurrying by
No time to stop and chat.
To and fro, here and there
No time to have a care.

Why can't the world slow down?
Children running, racing, quick.
No time to walk or look around.
Riding bikes too fast a pace
Urgency on every face.

Lorries, vans speeding past,
Time is slipping, hurry on.
Buses roaring down the street
Each its own deadline to meet
Why can't the world slow down?

High speed trains thunder on
Must get there on time.
Commuters in their fast, fast cars,
And jet planes heading for the stars.
Why can't the world slow down?

Elaine Rendell, Wiltshire

THE CISBURY RING

Standing on the Cisbury Ring
Watching birds upon the wing
Grassy workings of Neolithic man
This then is where our world began.

High up on the South Down
Looking down on Worthing town
Here is peace and ancient lore
Well above the traffic roar.

When all these men were working
With deer horn and bone for digging
For all the world like ants or bees
In and out holes on hands and knees.

And are their ghosts wandering still
Around and about on this grassy hill?
Can they see me standing here
Enjoying the air so fresh and clear?

Mary Mackinnon, Surrey

COME TO THE CEILIDH

The smoke doesn't harm,
They said so.
It spirals from the centre
In a haze of fragrance
Wafting curtains round the sleeping children.
The animals slept too in the byre nearby.

This was the day of the 'black house'
The day of the traditional 'Ceilidh',
More peat, more smoke, more gossip.
The rattle of teacups,
The clink of the wee dram glasses
Vied with the gyrations of the dancers,
And the songsters who raised the roof
With their old ballads.

The grey light of dawn,
The gentle lowing of the cattle,
The cries of the youngest member
Herald the new day.

But what a lovely 'Ceilidh' it was.

Isobel Scarlett, South Humberside

OH BABY!

It's no fun being a baby, especially when they put you on your tummy
And you cry for love and cuddles and all you get is a dummy.

It's no fun when you're little and they put you in your cot
And you kick the clothes right off the bed, 'cause you're too
blessed hot.

Now what about the playpen, well that's a sight to see
They put you there behind the bars until it's time for tea.
Then they give you mushed up food, followed by a drink
Then they change your nappy cause you're causing quite a stink.

Now what about when Granny calls and coos and holds you tight
And says 'Who's my little darling' and sings lullabies all night.
It's not that I don't love her and it's not that I don't care
But she treats me like a baby and she ruffles up my hair.
She buys me little presents like rompers and new vests
I wish she would stay away sometimes and give my ears a rest.

It's no fun being young
But then it's no fun being old
So I will sit here and drink my bottle
And do as I am told.

Lynn Barry, East Sussex

JUST A THOUGHT

When you don't know what's right or wrong
Having feelings so deep, so strong,
Thoughts hit you from you know not where
Where can you turn, these things to share?

Are they thoughts of a spoiling child,
Actions of youth just running wild?
Are they something beyond control
Eat at your heart - tear out your soul?

If you reach out - touch new-born face
Do you feel thrilled, your pulses race?
See young or old in hopeless state
Think 'I must help' - or stand and wait.

Why in supposed superior time
We see such torment, grief and crime?
Do these decades tell yours and mine
Greater knowledge is wasted sign?

Ron Forman, Denbeighshire

MILLENNIUM DAWN

Time for all to celebrate
On the New Millennium dawn,
As we plan for our future
New technology is born.
Exploring deeper into space,
Working on the moon,
Meeting aliens from outer space
It may happen very soon.
Let Earth become pollution-free
Life and Earth need this protection,
End of terminal illness
New drugs to fight infection.
Nuclear war could happen
If the tyrant gets his way,
Unite to beat the tyrant,
Madness must not win the day.
Dawn of the New Millennium
A new path for all to follow
Walk it wise and safely,
New hope, a new tomorrow.

Dave Maxfield, South Yorkshire

THE CHRISTMAS GIFT
(To my wife)

'To buy or not to buy'
That was the question,
'Should it be that animal so
Large and white that the very
Purpose of the gift be lost
From sight?'

Alas, I tremble at the very
Thought of such a deed when
Even less, 'haps better meet
Thy needs.

''Tis better ye this illusive
Gift do get, thence I your
Humble spouse so meet thy debt.
My heart is thine and no greater
Gift have I, 'haps this Xmas morn
Forgiveness in your heart might lie?'

R G Rudd, Suffolk

CHILDREN

Little arms that hug you tightly,
tiny fingers which prod you lightly,
dribbling chins, infectious laughs,
welling tears and bubble baths.

Toys and books at every turn,
each new day - lessons to learn
exploring places that they oughtn't,
ending up with bleeding forehead.

Quivering chin with bandaged knee,
lollipops and shouts of glee,
sticky buns and three-legged races,
shining eyes and happy faces.

Angels when to sleep they're bade,
golden tresses that cascade
Darling babes, at last in slumber
visiting the Land of Wonder.

Christine C Jones, Mid Glamorgan

WOODEN ROAD

My kingdom had a wooden road
That crossed itself upon the mat.
The snips were multicoloured grass,
And, as I sat,
The leaden-blue clouds snowed
But did not block my road.

The fire roared;
The tomcat snored;
The black-lead oven glowed.
I counted tassels in my den,
As in some big, four-poster bed,
With all the table overhead
And my crossed wooden road.

That road has run for sixty years
Thro' glass that's decked with rime.
That feel of warmth is with me yet,
Under the tent of time.

John Adams, West Yorkshire

WHERE HAS THE DAY GONE?

I think it's seven-thirty but no, it's near nine
I meant to rise early and for once be on time.

I think it's nine-thirty but I see it's near ten
I must write a few letters - but goodness knows when.

I think it's ten-thirty but no, it's past noon
The day is passing much, much too soon.

I think it's twelve-thirty, but it's really near two
Where has the time gone? I wish I knew.

I think it's two-thirty but no, it's gone three
Just time for a biscuit and a sip of hot tea.

I think it's three-thirty but no, it's near four
I'm late for the hairdresser, must rush out the door.

I think it's four-thirty but no, it's past five
No time for a cuppa, I hope I'll survive.

I think it's five-thirty but it's now well past six
I've my make up to do and my nails to fix.

I think it's near seven but it's actually eight,
The doorbell is ringing, I'm late for my date.

It feels it's eleven but it's really past one,
Time I was abed - where *has* the day gone?

Joanna Pickett, Bristol

CASTLETOWN DENE

There's a place I love to wander
In a spot not far from home
Where my spirit finds its longing
No matter where I roam

Where the trees are green and shady
And they reach up to the sky
Where the birds sing bright and gaily
To my heart a lullaby

I can wander through the flowers
It's so very peaceful there
I can learn to face my troubles
And throw away my cares

I am never, never lonely
Mid the birds and flowers and trees
And I thank God for his garden
Just like Gethsemane

Castletown Dene
Castletown Dene
Lovely Castletown Dene
It's a garden so fair
Full of beauty and prayer
My lovely Castletown Dene

R Colvin, Tyne and Wear

FERNANDA, THE PRINCESS OF BRAZIL!

A princess of Brazil I've found
And with a garland has been crowned,
She's beauty kissed by sun and rain
My sweet Fernanda is her name!

She's gentleness that moves the lake
And purity of winter's flake,
So springtime birds they rest their wings
And listen when their princess sings.

Her voice can bring the joyous dew
Upon the heart and faces too!
With movement of majestic play
A dancing bloom in graceful sway.

I've breathed the fragrance of her deep
So happy are my dreams to keep,
And like the stars of tranquil sky
Fernanda's beauty fills the eye.

No rose or star can give delight
Like my princess that graced my sight,
So love and prayers each day I send
Across the waves to my dear friend!

Peter James O'Rourke, Staffordshire

THE RAINBOW WIZARD

Long ago there was a wizard,
Who wanted to own a rainbow.
He travelled the new and shining Earth,
And when at last he found one,
He reached out his hand
To feel the glowing colours,
And steal it from the sky.
He pitted all his strength
To catch and hold it, but failed.
Then he roared in fury,
And the rainbow vanished.

When you said 'I'm sorry,'
Your eyes hiding tears,
You, who never gave a kind word
In all of thirty years,
It was as though you gave me
A piece of rainbow,
But it was all broken,
The pieces shattered -
By your anger, my unhappiness.
I cupped them in my hands,
Then let them fall.

Margaret Black, Humberside

THE FORTUNE TELLER

Pulling back gold tousled thread
I wondered, just what lay ahead.
Gazed at suns and moons, on wall
While she gazed into crystal ball
Closed eyes meditating into a trance
She said 'I see you at a dance'-
She saw a tall man, darkly dressed.
She saw me in my Sunday best
She could see me laughing - throwing back my head
I asked if it was him I'd wed?
She saw me asleep dressed in lace.
But still she could not see his face.
Her brass bangles made a jangling sound.
She said he still hadn't turned around.
She seemed to go into a daze
and said the picture was a haze.
She told me I don't understand,
What is he holding in his hand?
She broke in a sweat shaking her head.
I'll read the cards, for you instead,
She cut the deck and spread them out,
She began to chant and shout
As she turned them over, I couldn't wait
for this next card will seal you fate.
I went cold, as I stared hard,
For staring back, was the Death Card.

C Mogford, Gwent

BIRD SONG

They fly through the air,
without a 'single' care,
Always a place to 'go',
'always' somewhere to be.

They sing, and 'tweet',
about 'what', I don't know?
Perhaps they're singing for 'joy',
or just thanking 'God',
for giving them wings to fly!

The cuckoo in 'spring',
and the robin in 'winter',
All beautiful birds
even when painted in a picture!

They settle in trees
and sing all day long,
you can rely on a bird
to keep you going,
with a 'happy' song!

So, to the skies once more,
they flutter and glide,
like 'rulers' of our skies,
who guard it with 'pride'.

K Grady, Clwyd

GOING HOME

Whene'er I travel near or far
I have a yearning deep in me
To seek out a westerly star
That leads me back to my Cymru.

Its rolling valleys not so green
Nor its mountains overly high
But to me the best I've seen
My resurrection when I die.

O splendid garden, blessed earth
Foundation of the Celtic race
Where the Lord's love was given birth
And His spirit fills all its space.

Between the Dee and the Conwy
Its golden beaches hem it in
By dark of night or light of day
Its Celtic charms invade your skin.

They say a land of bards and song
But this does not give justice fair
Its girth is short, its length is long
And many wonders you can find there.

Cymru, Wales, in the pagan tongue
Land of joy and home of the free
This is the place where I belong
Cymru is in the heart of me.

W Hayles, Clwyd

SPIDER IN THE BATHROOM

Don't consider yourself an intruder
Or even an unwelcome guest!
A mother's lore taught us straightly
That we must not kill people of your kin
Rest content where you are.

I'll edge out wandering woodlice
With soft paper, utter invocations
To forbid them this house.
Place cups over everlasting wasps
Scrabbling on windowpanes. Say
'Out you fly -back to freedom!'

But you, alien black thing, huddled
Like witches' knot in hidey holes -
Cracks that are your home, or strutting,
Unhurried across your palace, the ceiling.
Do you read my thoughts
With spider mind, sense with prescience
That this bulky shape had no ill intent
To you?

This bath's your pub. Drink water to the full,
You many-legged Falstaffian drunkard.
Yet men, who peer through microscopes
At your drugged face, declare
You're terrible to behold.
Let them think so,
I'm still your unknown friend!

Harold E Nottridge

CIRCLES OF TIME

Dawn of life as the year awakes
Spring flowers cover the ground
Buds burst forth to clothe bare trees
As the circles of time go around.

Summer days heat up the earth
Blessed with a clear blue sky
Holiday destinations reached
As the circles of time tick by.

A mass of multicoloured leaves
Herald the autumn date
Bonfire smoke pollutes clean air
As the circles of time rotate.

Cold winds and chilly temperatures
Keep us under wraps
Winter months have taken hold
As the circles of time elapse.

Four seasons of the years complete
Ninety nine has all but gone
Forward now to millennium
As the circles of time spin on.

Kathleen H Allen, Wiltshire

WHO WANTS TO LIVE FOREVER?

The world is simply going insane,
Litter on the streets washed away by the rain.
Murders, robberies, violence and rape,
A hero is needed, Clark Kent and his cape.

Leaseholders on Earth that's all we are,
Choking to death by the fumes of a car.
Prisons overcrowded and hospital queues,
Syringes found in public city loos.

Millions on Earth in need of money,
Tramps on the street, their next meal a worry.
Old people afraid to open the door,
Thieves await them, shouting for more.

Questions and answers from Clinton and Blair,
Peace deals are broken, the guilty don't care.
Dreams of the day when we shout and sing,
That stunning speech from Luther King.

Until that day we all grind on,
Piggy banks smashed, savings gone.
Release the pressure, no more hurt,
The evil to remain with their faces in the dirt.

Damien Brennan, West Midlands

GRANDMOTHER

Grandma or Nanny, to choose you may,
Feel proud my dear on this your day,
The little Beauty, meek and mild,
A Grand-daughter now, a little child. (Grandson)

Pleasures for you, just time will tell,
With Mother and Baby doing well,
The care you give with each to share,
With Grandma, there's naught can compare.

Now what are Grandmothers useful for,
To nurse and clean, another chore,
A little tickle will make me smile,
Then off to sleep for a little while.

When tummy aches, and tears flow,
Grandma is there, with a kiss they go,
And if I burp, a smile will tell
A little cuddle and I feel quite swell.

With pride you take me in my pram,
And help in every way you can,
Time to chat with friends you meet,
Who look and say 'She is so sweet.' (He)

With tired feet you wend your way,
'Not used to this,' is what you say,
To get back home is your desire,
With a pot of tea, placed near the fire.

Dear Grandma, life is very sweet,
You've earned a rest, now raise your feet,
With hope that years to come will see,
A *happy child* and trouble-free.

Lee Thompson, West Midlands

ON MAY DAY MORN

A feathered songster sings his solitary note
before the dawn.
The choir swells to greet the day
On May Day morn.

A green carpet mottled with starry-eyed daisies
spreads before me,
celandines and violets vie for coolest place
in shady bower.
The daffodils are almost gone,
in their place stand tulips in rainbow hue
on May Day morn.

May Queens in pink and white,
dip and curtsey in the breeze to shed their gowns
like summer snow.
Beside the path, smart felines
stand sentinel.
Each yellow helmet, flat and wide,
shining and sparkling in the sun,
for May Day's come.

Chestnut candles shed their light
on aromatic waves, dancing on a bluebell sea.
Weird spindly shapes, thinly clad,
emerge like ghosts through a misty haze.
The once proud felines, now turned white,
await the innocent
puffing time away,
to live again another year
On May Day morn.

Marjorie Upson, Yorkshire

MILKY'S DAILY GRIND
(Golden Eages MCC)

Assertive are the clouds, their yields harshly driven,
As the wind and the rain will now be the rhythm,
Percussion from the horses' iron on craggy, cobbled roads,
To each awaiting doorstep, delivering heavy loads.

Stern creaks from ageing timbers, as to a halt, wheels drawn.
Wearily in pain they trudge, to the chorus of the dawn.
Delivering dewy bottles to each house along the line,
Briskly pacing mossy paths, in attempt to keep good time.

As honourable her conduct, the noble shire awaits,
Whilst, with heedful tolerance, the master locks each gate.
Returning to the laden cart with empty bottles, stained,
Lightening the heavy load, as fewer streets remain.

Over the hill and on beyond they struggle as a team,
Repeatedly delivering, fresh pints of milk and cream.
Blue, his shaking fingers, as notes of request are read,
Returning to his shire friend, and down the road she's led.

Highly seated on his cart he doffs his hat to greet,
Drowsy ascending customers, walking the foggy streets.
When returning to the dairy, their aching muscles feeling torn,
Slowly fade the bottle chimes, until the following morn.

Sara Russell, West Midlands

AYSGARTH FALLS

Three hundred million years ago
A path was carved for H_2O
The water answered nature's calls
As melting ice formed Aysgarth Falls.

The limestone rocks along its course
Upper, Middle and Lower Force
Outcrop from the valley floor
Through which the swirling currents pour.

The raging torrent swiftly moves
Across the pebbles, potholes, grooves
And races down the ragged face
Cascading like a fall of lace.

Resounding all along the shore
The echo of that mighty roar
Is deafening to every ear
And amplifies your sense of fear.

The colours of this awesome sight
Combine to make the scene ignite
A firework show which never fails
At Aysgarth in the Yorkshire Dales.

Charlie McInally, North Yorkshire

THE PERFORMER

The lady makes her entrance
Her audience applauds
And as she glides to centre stage
Her arms embrace the roars

The orchestra is playing
Familiar opening bars
To her captivated audience
She is the star of stars

Each high note breathes emotion
They hold it to their hearts
And recognise each number
Just as the music starts

The spotlights bathe her body
That shimmers as she moves
Before the music fades
She knows her audience approves

They thrill to every movement
And know their parts as well
Each power-packed performance
Keeps them locked under her spell

The chant for more grows louder
They all demand her now
Then stand in salutation
As she takes her final bow.

T Johnson

A WALK IN WONDERLAND

While walking down a country lane,
I spied among the trees,
A village church with spire heavenwards,
The sounds of a choir on the breeze.

As I meandered onwards, covering many a mile,
Across fields, past hedgerows and over wooden stile,
When there in a clearing in the shade,
A beautiful green wooded glade.

There nature's magic born anew,
A wonder to behold,
The colours of a picture book,
Started to unfold.

Hues of lavender, shades of blue,
What a joy to see,
Hundred of bluebells lying
In a carpet at my feet.

A pathway winding through the trees,
Fringed with cowslip and celandine, and
in a cluster were poppies red,
Daisies white, and wild woodbine,

While overhead the leafy branches,
Bending to entwine,
Trees that made an archway,
To a wonderland in time.

Joyce May, Birmingham

THAT SPECIAL PLACE

I wish I were in that special place,
So quiet and calm,
So alone and still.
Just the sound of the waves rippling over the shore,
To reassure my mind,
Restore my will.

I wish I were sitting on the water's edge.
The edge of the world,
Where nobody goes.
Just the moon and the stars in the darkened sky,
To keep me company,
To cure my woes.

I wish I could smell the salty night air,
To breathe it in,
To feel its power.
Inhaling the vapours of richness and health,
The only breath
In a midnight hour.

I wish I were in that special place.
So quiet and calm,
So alone and still.
I wish I had only the moon and the stars,
Instead of this life
Which is making me ill.

Frances Pallett, West Midlands

WEST SUSSEX

West Sussex is the place I live,
A Parish known as Worth.
Uncluttered rural landscape,
And a magic place on Earth.
Less crowded than the east side
And without the urban sprawl,
With river bends meandering,
Accessible to all.

The setting of the Downlands
Dipping gently to the sea,
With tiny Norman churches
Flint-stoned towers, along the lea.
The softly swaying grasses
In the shadeless summer sun,
As evening turns to twilight
When each golden day is done.

And this is where we choose to live
My life, each passing day.
A perfect style of living,
And in such a simple way,
A place where time is slowed,
With just your neighbour as a friend,
To travel on Life's highway
Till you reach your journey's end.

L Coleman, Sussex

THE ENIGMA REVELATIONS

And lo . . .

Up in the heavens
'Quite absurd!'
Came the biggest bang!
'That no one heard!'
And from the shrapnel
'No one saw!'
Came everything
'Not here before!'
Now
In the space been left behind
Exists a void
'No one can find!'
A place of angels in the sky
'Where to live . . .
You first must die!'

Barry Howard, Surrey

RACE

What is *race?* - deep down it is nothing,
just a face different from each other.
All we really are is sister and brother.

We have differences of opinion that we are
allowed, but not to rape and maim and kill
and ruin everything over plain and hill.

What is *race?* -just people who live in
other lands, we all have faces, bodies and hands.

Let us reach out to each other and live as mother,
sister, father and brother.

M Pullan

EVENING SHADOWS
(At Scarborough)

Red sunset tints the western sky
with gilded fingers reaching down
and orange clouds are riding high
to paint the roof tops of the town.

A thin dark line far out at sea
spreads swiftly in toward the land.
Evening shadows stain the beach
and softly shade the golden sand.

Gentle wavelets lap the harbour wall,
swishing as they backward flow.
Dark shadows creep, embracing all,
diffusing twilight's gentle glow.

A single star hangs, shining high,
a herald of the coming night.
A pale moon climbs the darkling sky
and bathes the town with silvery light.

Bright stars begin their nightly show,
a myriad lanterns shining down;
street lights set the town aglow
as evening shadows clothe the town.

John S Bertram, North Yorkshire

THE SEED AND THE SUN

Darkness. My own warm bed.
Time passes. Dampness soaks through
the crisp barrier to my heart.
My gathered energy,
focused, reaching upwards.
The earth moves with my growth.
A tiny glimmer, then
your wild glow rushes to my heart.
My green fingers caress
the light you sacrifice for me.
My provision of love and power
shoot lavish red petals
into your world.
The sight of your bright eye
warms my soul.
You give me life. Without you
my germination fails
and my beauty wilts.
I reach towards your heart,
I feel you next to me.
Your warm breath kisses my spirit,
before you slowly fade away.

Claire C Dick, West Yorkshire

A MIRACLE

Beautiful flowers in scenes enchanted
Treasures of Earth we take for granted
Of all the joys in all the world
A miracle I've seen unfold

The miracle is my new-born child
Born into this world so wild
And everyone will wait and see
Our boy gain his identity

For in this world he needs a name
He'll bring it joy or bring it shame
With love and knowledge he will grow
Into a life we don't yet know

One thing's for certain - when we're gone
Our name our boy will carry on
We hope he makes a name in life
Learns to love and finds a wife

Then when the circle has full turned
We hope in life they may have learned
Have their own children- share their pain
And life will start all over again.

Michael B Powell, South Yorkshire

My 'Gentle' Man

When I was young and foolish
You loved me from the start,
But you were quiet and gentle
And locked me in your heart.

Another's charms enticed me,
And that man was your friend,
He left me with a broken heart,
I thought would never mend.

You watched me in the shadows,
With my lovely baby boy,
Taking both our hands in yours,
Turning sadness into joy.

Suddenly the friend had gone,
There standing in his place
A man whose special love for me
Was shining from his face.

Suddenly at once I knew,
I'd loved you all my life,
This special shy and gentle man,
Asked me to be his wife.

My life is yours, my darling,
This is my only plan,
To be held fast forever
In the arms of a *'Gentle'Man*

Mary Hutson, South Yorkshire

A SEASIDE OUTING - 1940s

There were ice cream vans and lollipops,
We jostled on street and pier,
Rode bumper cars and carousels,
Thrilled in houses of fun and fear.

Spades and buckets for us kids,
And donkey rides on sands.
Fish and chips in paper bags,
And Punch and Judy stands.

Dad's trousers rolled up to his knees,
Knotted 'hankie' on his pate,
Mum in a deckchair, taking her ease,
Laughed at the sight of her mate.

Candyfloss and sticky cheeks,
Braced by fresh sea air.
Cockles and whelks and salty reeks,
Souvenir shops everywhere.

Laughing policemen, in glass box,
Sand between our toes.
Fortune tellers, with gypsy-black locks;
Golden earrings, golden clothes.

At day's end, we dragged our feet,
While our parents bumped and heaved.
Buses spat out fumes and heat,
One last look; it was time to leave.

Betty Morton, South Yorkshire